LOVE & DECEIT
UNFINISHED BUSINESS

SHANEKA M. JOHNSON

This is a work of fiction. The events and characters described herein are imaginary and are not intended to refer to specific places or living persons. The opinions expressed in this manuscript are solely the opinions of the authors and do not represent the opinions or thoughts of the publisher. The author has represented and warranted full ownership and/or legal right to publish all the materials in this book.

Love & Deceit
Unfinished Business
All Rights Reserved.
Copyright © 2013 Shaneka M. Johnson

Cover Photo © 2013 Marrio Marshall. All rights reserved – used with permission.

This book may not be reproduced, transmitted, or stored in whole or in part by any means, including graphic, electronic, or mechanical without the express written consent of the publisher except in the case of brief quotations embodied in critical articles and reviews.

Affairs of the Heart Publishing

ISBN: 978-0615852362

PRINTED IN THE UNITED STATES OF AMERICA

CHAPTER 1
LA'TIA

As I sat in the crowded lobby of family services, I was filled with disgust regarding the downward spiral my life had taken. I went from being financially independent to subjecting myself to government assistance. I looked around the room at mothers yelling after their kids; men impatiently walking in and out; and others, like myself, annoyed by the long wait times. I tapped my foot as I looked at the clock in irritation that my appointment was officially forty-five minutes late.

I'd left home nearly an hour ago and as soon as I felt my phone vibrate, I cursed knowing whom the caller could potentially be. I searched through my purse and rolled my eyes as I saw his name on the caller ID.

I took a deep breath before answering.

"Yes, Marcus," I said with attitude.

"How long are you going to be?" he asked in his deep raspy voice.

I looked around the room and back at the clock.

"I don't know," I answered. "Why, what's the problem?"

"I need to make a run to the A. I'm planning on hitting the road by eleven."

I shook my head in anger. There was always "something" when it came to Marcus watching Noah.

"I've previously missed two appointments and I can't afford to miss this one. You always have an excuse when I need to handle business. What you have going on can wait."

I could hear him breathing heavily through the phone. "I don't have time to argue with you right now. Why can't I bring him to you?"

I tried hard to remain calm in the presence of others, knowing deep down I wanted to unleash a few choice words at him.

"This lobby is full and Noah will not sit still with all these kids running around. I'm handling business that affects our livelihood, which is more im2portant than what you have to do."

"I don't have time for your nonsense right now, so either I'll bring him there or drop him off at Ms. Garrett. Which do you prefer?"

I hung up and wished it were a landline so I could've slammed down the receiver for emphasis. There was no reasoning with Marcus; he simply did what he wanted to do. It bothered me that despite doing jail time he still preferred the hustler lifestyle versus being a positive role model to his son. This only made me regretful of him relocating to Charlotte. While I loved him, his lifestyle and lack of responsibility as a father was unwanted.

I called Ms. Garrett, my neighbor, to see if she could watch Noah. I hated asking her as she watched him three times a week while I worked. She agreed to watch him as long as I picked him up by two o'clock.

I reluctantly called Marcus back. He answered on the first ring and began talking.

"I've already taken him to Ms. Garrett. I went over to ask her and she said you'd already called."

Amazing, it wasn't even eleven yet and he'd dropped Noah off.

"You really need to get your priorities straight. You get on my fucking nerves and—"

He abruptly cut me off. "Yeah, whatever," he said, then hung up the phone.

I looked at my phone in disbelief as I threw it back in my purse, fuming at his disrespectful behavior.

M2y best friend, Rachelle, introduced me to Marcus since she was dating his friend. I still cursed her out to this day for bringing him into my life. While he was 6'2", dark chocolate, with a nice physique, his mentality was all fucked up. But of course, in the beginning, you get blinded by the physical and don't take note of all the negatives until you're in too deep.

My head started to pound as I once again glanced at the clock.

I'd been in Charlotte for a year after leaving Atlanta. My life changed when I lost my job over a year ago. Finding out I was pregnant sent me right over the edge. I'd gone from living in a luxury apartment to nearly being evicted. I couldn't maintain my lifestyle and needed an easy out.

Initially Marcus's street life had its perks and thrills. After having my car windows busted out, enduring harassing phone calls, and getting my front door shot through, that life quickly became unappealing. Even though I voiced my concerns about his lifestyle and encouraged him to get a job, I never turned down what he had to offer.

Our relationship was a roller coaster of breakups and makeups. Right before I found out I was pregnant, we were once again on the outs. This time, instead of dwelling on us being separated, I took interest in another man. After being with Marcus for five years, being with someone totally different was refreshing.

Darnell and I met at a bar and after nearly three weeks of conversation, our relationship turned intimate. Our conversations were thought-provoking; I loved his style, charm, and professionalism as a successful businessman. He was the epitome of what I needed in a man; however, he was married. I'd never been with a married man, but the thrill and convenience of not being committed was favorable for me. Even though Marcus and I were going through the motions as usual, I knew that we would eventually get back together.

I didn't see Darnell leaving his wife, even though I sometimes wondered how things would be if we were a couple. After dealing with Marcus and all the other losers before him, Darnell was an upgrade. Things were going well between us and yet Marcus was still in the picture. His "business" kept him in and out of town, which gave me the freedom to see Darnell.

I remember setting up a romantic evening for Darnell. I opened the door for him wearing a black lace bodysuit with a garter and red high heels, and a look of seduction on my face. My whole mood changed by his reaction, as my appearance didn't prompt the eagerness I thought it would.

When he came in, he didn't bother to acknowledge what I wore or the romantic ambiance. He immediately sat on the couch and put his head in his hands. I shook my head and blew out the candles; the look on his face let me know the night wasn't going to go according to plan. I went to my room for my robe.

When I came back to the living room, he told me he could no longer see me. I was crushed. Somewhere in my head, I thought our affair would be ongoing and I'd accepted it because I liked him so much. Out of anger, I asked him to leave and threatened to tell his wife. I felt hurt, even though I knew the consequences of such an affair.

Once my pregnancy was confirmed, I immediately thought about Darnell and our sexual encounter weeks prior when the condom broke. However, when the doctor told me how far along I was, I knew it had to be by Marcus. He was once again locked up, so I told him of my pregnancy on one of my visits to see him. He cried tears of joy and promised me that he would get his life together when he got out. I believed him, considering I'd never seen him break down in such a way. But the truth remained, that with Marcus being in jail, I would financially struggle.

After months of draining my savings and 401k, I couldn't live off unemployment alone. I had to come up with a plan that would get me on my feet. When the thought hit me, I couldn't fathom carrying out such an act, but the more I convinced myself why I couldn't do it, the more bills piled up.

One night I called Darnell so we could meet up. Not only did I plan on telling him I was pregnant with his child, but I needed to see him in person so I could sell him on why I didn't tell him initially. My survival depended on this stellar performance I sought to pull off.

He insisted on being told over the phone, but even after I told him, he didn't believe me. I knew I had him thinking as he basically went silent. He agreed to meet me the next day. From that point on, he gave me money, which I needed to pay off bills—namely my car. But things came to a screeching halt when his wife found out about my pregnancy.

I knew my lie would catch up with me, so with all the money I'd managed to collect from Darnell, I broke my lease and moved. I needed a quick escape where I could live comfortably and raise my son without dealing with the aftermath of my lie.

Once I got settled in Charlotte, I thought about my actions and felt empty inside. Even though I'd managed to escape with a new number in a new city, I couldn't escape the resentment. I'd created a mess and was left alone to figure out how to right my wrong.

Rachelle didn't understand why I would up and make such a move. I was too ashamed to share with her how I'd managed to bamboozle another man into believing I was pregnant with his child. Even though she disagreed with my move, she still supported me by being the friend I desperately needed.

Giving birth to Noah Tyree Daniels gave me a feeling of joy I hadn't felt in years. Holding him in my arms, all I could do was smile at my greatest creation.

Once Marcus was released from jail and moved to Charlotte, I felt as if things were finally coming together. I thought about the promise Marcus had made to me and knew that being in a new city would allow him to make a fresh start. He had so much determination and started looking for a job immediately. As time progressed, he stopped looking and started staying out late. It was then I realized he'd reneged on his promise and gone back to the lifestyle that sent him away in the first place.

At that point, I started focusing on raising Noah as a single mother. Noah gave my life new meaning and I couldn't bother trying to change someone who didn't want to change.

It became apparent to me that in order to free my conscience, I needed to rectify the situation with Darnell. I knew the situation left Darnell with the agony of wanting confirmation on whether he had a child. With social media being so prevalent, I felt that would be a sure way for him to find me.

Sure enough, months later, his wife reached out to me on Facebook and I called her. While nervous, I agreed to come to Atlanta to do a paternity test. Once the test was done and the results were in, it revealed what I knew all along: Darnell was not the father. I deactivated my Facebook page and changed my phone number again. At this point there was nothing further to discuss and I couldn't bear the ridicule from my deceit; the truth being revealed was all that mattered.

I snapped out of my thoughts as I heard the receptionist finally call my name. Thank goodness my long wait was over.

After my appointment, I went by the store to grab some things. My cell phone rang; it was Rachelle.

"Hey, lady. What's going on?" I answered.

"Same ole' stuff, different day. When can I come for a visit?"

"You really want to come here," I said. "You know you need no invitation."

She smacked her lips. "Girl, you don't live by yourself. Don't you need to run this by your boo?"

Clearly she was in a joking mood. "Marcus is one step away from getting the boot. He has no say-so when it comes to my household."

"Ah, look at you being all hard," she said, chuckling. "Well I'll be up there Friday."

Considering today was Wednesday, it left me little time to prepare.

"Damn, most people would at least give a two-week notice," I joked.

"Girl, I'm not company; no need to pull all the extra gimmicks with me. I'm not coming to critique your place."

"That's cool; it'll be nice to have you here. Are you bringing the kids?"

"Are you kidding me? Hell no! Between them and their daddy, that's why I need an escape."

I couldn't even remember the last time I had a break. My life consisted of working and taking care of Noah.

"I heard that. I'll see if my neighbor will be able to watch Noah Saturday night so I can at least take you out kid-free."

We talked longer as I headed home. I pulled up to a number of police cars with flashing lights at the front entrance to my building. Nervously, I ended my call with Rachelle and illegally parked in the only spot I found available. I jumped out my car without grabbing any of my belongings and jogged towards my building.

I could see a crowd of neighbors surrounding the other side of the entrance. Crime tape blocked off the area in my path, making it hard to view the entryway. I made an attempt to go under the tape when an officer rushed over to me.

"Ma'am, this is a crime scene. You have to stay behind the tape," he said as he pointed to the crowd.

"Sir, I live in this building and my neighbor is watching my baby. I need to know if they're OK."

"Which apartment do you live in?" he asked with a perplexed look.

"232," I said.

His eyes lit up. "Ma'am, please wait right here, I'll be right back."

He went over and interrupted two detectives who were talking off to the side. The officer pointed in my direction as the detectives walked towards me.

"What's going on? Please tell me my son is OK," I said as tears fell from my eyes.

One of the detectives looked at me with a half smile. "Ma'am, your son is fine. Your neighbor and son went to another neighbor's house in the next building. Can I have your name please?"

"La'Tia Daniels," I said with a bewildered look. "Why? What's going on here?"

The detectives looked at each other as if to see who would be the first to speak up.

"Ma'am, I'm Detective Williams." He hesitated before proceeding. "There was a shooting about thirty minutes ago here, in front of your apartment. Do you know Marcus Taylor?"

I instantly started shaking at the mention of his name. "Yes, that's my boyfriend."

"I'm sorry, Mrs. Daniels, Marcus Taylor has been the victim of a homicide. He was pronounced dead on the scene."

I stood like a deer in headlights as tears streamed down my face.

"No, no, no," I screamed as I pushed my way past the detectives.

They grabbed me by my arms as I fought to get away from them. I needed to see for myself. Why was this happening? Before another thought entered my mind, before another tear fell from my eyes, my world suddenly faded to black.

CHAPTER 2
KELLY

"Swing left, swing right, step forward, step back," said the drill sergeant/aerobics instructor.

Since giving birth to Kimora, I'd turned into the ultimate gym rat to get my body back in shape. I worked out four times a week for two hours and stuck to a strict diet. My determination to get back to my post-baby figure was in full swing.

Life since my precious baby girl made her debut had been an emotional roller coaster. When I came clean with Derek about Kimora's pending paternity, I knew at that point that my chance of a relationship with him was slim to none. When it was determined that Derek was Kimora's father, I was relieved, but knew even that couldn't mend what had been broken.

After some time passed, Derek admitted he wanted to slowly work on rebuilding our relationship. I didn't exactly know what that meant, but I went along with the program without question. I quickly learned that "taking it slow" meant no intimacy. We would go out on dates and he would escort me to my door and give me a peck on the lips as if it were our first date. At first I thought it was cute, but date after date, I found myself getting more frustrated. I would purposely wear sexy outfits, give him seductive looks, and at one point flat out asked for sex, but he wouldn't budge. I tried not to think about him possibly having someone on the side, but it left me wondering.

We'd decided to attend my best friend and his sister-in-law Jessica's gala for her non-profit organization. This would be our first date in the presence of family who weren't aware of our prior breakup. He held my hand throughout the night and while I tried not to read too deep into it, I felt like maybe this could be a breakthrough.

After the event, I expected nothing more than the same routine of previous dates. I opened the door to my place and, once inside, he pushed me against the wall where we engaged in a passionate kiss. From there, things flowed naturally and we left a trail of clothes from the foyer to the bedroom as we let go of our built-up sexual frustration. The lovemaking was the best we'd ever experienced together. I slept in his arms the whole night, and the next morning, I didn't want him to leave.

Snapping back to reality, we were in the cool-down stage, which meant the torture for today was over. I looked around the gym in search of my co-worker, Gigi. She kept me well entertained, as her gym motivation had nothing to do with working out itself but to look cute and attract guys.

At thirty-nine her goal consisted of having a kid and getting married—in that order. Being of Puerto Rican descent, she had curves with the assets to match. Her tanned complexion and long jet-black hair accented her look. Gigi had natural beauty, but she allowed excessive makeup and outrageous extensions to distort what came naturally. I'd tried to convince her on numerous occasions to go natural, but it fell on deaf ears.

I grabbed my gym bag and headed to the treadmill section where I spotted Gigi having a conversation with a man next to her. While he seemed focused on his workout and uninterested, Gigi was enthralled in conversation as she slowly walked on the barely moving treadmill. I shook my head at her as I walked up and tapped her on the shoulder.

"Oh hey, girl," she said and smiled.

"Who are you really fooling?" I pointed to the slow setting on the treadmill. "There's a line of serious people waiting to get on these treadmills and you holding folks up so you can casually walk and talk."

Gigi waved her hand at me. "I pay my dues to be here like everybody else. They better wait their turn," she said as she whipped her hair.

I laughed. "I'm beat and I have to pick up Kimora, so I'll see you at work Monday."

She stopped the machine and told the man beside her to enjoy his workout; he seemed relieved.

"I have a date tonight so I'll leave too. Let me go grab my bag from my locker."

I walked towards the exit with my head in my bag to retrieve my cell phone and keys. I carelessly bumped into someone coming around the corner. I looked up apologetically and my mouth flew open, but no words came out. I stood face-to-face with a familiar face I never cared to see again.

He looked at me with a mischievous grin. "Well, well, well, if it's not the beautiful and sexy Kelly. Last time I saw you, you were pleasantly plump."

I rolled my eyes. "Sorry for not paying attention," I said, walking around him.

I guess he felt like annoying me as he followed me outside.

"Is there a reason you're following me? I've apologized already."

He held up his hands. "Apology accepted. It's amazing even after time has passed you're still bitter. Hell, I explained why I did what I did. What's so wrong with me being a responsible party? Obviously you had something to hide in the ordeal, but I had no hidden agenda."

"John, I told you my baby wasn't yours to begin with and you persisted, which was totally uncalled for. You were being a complete asshole about it and causing unnecessary drama."

"So I'm an asshole for confirming paternity? No, I think I was protecting my livelihood by ensuring it wasn't mine. I've seen a lot of my friends get caught up in situations without taking care of matters on the front end. I'm sorry for the anguish it caused."

Honestly I'd forgiven John, but I still didn't like him for reasons that went beyond his paternity-suit tactic.

I sent Gigi a text to let her know I was outside. She came out by the time I had hit "send."

"I was looking around the gym for you, but now I see what had your attention." She smirked as she sized up John.

I shook my head. "I ran into him as I was heading out. John, this is my friend Gigi."

They shook hands and exchanged pleasantries as he excused himself to enter the gym.

Gigi proceeded to watch him as he walked into the gym.

"Girl, he is fine. Please tell me he's some long-lost friend."

"He's a former acquaintance that had occasional benefits."

"Damn, ain't that a pity," she said, shaking her head. "I need a brother like that."

"Trust me, he's not your type. Way too egotistical."

"Ummm hmmmm. Oh well, dear, I'm off to get ready for my date. I let my sister play matchmaker. Say a prayer for me."

I grinned. "Hopefully she's better at that than your cousin."

She shivered in disgust thinking about her matchmaker date from hell. We exchanged hugs as we walked to our vehicles.

I hit the remote to my black Lexus GS300 and threw my bag in the backseat. My backseat was a constant reminder of my shift from the single carefree life to that of motherhood. Besides Kimora's car seat, her toys and food crumbles covered the seat and floor. I remembered the days when I wouldn't let anyone drink or eat in my car and I kept it freshly detailed every week. Those days were long gone.

I got in the car and headed to Derek's house to pick up Kimora. I'd been doing a better job of staying at his house, but it still felt strange. With us moving forward in our relationship, I hoped he would one day be open to buying another house. A new chapter in life meant creating new memories in a new environment. Considering the house was filled with memories of his deceased wife, I wasn't trying to build on what she'd established there.

Derek still worked at his father's company, Walker & Co., as the CFO. He now worked only four days a week so he could have more time to shuffle the kids to their practices and attend games and recitals. With Kaylee in ballet and Kayden playing soccer and swimming, Derek definitely had his plate full. But even though helping the kids do their homework and extracurricular activities took up a great deal of time, he never neglected to spend time with Kimora. Derek was the epitome of a great father, which I loved about him.

I pulled in Derek's driveway and noticed an unfamiliar vehicle parked in front of the house. Normally I would call to let him know I was on the way, but I neglected to do so this time. I get out the car and walked up the cobblestone walkway to the front door. I stepped on the porch as Derek, with Kimora in hand, opened the door.

"Hey, babe," he said, smiling.

"Hello," I said as we shared a peck.

I grabbed Kimora and started loving on her as she leaned back and giggled.

"Do you have company?" I asked.

"Yes, Karen's parents are here for the weekend. Saturday is the anniversary of Karen's death so we are going to the cemetery to lay flowers. They came early to spend time with the kids."

I'd totally forgotten about it. "I didn't know they were coming in today. I would've left the gym earlier."

"It wasn't a big deal; besides, they didn't tell me until the last minute. Kayden is having field day tomorrow, so they wanted to come watch him since I won't be able to make it."

We proceeded to the sunroom where Mr. and Mrs. Jackson were hugged up with their grandkids. Kaylee jumped up from the sofa and ran to me for a hug, which she normally did.

"Hey, Mama," she said as she hugged me.

As all eyes turned to me, I didn't know how to respond. Kaylee had never addressed me as such; she normally called me KK. I could see a look of shock on the Jacksons' faces. I wanted them to understand that her addressing me this way was clearly unexpected and something new.

"Well that's definitely shocking. Hey, Kaylee," I said as I stroked her unruly hair.

The uncomfortable silence that plagued the room made me nervous, but I remained personable.

"Hello, Mr. and Mrs. Jackson. How was your drive down?" I said.

They both spoke in unison that it was fine. Mrs. Jackson gave me an intense stare as if she were trying to read my thoughts. Kimora grew quite heavy in my arms, so I excused myself and went upstairs to Derek's room. I sat Kimora on the bed as I rubbed my temples. Derek came in and closed the door.

"Are you OK?" he asked with a concerned look.

"Yeah, but things started feeling awkward after Kaylee's shocking greeting."

"I know that was uncomfortable, but don't worry; we know she said that on her own. They have to understand that you're the only mother figure she has in her life."

"We know that, but they don't."

He frowned. "I'm not worried about that; they'll be all right. By the way, Mrs. Jackson wants to take you to lunch tomorrow."

Take me to lunch? Oh great. I guessed with Kaylee addressing me like that and her seeing Derek and me getting serious, it was interrogation time.

"I don't have a problem with it, but I don't do well with intimidation tactics. I respect her as your kid's grandmother, but I'm just saying."

"Well I trust you will handle yourself tactfully. She can be a pretty cutthroat woman. She and Karen were always going at it, but trust me, she knows her boundaries."

I'd never asked Derek what his former in-laws thought of me because, honestly, it didn't matter. When I had initially met them, they were polite, but it was a rather brief encounter considering we only dropped the kids off.

I glanced over at the bed and Kimora was knocked out. I didn't want her to sleep too long and walked over to wake her up.

He grabbed me by the arm. "Let me talk to you for a minute," he said. He patted the seat next to him on the bed stool.

"What's up? Is everything OK?"

"No need to be alarmed; everything is good. I've been thinking about this for the past few months and going back and forth with it. But I'm ready to buy a house."

Damn, was he reading my mind or what. I wanted to jump for joy, but figured that wouldn't be the best reaction.

"Oh really," I said with raised eyebrows. "What brought this on?"

"Well, I think it's time for me to move on. We're progressing in our relationship and the kids are getting older; we need a bigger space. My plan is to rent this house out to Karen's sister since she's planning on moving here soon."

"Is she moving here with her family?"

"It's just her and her ten-year-old daughter. While I'm ready to move, I'm not ready to sell yet. And by renting it out, I'd rather it be to someone I know and trust."

"It seems like you've got a well-thought-out plan. Go for it."

"I don't want to go into this alone. I want us to go into this together."

I stared at him, as inside I was overjoyed he was ready to take such a major step with me. I loved my townhouse and took great pride in it being my first investment without the help of my parents. It scared me to think about taking such a financial leap with Derek without us being married; I didn't feel comfortable with agreeing to it at this point.

I fidgeted with my fingers as I tried to come up with the right words to say versus flat out saying "put a ring on it first."

"I know you've given this a lot of thought and I'm glad to know you are preparing for the future. I definitely didn't see this coming," I said. "How do you think the kids will take it?"

He lowered his head. "For Kaylee, she's too young to care. All she wants is her princess house bunk-bed set." He smiled. "Kayden wasn't thrilled initially, but when I took him with me to look at some houses, he got a little excited. Deep down I think he's ready for something new. I'm keeping him in the loop because I want him to feel a part of this decision."

I loved Derek so much for his compassion and his willingness to sacrifice his own needs for his kids.

"I commend you for all that you're doing. Your kids are so blessed to have a father like you."

He smiled. "So, are you blessed to have me as your man?"

"Of course I am." I blushed.

"OK, so again, what's up? Are we you ready to do this with me?"

I leaned my head back on the bed. "Derek, I want nothing more than to take this step with you. But," I hesitated. "I would like to be married first."

"Just because we go into this unmarried doesn't mean that it won't eventually happen."

"I hear what you're saying, but when we start going into things jointly, I prefer to be married. I mean we are practically living with each other on a part-time basis now. We both love each other and want a future together. What's holding us back from getting married before buying this house?"

He was saved from responding by a knock on the door. He got up and opened the door.

"It's getting late and I know the kids have to get ready for bed, so we're going to head on over to the hotel. Thanks for allowing us to intrude on you with such short notice," Mrs. Jackson said from the doorway.

"Not a problem. The kids are always excited to see you all."

Mrs. Jackson smiled and turned her attention to me.

"Kelly, I don't know if Derek mentioned it but I would love to do lunch with you tomorrow."

"Yes, he did. That's certainly not a problem."

"We're staying in Buckhead at the Marriott, so I know there's plenty over there to choose from. Pick a place in that area and I'll meet you there after we come back from Kayden's school."

We agreed to meet at Maggiano's and exchanged numbers. Derek left to escort them out and get the kids ready for bed. I watched over Kimora as she slept peacefully.

Kaylee and Kayden came in the room to give me a good night hug before retreating to their rooms. Kayden was starting to warm up to me better, but he still had moments where he was distant. As the big brother, he took great care with Kaylee and Kimora. He had a maturity about him you wouldn't normally see in an eight-year-old.

Derek returned to the room and slightly closed the door. I looked at my watch to remind him that I needed to get home.

I stood with my arms folded. "As I was saying, what's holding us back from marriage?"

He sighed. "I'm trying to get over one hump at a time, baby. I'm not saying I'm not ready to commit. I still have the ring, we can be engaged, but let's not push the marriage issue right now."

Push the marriage issue? It wasn't as if I wanted him to propose and set a date tonight. His response didn't sit well with me and I tried not to let it show. I never wanted him to feel pressured to do anything because some men will propose to their woman just to shut them up. That's not what I wanted.

"Give me some time and I'll think about it," I said without making eye contact. I gathered Kimora's things as he scooped her up from the bed. He walked us out to the car and secured her in her car seat. Then he walked around to my door and stuck his head through the driver side window for a kiss.

"If the Jacksons hadn't come through, it would've been on tonight," he said in a seductive voice. "Tomorrow, let's make that happen." He winked.

As much as Derek had my nose wide open when it came to sex, tonight his seductive tactic was unappealing. I gave him a fake smile in return as I pushed the start button in my car. I backed out the driveway without looking in his direction. The ride home gave me time to clear my head and think about what we'd discussed. I wanted nothing more than a life with Derek, but taking on a house and the responsibility of his kids seemed like a major jump without a total commitment.

CHAPTER 3
JANEN

As the bright sunrays entered through my bedroom blinds, I rolled over to look at my husband, Tony, sleeping so peacefully. We'd been married for eight months now and things were only getting better for us. Six months ago we had relocated to Miami, which was a better city than the initial destination of Puerto Rico. I truly enjoyed the Miami life, from the sunny skies to the beautiful ocean views from our twelfth-floor condo.

I gently kissed Tony on the lips as he lay unmoved by my touch of affection. I drew the covers back and decided to give him a real morning wake-up that would surely make him move. As I playfully stroked his penis, a smirk came upon his face. He still didn't bother to open his eyes or speak. I slowly put my mouth over his penis, so he could feel the heat of my breath. He hardened in anticipation of what was to happen next. I further aroused him as my tongue went up and down his shaft. He moaned as he stroked the soft curls of my short hair. His moans increased in delight as I took all of him in, moving my mouth up and down.

After minutes of me pleasuring him, he leaned forward and flipped me on my back. He pinned down my arms as he climbed on top of me and engaged in a deep kiss. He lowered himself as he sucked on my ample breasts and made his way down to the soft spot nestled between my thighs. He lightly flicked his tongue over my clit as I moaned and jumped in excitement. He ignited every inch of me with the tender touch of his tongue. Once I'd reached a level of wetness, he abruptly stopped and hopped off the bed as he reached for me. I took his hand as he led me into the living room with its floor-to-ceiling window. The good thing about the view was that it faced the ocean and our windows were tinted so we could see out, but not in.

He led me to the chair near the window and bent me over the backside of it. He entered me from the back and with each stroke, I cried out in pleasure. People were so stereotypical when it came to interracial relationships and made it seem as if all white men were packed with small penises. While Tony was my first, he surely didn't lack in his size, endurance, and freakiness. He was a true romantic and knew exactly what it took to get me to the point of climax.

He flipped me around and lifted me onto him. We passionately made love in front of the window as he moved with bended knees to lean me against the adjacent wall. We were both so wrapped up in each other that we didn't hear the phone ringing. We ended up on the floor as I rolled him over and straddled him. I rode him from the back as he playfully spanked me and admired my curvy physique. He tapped me to let me know he was ready as I rapidly grinded on him to reach the point of climax. As we both cried out upon reaching orgasm, our erotic moment was interrupted by a knock on the door.

I quickly rolled off him as he attempted to gather the energy to get up from the floor. He got up and tiptoed to the door to look through the peephole. He shook his head as he mouthed it was his sister. I rolled my eyes as I got up and went to our room to gather our robes and a warm towel. I could hear Tony spraying air freshener to disguise the present sex smell. I wrapped my robe around me as I walked in the living room and handed him his robe and towel. He yelled through the door that he'd be right there as he quickly wiped himself off. My only question was why the hell did she not call? And even if she did, why come by if no one answered?

His sister, Carrie, was not a biological sister, but the daughter of a family friend his parents had helped raise. I didn't particularly care for her with her over-the-top antics, which is why her showing up today didn't come too much as a surprise. It was so typical of her and it annoyed me that Tony wouldn't put her ass in its proper place.

I walked in the kitchen to start on breakfast. Something I didn't normally do, but felt it would be the best thing to do to keep me occupied. As Tony opened the door, Carrie walked in and hugged him.

"Hey. I'm so sorry to pop in on you guys, but I tried calling," she said as looked around.

Tony closed the door and walked over to sit in the chair we'd minutes ago used as a prop during our lovemaking.

He scratched his head. "Well, if we didn't answer, why didn't you wait until you got a response? Unexpected visits are rather rude."

She rolled her eyes and shooed him with her hands. "Oh please, we used to do it all the time to each other when you were in New York. I'm family, not some random stranger."

I shook my head hearing her response. This was one reason I didn't like her; she was inconsiderate and rude.

Carrie walked over to the breakfast bar to greet me.

"Hi, Janen. How's the married life treating you?" she said, looking me up and down.

"It's treating me damn good," I said, giving Tony a devilish grin.

She looked at me and Tony. "Well we all can't be so fortunate. I see I came at the perfect time."

"Not really," I said, straight-faced. Even though the response slipped out, I wasn't sorry for saying it.

The look on her face was priceless as she turned to walk back to the living room without further comment.

I made sure to make just enough breakfast for Tony and me. Once I was done, I made my plate, sat his on the breakfast bar, and headed into my bedroom to eat in peace. I didn't care to sit with her and pretend she was a welcomed guest that I enjoyed.

My phone rang. "Hello," I answered.

"Hey, sis. How are you?"

"Oh hey, Jess. I'm doing good, girl. How is my beautiful niece doing?"

"She's great and doing what she loves to do—eat," she said and chuckled.

Jessica and her husband, Darnell, had a baby girl, Tianna, four months ago. They named her after Disney's first black princess—go figure.

"So what's going on with you?"

She sighed. "Girl, my plate is extremely full, but it's going good so I can't complain. The organization is in full swing; our grants are rolling in and we have a good number of clients we're working with. I called you because I need your help. I'm being featured in *Atlanta's Best* magazine. I'll be doing a photo shoot with the family and they were trying to get me to use their in-house stylist, but to me this is too major of a deal to half step on. I need you to come work your magic."

I was honored by the opportunity to contribute to the project with such a reputable magazine.

"That's big, sis. Of course I will be there with bells on. Just tell me when and where."

"It's in two weeks; sorry for the late notice."

"Girl, that's nothing I can't handle. I'll start pulling together some pieces now for you and Darnell to look at. I'll email them to you by Tuesday."

"Great! So what's new on your end?"

I sighed heavily. "Would you believe Carrie came to town without notifying Tony and had the nerve to pop up at our place? Girl, we were in the middle of getting our freak on when her ass rudely interrupted."

"OK, that was too much information," she said, chuckling. "Yeah, that was rude of her not to announce she was coming prior. Tony is a good one cause she would've stayed outside the door. What is she doing there?"

"Girl, hell if I know. I'm in my room with my door closed. I'm sure he'll tell me once she leaves. You know I'm ready to give him a mouthful."

"Oh I'm sure of that. Have you talked to Mom?"

"Not this week. Is everything OK?"

"Yeah, she and Mr. Frank are doing well. I think she's decided to rent out the house to Mikey and his wife."

"That's good. I know she didn't want to sell it and what better way to keep it in the family then rent it to her only son. I need to give her a call and let her know I'll be there. I'll more than likely come a few days earlier before the shoot."

"I'm sure she would like that. Well I'll let you get back to your company..."

"Talk to you later."

I hung up the phone as Tony opened the door to the room.

"She's gone." He sighed.

"What the hell did she want?" I asked.

He fell back on the bed. "She's down here on vacation with some dude."

"I don't have to tell you how irritated I am by her popping up. That's rude to know you coming somewhere and don't at least give someone advance notice before showing up on their doorstep."

"You were in there when I told her that and, trust me, through your actions, she knows."

"The question is does she care. I know she doesn't like me and that's fine, but she will respect our household. She pulls that shit next time, I'm going to cuss her out as I slam the door in her face."

"Well hopefully there is no next time. And who says she doesn't like you?" he said.

I give him a "yeah right" look. "Please, she's never given me a fair shot. From our initial meeting she never tried to get to know me and she says the bare minimum to me and it's always some slick-ass comment."

He turned over and looked at me. "What steps have you taken to get to know her? Stop putting the blame solely on her. I think you both are misunderstanding each other because she thinks you don't like her too. You damn women," he said, shaking his head.

"Women just know these things; but anyway, I'll be doing some work for Jess in about a week. She has a major photo shoot coming up."

"That's great, baby."

I really loved the support I received from Tony. He was always boasting about my work to his friends and clients.

I needed to talk to him about something that had been on my mind for a few months now. Since my mom and I had mended our relationship, it only sparked my curiosity on finding my biological mother. Every since I found out my stepmom had adopted me as a baby out of an affair between my dad and a neighbor, I felt like I needed to find out who I truly was. My upbringing hadn't been difficult, but I had made it that way out of my own anger towards the situation. I needed closure to years of wanting to know this woman.

"Baby, we need to talk," I said as I tapped his arm.

He opened his eyes and sat up, giving me his full attention.

"What's on your mind?" he asked with his head propped on his arms.

"I want to find my biological mother."

He straightened his posture as he stared at me without emotion.

"Well, if you see it's something of importance to do, then go for it."

I give him a sidelong stare as I could tell he was holding back his thoughts.

"Do you understand why this is important to me? I mean, tell me what you really think, Tony, because your expression is saying a lot more than your mouth."

"OK, I see it like this. She didn't want to be a part of your life and never made an effort to get to know you, so why bother? I don't want to see you hurt through this process. I think your parents did a good job raising you without her. How do you think this will make Mrs. Joann feel?"

I lowered my eyes. "I know this is a huge step mentally, but I feel it's something I need to do for myself. I am made up of this woman; even though she's never been a part of my life, I need to know. That's important to me since we are looking to start a family of our own. As for Mom, I don't know how she's going to feel about it, but I know she will respect my wishes. I'm not out to hurt her or Dad; it's simply a way for me to heal and move on."

He ran his hand over his face. "Personally I don't want you to. But if you feel doing this will give you the clarification you need, then you have my support. However, I'm pleased with the woman you are. Now I'm about to take a shower."

He disrobed and walked into the bathroom. I heard the shower turn on as I sat in the same spot in deep thought. I understood how Tony felt, but he was not in the situation. I've always felt incomplete because I didn't know the woman who birthed me. So many questions came to mind that neither Mom nor Dad could possibly answer. I needed to speak directly with the source. I didn't know where to begin with this journey, but I figured the first start would be getting the reassurance from my parents.

I pick up the phone and call my dad. He answered on the second ring.

"Hey, sweetie pie. How are you and Tony doing?"

I smiled at the warm greeting my dad has used since I could remember. "We are doing good, Dad. How's Taylor and Camry?"

"They're both doing well. Taylor's mom is here for a few days so they went shopping."

"Oh, OK. What you doing for the day?"

"Enjoying this peace. Camry has been quite fussy lately and with Taylor's mom here, it's just been nonstop chatter and noise."

"Well I can understand that. You know whenever you need a break, it's only a four-hour drive."

"Trust me, it's been a real thought. So, what is new with you? How's work?"

"I'm staying busy, that's for sure. I'm going to Atlanta in about a week and a half to do some work for Jess. I'm super excited."

"That's great, baby. I'm so proud of all of you for doing so well in life."

I prepared my words carefully for what would come next.

"Dad, I wanted to call to get your opinion about something that's been on my mind."

"Sure."

I sighed. "I'm not going to beat around the bush. I want to find Naomi."

If I didn't know any better, I would think he'd hung up the phone. I knew such a revelation after nearly twenty-four years would be a shock to him.

"Dad, are you there?" I asked.

"Yes, baby. I'm a bit shocked though. Why now? I would think at this point you wouldn't care."

"That's just it. I've tried to block it from my mind for years, and considering it's still a lingering thought after all this time, I need closure."

"You know I'm supportive of your efforts, but this is one that I disagree with."

I shook my head in frustration. "This is my life here; a missing part of my existence."

"A missing part that you've done well without, Janen. Have you talked to Tony about this?"

"Yes, and while he's being supportive of me, honestly he doesn't want me to either. I don't think either of you understand how unsettling this whole situation is even today as an adult."

"Do you understand how this may affect Joann?"

"Of course I've considered that. This isn't to defy her or open old wounds; it's for my personal gratification. I'm telling her when I go to Atlanta. I didn't want to go behind you guys' back and do it. I might even need your help in trying to track her down."

"Well, sweetie, I in no way want to stand in your way, but that's a part of my life I choose not to relive. Naomi chose not to be a part of your life and we accepted that."

I leaned my head back on the bedpost and closed my eyes as a burning sensation formed in my throat.

"I understand your point of view, but will you do me a favor? I will ask nothing more of you."

"What is it?"

"Can you give me her name and the apartments we used to stay in back then?"

He sighed and hesitated before responding. Then he reluctantly gave me the information as I wrote it down on the notepad on my nightstand.

I got up from the bed and went to my drawer to find something to put on for the day. Tony came out of the bathroom with the towel wrapped around his waist. His muscular physique, which he worked hard to maintain, made me smile; my husband was simply fine.

"What are you smiling about?"

"You, of course. You look so damn fine."

He blushed as he walked past me and patted me on the behind. "If I want you to stay fine, I gotta hold up my end of the bargain as well. Listen, I'm going to meet up with Carrie and this dude she's here with," he said, rolling his eyes. "Do you care to join me?"

I put my hand on my hip and gave him the "whatever" look.

"As much as I enjoy spending time with you, I'll pass. I think I'm going to go to some boutiques and gather some ideas for Jessica's photo shoot. Let's say we meet back here at the house by eight and go downtown to the new lounge that just opened."

"Cool, we can do that." He smiled and kissed me on the forehead.

As I stepped in the shower and turned on the water, I thought about my life and how things had worked out for me in the past three years. I stepped out on faith and moved to New

York; took a chance on love with a man outside of my race; made peace with Mom; got married; and made yet another transition to Miami. Even through all the trials, I was proud of my humble beginnings and where I was now as a woman. However, I needed closure to the lingering questions in my head related to my biological mother.

CHAPTER 4
DEREK

When I married Karen, we were so in love and inseparable. She had sass, style, charisma, and a beautiful smile. I remembered going on our second date. We'd hit it off so well on the first date I just knew sex would come easy. We went back to her apartment, and after hours of talking, we ended up falling asleep in each other's arms. I realized that while I wanted her sexually, I was intrigued by her and wanted things to happen naturally. Simply put, we had chemistry—something I'd never experienced before with another woman and deemed what we shared as special.

We'd dated for nearly two years before she gave birth to our son, Kayden. I'd thought about marriage before we found out she was pregnant. However, seeing my son being born made me realize how worthy she was of sharing my last name. We married two months later.

Once Kaylee was born, we felt our family was complete. Karen was such an attentive, hands-on mother, and never let a day go by without letting them know she loved them. That dreadful day when she set out for work, Kaylee was sick, but I didn't want her to take off work to care for her as she normally would. With Kaylee in arm, I walked Karen to the door and gently kissed her on the forehead. She turned and blew kisses as she smiled and headed for her car. After I laid Kaylee down for a nap, I ended up drifting to sleep. I was awakened by the phone ringing. I frantically searched for the missing cordless phone until it stopped ringing. My cell phone rang next.

I answered the phone to the sound of screams and crying from Karen's mom, Marilyn. In that instance, I thought maybe it had something to do with her husband. I tried my best to calm her down as the home phone once again started ringing. All the commotion had awakened Kaylee and she instantly started crying. I found the house phone in the bathroom and when I answered, an unknown female on the other end asked that I come to Grady Memorial Hospital immediately. When she stated this was in reference to Karen, I hung up both phones without a second thought. I scooped up Kaylee and placed her in her car seat. We were out of the house in less than five minutes.

When I got to the hospital, I was met there by my mom and Darnell who watched over Kaylee while I met with the doctors. The detective on the scene stated that Karen was the victim of a robbery. She was shot in her side and tried to drive herself away from the convenient store; but with the amount of blood lost, she fell unconscious and crashed into a telephone pole. To see Karen severely swollen beyond recognition with tubes and monitoring devices everywhere made me sick to my stomach. She had internal bleeding and damage to her liver and lungs. I couldn't believe less than three hours ago, I had kissed my wife as she headed to work, only now to witness her fighting for her life in critical condition.

I shed tears as I stroked her hand and repeatedly told her how much I loved and needed her. Her wedding ring that once adorned her finger had been removed per the nurse's request and reflected only an imprint. I kissed her hand and prayed that God would restore my wife; that she would pull through this storm and continue to be the great mother and wife she was to us. I couldn't stand the sight of seeing such a strong woman in a helpless position and me not being able to do anything for her.

The next two days after the accident was spent at the hospital listening to the doctors and their prognosis that grew grimmer by the day. I was crumbling inside and didn't know how I was going to move forward without Karen. I prayed that God would bring her back to us stronger than before. I didn't know how to tell my kids, mainly Kayden, about the possibility of his mother not making it. Kayden was an inquisitive kid and knew something was wrong considering he hadn't seen his mom in days and I was spending all my time at the hospital.

The day I had to make the decision to take her off life support was the worst day of my life. I consulted with her parents and they felt it was best to let her go. I wasn't ready to make that call, but I couldn't stand to see her suffer any longer.

After her death, I had to be the pillar of strength for the kids; Karen would've wanted it that way. There wasn't a day that went by that I didn't think of her. I hugged her pillow at night, as I could still smell the scent of her hair and the body oil she loved to use after her bath. While Kaylee was her normal jolly self, my son was suffering. I'd made an appointment for us to start grief counseling because while I wasn't showing it on the outside, inside I was falling apart.

Months following, we were getting back to some normalcy. I found myself at night talking to Karen, hoping to hear her voice, her laugh, or see a faint image of her beautiful smile. I missed my wife tremendously, but I was thankful for the two lights she'd placed in my life. My kids meant everything to me and looking in their faces every day reminded me of her.

Moving on hadn't been a thought; I couldn't see myself with anyone else. I remember talking to my mom after a year had rolled by and her telling me I needed to live my life. At that point I didn't know how to live because my kids were my main focus. I never wanted them to feel as though I was neglecting them by putting them off on others. They'd lost their mother and I never wanted them to feel as if they were losing me too.

My brother, Darnell, got me out for the first time and it felt weird. I tried to be out as much as I could, but all I could think about was being at home with my kids. When I saw Kelly at the bar with Casey, it was refreshing to see a familiar face.

I'd known of Kelly through Jessica, my sister-in-law, but I didn't know her personally. She came over and made small talk with me. From that day forward, we talked more and got to know each other better. We started seeing each other on an intimate level. Initially I felt as though I was cheating on Karen, but I'd been on a sexual drought for so long, I needed a release. I'd made it clear to Kelly that I wasn't looking for a relationship and she accepted it.

I couldn't deny Kelly's sex appeal. She wasn't Karen, but there was something about her that kept my attention. The more time I spent with her, the more I found myself wanting the same thing I was trying to steer clear of. When she told me she was pregnant and considered having an abortion, I cringed. While I didn't know how my family would respond, I knew that I liked her and wanted to see where things went between us. As a man I'd always took great pride in taking care of my responsibility, and while the situation wasn't planned, I saw it as a meaningful purpose.

When Kelly confessed after Kimora's birth that she wasn't sure of her baby's paternity, I was furious. How could she have deceived me in such a way where it affected not only me but my kids? I'd finally gotten to a point where I was ready to start a new chapter in my life by proposing to her. It angered me more than anything because she was the first woman outside of Karen I'd let into my heart and around my kids.

When the test results confirmed I was Kimora's father, I was relieved. However, I couldn't get over the fact of how Kelly lied to me for months when she could've been honest from the beginning. Even though it was a hard pill to swallow and I did everything I could to steer clear of her, in my heart I wasn't ready to give up on her. She had made a mistake and I had to search within myself and forgive her.

As of present date, things between Kelly and I were going well. I started thinking about the next move, which led me to the thought of buying a new house. I stopped by Darnell's office one day before leaving work to get some feedback from him. My brother was my best friend and I trusted his advice.

Darnell was in a much happier state of being since he'd reduced his schedule at the company and became a father. I walked into his office where he had framed pictures of his daughter and wife throughout; it felt almost like a shrine. He'd just finished up a phone call as he leaned back in his chair.

"Rough call," I said as I sat in the chair in front of his desk.

He rubbed his forehead. "I've been working with Carlton on closing out this deal with the Marriott and it's been one issue after another. But anyway, what's up with you?"

"I'm finally looking for a new house."

He sat up and intertwined his fingers as he leaned on his desk. "Well that doesn't sound like a bad thing. Why the gloom-and-doom look?"

"Because I want to do this with Kelly and she's making it harder than it has to be."

He raised his eyebrows in surprise. "Like what?"

"She wants to be married first."

"Well?" he asked.

I leaned forward with my elbows on my knees. "Not yet. I want to get things settled with the house first."

Darnell gave me a puzzled look. "OK, so why not marry first and then get the house?"

"Why does it matter when we've done everything else out of order? The house is more important and it's a way for us to adjust as a family beforehand."

Darnell smirked. "And you really think headstrong Kelly is going for that? You know damn well she wants to get married. OK, so buying a house is a big step, it says something. But that's a major responsibility, D."

I sighed. "I need to straighten some things out first before I think about marriage."

Darnell threw his hands up. "Is the mafia after you or something? You holding back on me; what's going on?"

"I'll let you know once I get things a bit situated," I said, standing up.

I left the office and headed out the side door. I'd hit the key remote to open my car doors when I heard a familiar unwelcomed voice call out to me.

"Well hello, stranger," she said.

"Hey, Lacey," I said as I continued to my car.

She followed behind me. "Why are you giving me the cold shoulder now?"

"Giving you the cold shoulder? I think I'm just walking to my car."

She smirked. "I've called you a few times and even texted, but you don't respond."

I put my laptop tote in the backseat and closed the door.

"Lacey, I have three kids; my time is very limited."

"Oh and don't forget a girlfriend."

I nodded my head. "Yeah, you're right."

"So I guess you used me to pass time until you got your life back on track," she said, looking down.

I didn't have time for her pity party and right now certainly wasn't the time I wanted to deal with her.

"Stop trying to come off as a victim here. I've always been up-front with you and never led you to believe anything otherwise."

She playfully slapped my arm. "Don't be so uptight, I miss what we shared," she said and smiled.

My cell phone started to ring, which was exactly what I needed to end this conversation.

"I need to take this call. I'll see you later."

"I sure hope so." She winked as she headed back in the building.

I got in my car and pressed the Bluetooth button. It was Darnell.

"You OK?"

"Yeah," I said.

"I walked in the conference room and happened to see you and Lacey outside having a conversation you didn't seem too interested in. What's going on with that?"

"It's not anything serious; not even worth discussing right now."

I could hear him close the door to his office.

"Don't give me that shit, D. I know you, and I'm not as dumb as you think I am. Remember, I've been there."

I leaned my head back on the headrest. "Darnell, I'm not having an affair. I'm not married, remember."

"You know exactly what I'm talking about, so cut the bullshit. This is a place of business, and fraternizing is a huge company liability. I'm not risking my livelihood because you can't control your dick."

I sighed knowing Darnell wasn't going to back down. "When Kelly and I were on the outs, I went out a few times with Lacey."

"Dude, don't you know you don't shit where you lay? It's suicidal to be intimate with someone you work with."

"Man, I know I messed up with that, but, hey, it happened. She's attractive, she was at the right place at the right time, and with everything going on, I wasn't thinking about all that."

"You were thinking, all right, just not with the right head." He sighed. "Is she harassing you? Do you need me to intervene?"

"No, Darnell. I don't need my big brother intervening in my personal affairs. She's not harassing me like that, but I don't want to deal with her and she still calls me every now and then."

"When was the last time you were with her?"

I felt as if I were going through an interrogation. I understood Darnell's concerns, but I wanted to handle the situation on my own.

"Darnell, let me handle this, bruh. If I feel things are getting out of control, then I'll let you know. I never led Lacey on to believe we would be anything more than friends with benefits."

"Women are sensitive when it comes to stuff like that. You can say you want nothing but a friendship with occasional sex, then they develop feelings and while they may not be vocal about it, deep down they want more. With her working here as a clerk and you as an executive, she can easily flip the script and claim sexual harassment."

"I don't see her taking things there."

"Don't underestimate the power of a scorned woman. Trust me, I know."

Even though Darnell was right, I didn't foresee things going that far. Lacey wasn't consistently blowing up my phone nor stalking me outside the building. I didn't see her as the threat Darnell spoke of.

I pulled up to the daycare to pick up my baby girl and ended my phone call with Darnell. I sat outside for a moment to collect my thoughts. Lacey was nothing more than a rebound after the situation with Kelly. However, even as Kelly and I decided to work on our relationship, I didn't end my sexual relationship with Lacey. I withheld from sex with Kelly so we could work on building our relationship, but in my selfishness, I held on to Lacey to satisfy my sexual desires.

Kelly and I were progressing and I wanted to make her my wife someday. I wanted a clean slate and a new beginning with her; not the lingering baggage I currently towed. I'd escaped falling into Lacey's trance for weeks now, but the images of her in my head hadn't dissipated. I could only hope that all that Darnell said wouldn't come back to bite me.

CHAPTER 5
LA'TIA

After Marcus's death, I had a hard time going back to my apartment. I stayed with my neighbor for two days unable to do anything but cry and drown in my own misery. With Rachelle already planning to come that Friday, she made arrangements and arrived Thursday night. Even then, I still was unable to move from my neighbor's couch.

By Saturday, I'd made it back to my apartment, but not without first having a breakdown where Marcus's body had lain when he was killed. I could almost visualize him there as I walked by. I knew at that moment there was no way I could stay here.

Rachelle was a lifesaver as she stepped in to do everything that I couldn't muster the energy to do. I didn't know the first thing about planning a funeral or even where to begin. The detectives were still conducting their investigation and therefore, the medical examiner's office hadn't released the body. I'd spent quite a few times down at the station giving statements and obtaining reports. The whole investigation process was mentally draining.

After Rachelle contacted her baby's daddy, Ryan, he took the responsibility of notifying Marcus's mom since he and Marcus grew up together. In the years that we'd dated, I'd only met his mother on two occasions. Their relationship was strained and he never discussed in detail the reasoning. I'd encouraged him to mend their relationship and he told me to mind my business. From that point on, I never brought up the subject and hoped over time the situation would work itself out.

Before Noah was born, I thought about reaching out to his mom for the sake of him having a relationship with his grandmother. Even with my own family there was distance. After years of dealing with emotional stress, I stepped away and never looked back. I felt it was important for my baby to at least have some form of family in the event something was to happen to me.

Once Ryan went over to deliver the news, she reached out to me hours later. I felt horrible that we would have to speak under the current circumstances. I had Rachelle take Noah to the other room while I took her call.

"Hello," I answered.

"Hi, is this Tia?" she asked.

"Yes, it is."

"I'm Sharon Michaels, Marcus's mom. How are you holding up?"

"It's been rough, but I have my best friend here with me; she's been a blessing. It's such a shame we have to be re-introduced on these terms. I can only imagine the pain you are going through right now."

"I know, honey; I feel horrible. I hadn't seen Ryan in months, so when I saw him on my doorstep with a sad look on his face, I knew it wasn't good." Her voice cracked as she spoke. "I'd not talked to Marcus in nearly three months. I guess you know our relationship has always been rocky."

"Unfortunately, yes. I never understood the issues nor did he discuss them. When I did, he was standoffish and defensive, so I didn't bother discussing them anymore."

"That's Marcus—stubborn just like his father. I did all I could to protect him from that street life. His father was a well-respected drug dealer in the East Atlanta area. He spent most of his life in and out of jail. I didn't want that for Marcus, but he idolized his dad and continued in his footsteps. His father died in prison from cancer and when that happened, Marcus went crazy. It's as if he blamed me because I wouldn't allow his father to come back after his third jail stint. I'd personally dealt with that life long enough and I had other children to protect. Our relationship had been strained for that reason; he felt as if I had abandoned his father when he needed me most."

It's always interesting to hear the other side of the story, as Marcus would only say his mom treated him like an outcast. We continued our conversation about the arrangements upon release of the body. Luckily she'd already made phone calls and arranged for the mortuary in Atlanta to handle his body. I gave a sigh of relief that I wouldn't be tasked to deal with that aspect.

"Last time I talked to Marcus, he told me he had a son," she said.

"Yes, his name is Noah Tyree."

"I love the name. I can't wait to meet him; when he told me about him, I told him I wanted to visit."

It delighted me that she took an interest in getting to know Noah. We continued to talk about Marcus and I told her that once I received an update from the medical examiner I would let her know.

I spent many nights thinking and wondering how my life could be at this point. I'd always feared for Marcus's life; each time he went to jail, I felt like that was the best place for him. Each time he got out, I prayed that his jail time gave him the eye-opener to change his life. It never happened. I hoped him realizing he was about to become a father would provoke the long overdue change. Eventually, I came to the realization that the street life was all he knew and he found comfort in the grind. He idolized his father and wanted that same respect; a respect he may have never received on a regular job.

I had nothing to stay in Charlotte for and decided to move back to Atlanta. With everything going on, I'd already quit my job, so my plan was to leave as soon as Marcus's body was released.

I'd put Noah down for a nap as Rachelle and I sat in the living room drinking glasses of wine.

"So what's next?" she asked.

I ran my fingers through my unruly hair. "I can't stay here. I'm moving back to Atlanta."

"I couldn't agree with you more. You and Noah are more than welcome to stay with me and the kids until you get on your feet. I told you that before you moved your ass up here."

I huffed. "Sometimes you've got to find your own way."

She hissed. "Put your pride to the side and do what's best for your son. Now that you've made contact with Sharon, Noah now has family that he can get acquainted with. You don't have to do this alone, Tia."

"I know, Rachelle, and you're right. I appreciate you being such a good friend to me. I accept your offer, but I promise you, it won't be long term."

She jumped out of her chair and came over to the couch to give me a hug.

"I know you won't wear out your welcome. Besides, the girls might be down each other's throats so much sharing a room, you'll want to move sooner," she said, laughing.

With a plan of action in place, we assembled boxes and started packing. While the circumstances weren't the best, I prayed that this would be the start of something positive in my life.

Two days later, as we packed, I thought about Marcus and how much I missed him. I'd been notified that his body would be released tomorrow. The thought of going to the medical examiner's office and seeing Marcus's lifeless body made me emotional. We'd been through a lot and while I hated his lifestyle and the fact he wasn't being the father he had the potential to be, I still loved him. My heart cried for Noah not having an opportunity to grow up with him. I felt like sons needed their fathers, and I prayed for my strength to fulfill both roles as best I could. I'd gone through so much within my own childhood that I didn't want Noah to ever experience such hardship.

Rachelle was yapping away on her phone as she packed when someone knocked on my front door. Since Marcus's death, I'd become leery of everybody in the complex and hoped that whomever was involved wouldn't come back to harm Noah and me in an act of revenge .

I looked out the peephole and saw a lady turned sideways looking down the stairs.

"Who is it?" I yelled through the door.

"Sharon Michaels."

I'd called her right after I gotten the call about his body being released, but she hadn't mentioned driving up. I unlocked the three locks and opened the door as she smiled back at me.

Sharon was a light-skinned woman; about 5'6" in height, with a slender build and shoulder-length honey-blond hair. The bags under her eyes reflected lack of sleep and mourning.

"Please come in," I said.

We embraced as she walked in.

"I'm sorry I didn't call to let you know I was coming. I wanted to make sure I was here first thing in the morning so we could go to the office together. That's my son, you shouldn't have to do that alone," she said. "It's been so stressful being at home;

the drive here with the scenery and peace alone gave me time to clear my head a bit."

"I can understand. Does anyone know you're here?"

She chuckled. "After I crossed the state line, I figured I'd best let someone know where I am. So I called my daughter Kima, my oldest, and told her to let my son Hunter know as well."

I knew Marcus had other siblings, but he never mentioned anything about them. That's one thing we both shared in common; we never talked much about our families.

"Well, glad you found me without complication," I said, smiling.

Rachelle walked in with Noah as he'd just awakened from his nap. I could see a big smile on Sharon's face.

"Rachelle, this is Marcus's mom, Sharon. Sharon, this is my best friend Rachelle."

They exchange greetings as Rachelle handed Noah to me. She took my car keys to run to the store.

Noah with eager eyes stared at Sharon as she spoke to him.

"You are absolutely adorable. I swear he looks like Marcus as a kid," she said. She reached out for him as Noah willingly went to her.

As tears formed in her eyes, I excused myself to give them some alone time together. I didn't know whom I hurt for more, Noah or Sharon.

Sharon stayed over for hours playing with Noah. It was getting late and I didn't know whether she expected to stay at my place.

"Sharon, would you like to stay here for the night?"

"Oh no, honey, I've imposed enough. I'm going to go check in a hotel I saw near the freeway."

"I can at least call and make a reservation for you. I would hate for you to go there and there's no vacancy."

"I would appreciate that," she said with a smile.

I grabbed my laptop from the bedroom to look up the hotel.

"Ryan told me you're moving back to Atlanta," she said.

"Yes, hopefully I can do everything before the services. This place is a bad memory."

She nodded her head as she looked at Noah.

"Would you mind if I took Noah back with me? At least it'll give you the opportunity to move without having him in the way. Plus it'll give us time to bond with him."

While I appreciated the offer and understood the logic, I couldn't wholeheartedly say I was comfortable with that.

"The idea makes sense, but let me think about it. I don't know how he'll react considering he's never spent the night with anyone."

I found a nicer hotel close by and let her know I'd reserved a room for her.

She stood up as Noah laid his head on her shoulder. "I'll be here tomorrow around noon."

She gave Noah a kiss and handed him over to me. She left as Rachelle walked back in.

"Geez, I thought you'd gone back to the ATL."

She chuckled. "After I left Target, I stopped to get gas and this dude started talking to me. Girl, body-wise he was a ten, but when he opened his mouth—ratchet. You know I love me a thug, but that gold-all-in-my-mouth look is not what's up. Anyway, how did things go with Ms. Sharon?"

"She seems nice and she absolutely adores Noah. She wants to take him back with her so I can get things moved."

"That's great, girl. See, that's what I'm talking about. That lady is going to be your ticket for some free daycare."

"I told her I'll think about it."

She bucked her eyes. "You'll think about it? Do you think this lady is going to run off with your baby? Come on, Tia, you're being a bit overprotective."

"Damn right, I'm overprotective. I've met her casually twice before and years later, I'm meeting her formally—I don't know this lady. I've never been to her house; don't know where she lives; and you expect me to freely hand over my son just because she's his grandmother."

"OK, OK, OK, I get your point. I guess I'm a bad parent then. But I hope you'll get to know her so she can spend time with him. Hell, that's a break for you. Anywho, you have any idea what you're going to do job-wise?"

I plopped down on the couch and leaned my head back. "I have no idea. The job market sucks right now."

She sat down beside me with a big smile on her face. "Well you know I got connections."

I've never been too keen on Rachelle's choice of people to connect with. Rachelle had a hustler's mentality, but not in an illegal sense. She'd done everything from selling hair to bartending to stripping. I didn't look down on her because she did what she felt she had to do to provide for her kids, but that hustling life wasn't for me.

I gave a smirk. "Connections in what, Rachelle? If it's not an office job, I'm not interested."

"Look, I know people that are grinding being their own boss and not sitting up in somebody else's company making them rich. Now I understand you got a degree, but you also have responsibilities. I'm not saying you can't find anything, but if you need something in the meantime, I got you."

"OK, so what's the job?"

"I work at an exclusive club. I bartend there, but it's more of a lounge with a variety of adult activities; only people with money get in."

"Adult activities? So what exactly would I be expected to do?" I asked with a raised eyebrow.

She threw up her hands. "See, you already thinking the worst; be open-minded, please. You're a grown woman, Tia, no one will force you to do anything. I can get you a hosting position. You'll be amazed what a smile and good attitude will do for you."

"OK, so where's this club?"

"I can't tell you that, it's a secret club for a reason. Listen, the hostess job is simply dealing with ensuring our members receive service to their liking. You have the shape, personality, and people skills to do it or else I wouldn't have mentioned it."

I definitely needed a job but I wasn't sure if this would be something I'd be comfortable doing. I'd never done anything remotely close to hosting and although my people skills were good, my patience level was on the decline these days.

"And how much does this position pay?"

"It varies per position, but if I'm not mistaken it's like $80 a night plus tips. When I bartend, I work Thursday through Sunday for five hours. We can start out on the same schedule if that'll make you comfortable."

I did the math in my head. "That's not a lot of money, especially if it means me stepping out of my comfort zone."

Rachelle shook her head. "It's more than your ass is getting waiting on a monthly check. At the club you're paid weekly and make your money off tips."

"I didn't mean to come off like that. I know I'm going to need to do something, and with tips, I'm sure I can pull in some money with that. Have you ever had any bad experiences there?"

"Not a one. Security is top notch and hood rats are not allowed. Our members are mainly politicians, corporate executives, and business owners. If anything, I've gotten some good opportunities presented to me," she said with a smirk.

I wouldn't say Rachelle was a gold digger because she worked hard for what she had, but she wasn't one to turn down any offerings either.

"Well I appreciate the offer; it's something I'll need to think on. Tomorrow is going to be a long day, so I'm going to call it a night."

"Since Sharon is here, I think I'll stay back tomorrow, watch Noah, and help you pack. Ryan said he would come up with two of his boys to help you move," said Rachelle.

Ryan was once heavily involved in the streets as well, but I always respected the fact that as a family man he never brought his dealings to his doorstep. When he changed his life and got an honest job, I prayed it would rub off on Marcus. I used to tell Ryan to talk to him about getting out of the game. He would tell me, '"Every man gotta find their own path. When a man is ready to change, he'll do it without anybody riding their back about it." I understood what he meant.

I said goodnight to Rachelle and headed to my room. I could hear Noah snoring from his crib as I tiptoed to the bed. I loved my baby so much and he truly gave me the motivation to keep pushing. I'd spent many nights in the dark crying over Marcus. Mainly out of guilt for being so angry with him during our last conversation. Now all I could do was think of all the things I wish I could've said to him. I never wanted things to end like this, especially without me letting him know how much I loved him.

I tossed and turned, trying my best to clear my mind and get a good night's sleep. I had so many things to sort out and work through, but my biggest challenge would be tomorrow. I prayed for my strength to get through this. Struggles have always been my way of life, but this struggle was no longer about me; I had to be strong and see it through for my son.

CHAPTER 6
KELLY

En route to my lunch with Mrs. Jackson, I gave myself a pep talk as I tried to control my nerves in anticipation of this awkward meeting. I pulled up to the restaurant and had the valet park my car. I walked in and spotted her waving me over as she sat at the bar. The restaurant was crowded due to Friday lunchtime as I zigzagged through waiters and patrons. When I approached her, she stood and we exchanged hugs.

"You look nice," she said with a smile.

"Thanks. You don't look like you've come from a field day. You look great yourself." I smiled back.

"Why thank you, dear. Our table should be ready shortly. Would you like a drink?"

Mrs. Jackson was a petite woman with a short gray bob and a nice set of dentures. She had a feistiness about her that came off as intimidating.

"Sure," I said.

As I awaited my drink, the hostess came over to inform us we were ready to be seated. Mrs. Jackson went to grab the table as I stayed back for my drink. I paid for my drink and headed over to the table.

"Gosh, this place is packed, but I love this area," she said, looking around.

"Normally I try to avoid this area during lunch, but it is rather nice." I smiled.

She intertwined her hands as she spoke. "So, I wanted to have lunch with you to get to know you a bit better. In an odd way, I still look at Derek as my son-in-law. He's done a tremendous job with the kids and that we're thankful for. Our grandkids are our remaining pieces of Karen—our pride and joy."

"I completely understand. Derek is a great father and I applaud him for all he's done in keeping his family together through such a tragic loss."

She gave me a side-eye stare as she took a sip of her drink. "Exactly how long have you known Derek?"

By her look, I assumed she perhaps felt Derek and I had something going on well before Karen's death.

"Well, I knew of Derek through his brother's wife, Jessica, who's also my best friend. We started dating a few months before I found out I was pregnant."

"How are the kids adjusting to you? I see Kaylee is quite fond of you," she said. There again, she gave the same side-eye stare while taking yet another sip of her drink.

I inhaled deeply and exhaled as I forced a smile.

"As to be expected, initially it started off a bit awkward. Kaylee warmed up to me in no time, while Kayden was polite but standoffish. Things are a lot better now; I don't smother them or put any expectations on them. I believe in letting things flow and allowing them to see me for who I am. When Kimora was born is when a breakthrough really came. Kayden has opened up more and, as you saw the other day, Kaylee is all over me."

"Yeah, it took me by surprise when she called you 'Mama,'" she said with a smirk.

I gave a half smile. "Let me just say that came as a shock. She's never addressed me as such nor have we ever asked her to call me that. I want to reassure you that as Derek and I progress within our relationship, I would never try to be a replacement for their mother."

She nodded her head as she took another sip. "I appreciate that. My daughter and I bumped heads a lot, but one thing I could never argue is how she cared for and raised her kids. She loved her babies. I don't need to tell you how important it is for those children to receive an abundance of love and attention after what they've gone through."

Thankfully the waiter came over to take our orders. I wasn't hungry at all; I was more interested in getting this lunch over and done with. Her side-eye stares were piercing, but I hadn't flinched or stumbled in my words yet. Once the waiter left the table, I felt it was now time for me to take charge of the conversation.

"Mrs. Jackson, I can see that Karen took great care of the kids and their environment. I in no way want to interrupt that. Let me assure you, those are great kids that deserve to be happy with all they've been through. I love Derek and I love them. They have a little sister now who they absolutely adore and I take great pride in watching them interact amongst each other and I want them to grow up and be just as close. Derek and I are progressing relationship-wise and my relationship with the kids has grown as well. I am confident that I can be that womanly figure in their lives, but I'm no replica of their mother. I can only give them love and be there as a co-parent to Derek. He's never once pawned his kids off on me; he's a hands-on father who does it all himself. So if you're checking to see if I'm a good woman, I am. Am I good enough for your grandkids? I've given them no reason to believe otherwise."

I smiled and took a sip of my drink. She stared back at me with a straight face, but after I stared right back at her with my smile, she lightened up.

She downed the rest of her drink. "Well I guess we are clear on that matter. So what is the next step with you and Derek? I see that spark in his eye," she said with a smirk.

I grinned. I didn't know if she knew that Derek had initially proposed.

"I think we have a good outlook up ahead," I said, blushing. "We're looking to buy a house together soon."

Her face went completely blank. "What?"

Oops. Obviously Derek hadn't shared his plans with them, but, hell, why would he need to?

"Ummm, we've discussed moving into a bigger house," I said with unease.

She frowned. "Interesting he hasn't mentioned this to us."

With a puzzled expression, I had to inquire on why it meant that much to her.

"Am I missing something? I mean the kids are getting older and, with Kimora, we need more space."

She leaned back in her chair. "Yes, you are missing something. My husband and I gifted that house to Derek and

Karen when they got married, but with stipulations. I would expect him to at least discuss this with us beforehand."

My head was starting to pound at this point now that things had taken a quick left. That would explain why he was hesitant on selling it. I was irked that Derek couldn't confide in me the real reason, which led me to think about what else he could be hiding.

By the time our food arrived, my hunger was nonexistent. I shifted my food around the plate, eating small portions. Whatever was on Mrs. Jackson's mind wasn't affecting her desire to eat as she took full advantage of her plate.

My cell phone rang, and when I looked down at the caller ID, it was just the person I needed to talk too. I excused myself from the table as I stepped outside.

"How's it going?" he said.

I wanted to blow up on his ass, but decided to remain calm. "It was going good, but now it's a bit awkward."

"Awkward? How's that?" Derek asked.

I sighed. "Well the conversation shifted to us getting serious by buying a house together and Mrs. Jackson's expression turned from pleasant to deer in headlights. Want to fill me in on why?"

He paused before responding. "I didn't think the conversation would be about us looking for a house. I hadn't told them about it yet."

"OK, so why would they need to know that?"

He sighed. "They technically bought the house—it was initially a foreclosure. When Karen and I married, they agreed to change over ownership to us. However, we have a written agreement about the sale of the house. That's why I can't sell it and thought to rent it out for the time being."

I shook my head and threw up my hand. "How could you even negotiate renting it if you hadn't even discussed it with them? Technically they partly own the house."

"Listen, I apologize for not filling you in on all the details, but it's not as complicated as it sounds."

"At what point was I going to be brought in the loop? Hell, we are going into purchasing a home, why wouldn't this be one of those important factors I needed to know?"

"I'm sorry things got brought up this way and you're right, I should've told you. Look, you're at lunch so we can talk about this more—"

I hung up the phone before he could finish. I took a deep breath as I walked back to the table. Mrs. Jackson was in the middle of taking care of the bill.

"Sorry about that," I said, taking a sip of my drink.

"Not a problem. Is everything OK?"

I nodded my head as I summoned the waiter for a to-go box. I could feel her piercing eyes on me. I didn't have anything else to talk about; all I wanted to do was leave. As I bagged up my food, I looked up and smiled at her.

"Thanks so much for lunch," she said.

"Not a problem. Sorry I have to rush off, but I've got to head back to the office. Hopefully I'll get to see you guys before you leave. Do you need a ride back to the hotel?"

She shook her head. "No, Tim should be on his way back here."

She stood up as we exchanged hugs. I made a beeline to the front door and handed the valet attendant my ticket. I waited in the long line as the two attendants on duty worked feverishly to bring the cars around.

Out of the corner of my eye, I caught a glimpse of a familiar face. She was going through the opposite entrance, but I spotted her well—it was Gigi. I was going to walk over and speak when I saw another familiar face walk in steps behind her. My mouth flew open seeing John. I wanted to shock them both by saying hello, but thought against it.

As the attendant brought my car around, I gave him his tip and smashed out the parking lot. What the hell were they doing together?

My cell phone rang and I thought maybe Gigi had spotted me too.

"Hello," I answered.

"Is there a reason you hung up on me like that?"

"Derek, I was pissed that you set me up for such an awkward conversation. You should've told me; therefore, I never would've brought it up."

"I'm sorry about it. It's no big deal though; I'll talk to them this weekend."

A whole week passed and I'd not talked to Gigi or seen her at the gym. I purposely went back to the gym where I had run into John to see if I would find them together; but no such luck. I wondered how long she'd keep me in the dark about her and John going out on a date. As much as I wanted to call her and ask what she'd been up to, I figured I'd just wait on her move.

Derek and I hadn't talked much due to his hectic work schedule. I had more questions regarding the house situation, but figured we needed a face-to-face conversation versus talking on the phone. With him being busy with the kids and their grandparents last weekend, I allowed them the opportunity to engage in their activities without my presence.

I'd given a lot of thought over the past week about moving with Derek. Since Kimora had turned into a crawling diva, my house wasn't the safest with all the stairs. My house wasn't by any means kid-friendly and it unnerved me any time Kimora got down to crawl or the kids came over.

Kimora was spending the weekend with my parents, while I did some house shopping with Derek. I couldn't deny the excitement of looking at new homes as I'd found two I thought would be a perfect fit for our blended family.

Derek was on his way over when my phone rang. It was Casey.

"Casey," I screamed. "How the hell are you, stranger?"

"Oh please, you act like it's been weeks since you last heard from me. I'm doing good. What's going on with you?"

"I'm heading out to do some house hunting with Derek."

She gasped. "You guys are finally moving in together. That's great."

"What's so great about it if there's no wedding date?" I said with irritation.

"Kells, you can't be serious. To get in debt with a house is a major commitment that you don't just make with anyone. You know damn well the man wants to marry you. With all you two have been through, you should see without a shadow of doubt that he loves you and wants more. Why are you making this difficult?"

Leave it to Casey to always flip the script on me.

"It's not being difficult, Case; it's about what I want."

She chuckled. "Look you have a good man by your side and you know that. Don't push him away with your attitude. You don't have him wrapped around your fingers like you do your parents. He wants to put your ass in a house; accept it or let him move on. What the hell is wrong with you?"

"Obviously you don't understand my point of view. Getting a house jointly is a huge step, a major responsibility. Derek has two kids, our household is now combined; they are now my responsibility. With all that, why can't I share the same last name as everybody else in the household? I'm sorry that seems petty to you, but I don't see anything wrong with my logic."

Casey sighed. "Well, why are you building false hope by going house hunting with this man?"

"Because I do want the house," I pleaded. "I know I'm spoiled, Case, but damn it, I think there's any easy solution. He said he didn't want to marry right now. Why the hell not?"

"He's dealing with what matters the most right now. Just trust the man on this, OK. You can't control everything. He knows that you don't feel comfortable being in his current home, so what's wrong with starting a new chapter, with a new home first?"

I sighed. "OK, you've made your point. How's Josie?" I said, getting off topic.

"She's OK. She went to see her mom in LA for the weekend."

"I'm going to visit you guys at some point. I've never been to Houston. How is it out there?"

"Hot as hell!! You think Atlanta heat is bad, girl, I'm ready to cut off my damn hair. But overall it's good. Josie is still looking for work, but we're good."

Casey's job got transferred to Houston, Texas, six months ago. She didn't want to leave Atlanta, but after she was promoted and got an increase, she felt it was better than being unemployed. I missed my friend, but I was happy for her advancement as well as her relationship with Josie.

I heard the front door open as I peeked out my bedroom window to see Derek's car in the driveway. I ended my phone call with Casey as Derek entered my room.

"Hey, babe," I said.

"Hey," he said with a puzzled look.

"OK, what's wrong?"

He sat down on the chaise by the bed. "I need to know if we are in this together. I don't want my hopes up for nothing since you're on the fence with the idea."

"I don't doubt what we have, Derek; bottom line is, I'm ready for marriage. I've had a reality check and I realize that I must allow you to be the man and trust in your way of doing things. It's not easy, but the importance of getting a bigger space for our kids and a place where they can grow up together is what matters."

He bucked his eyes as if he couldn't believe what I'd said.

"Wow, I wasn't expecting such an easy compromise," he said with a smirk. "But I thank you for allowing me the opportunity to go about things my way. Again I apologize for last Friday with Mrs. Jackson. I've talked to them both about my plans."

"I don't understand why they are so involved if it was a gift."

"They sold two homes they had here before moving to North Carolina. Our house was a foreclosure so they got it for cheap. However, they gifted to us with a stipulation; if we ever sold the house, we would give them half of the sale. What they didn't know is we took a second mortgage out for remodeling."

"So that's why you can't sell?"

"Yes. I could pay most of the loan off, but then it would totally screw up my plans with the new house."

"Is the sister interested in renting it?"

He shrugs. "I mentioned it to her and she seemed rather hesitant, so I'm not sure."

"Are you sure moving forward with this house is a good idea?"

I didn't need the financial strain of his current house haunting us and spilling over into my finances.

"We'll be fine. Let's get going," he said, standing up.

We left the house. As we were on the way to the first house for viewing, my cell phone rang—it was Gigi. I thought about hitting the "decline" button and calling her back later, but I was anxious to hear what she had to say.

I answered the phone and tried to sound as upbeat as possible.

"Hey, girl, what's up?"

"I wanted to see if we could meet up later for some drinks. Girl, I've had a workweek from hell and could use an escape."

"Around what time? I'm handling some business right now."

"Let's say around eight-ish. I'll call you before then."

I hung up the phone. Maybe tonight I would get the truth from her. While our friendship didn't run deep, I considered her to be someone I could trust. If she could betray me by dating one of my ex-factors, then who knew what else she was capable of doing.

CHAPTER 7
JANEN

As I picked up my luggage from baggage claim, my cell phone rang. Perfect timing! I struggled as I rushed to the nearby bench to find my phone before it stopped ringing. I pull it out of my purse and frantically answered.

"Have you gotten your luggage yet?" she said before I could even say hello.

"Yes. I was about to call you once I got outside."

"I'm circling back around. I should be there in ten minutes, so stand outside."

I smiled, thankful that I didn't have to wait for my ride. Normally on visits I would rent a car so as not to inconvenience anyone and to have the freedom to go as I pleased. However, Jessica insisted that I use her car during my visit to cut down on expenses. She'd invited me to stay at her house, and Mom extended an invitation as well, but I opted to stay at a hotel. I'd not only planned on spending time with Mom and helping Jess on her photo shoot, but I wanted to start the search for my biological mother.

My dad provided me with her name and where she was last living, but he was certain she probably didn't live there anymore. He gave me the name of an old neighbor from the apartments we used to live in who still lived in that area, so I was determined to see if I could find her to get further information.

As Jess pulled up in her new hunter-green Range Rover, we both beamed smiles at each other. She put the truck in park and climbed out. We ran to hug each other like we were Celie and Nettie from *The Color Purple*.

"Sis, you look great," she said, pulling back to give me a look over.

I shooed her off. "Girl, please! It doesn't even look like you've had a baby."

She helped me with my bags as we loaded them into the back of the truck. We got in and I was met by the new car smell and fresh leather.

I looked around in the backseat. "This is nice."

"Thanks, girl. I had to beg Darnell for it. So how was the flight?"

"It was good," I said as I texted Tony to let him know I'd arrived.

"So what's on your agenda besides hooking us up for the shoot?"

I looked out the window wondering if this was a good time to let her know my intentions. I figured I might as well get her insight before letting Mom know.

"Well I've been dealing with this thought for months and I've talked to both Tony and Dad about it," I said with hesitation.

Jess looked over at me as we pulled up at a traffic light. "Is everything OK?"

I nodded my head. "Everything is fine; no worries. I'm going to search for my biological mother. I wanted to talk to Mom first, but I have a few leads that I plan on looking into while I'm here."

Jess had a tense expression as she directed her attention back to the road as the light changed. There was silence between us.

"I understand why you would want to do it, Janen. I thought it would've happened sooner, to be honest."

I was happy for once someone understood how important this was for me.

"With my relationship being as it was with Mom at the time, I didn't want her to think I was doing it out of retaliation. I'm at a happy place in my life and I need closure on this. I need to know who she is; who my siblings are. I have a lot of open-ended questions that only she can answer."

Jess grabbed my hand. "I understand, Janen; I really do. You have my support, and if you need anything, let me know. I'm really interested in what Mom has to say about all this."

"Dad made me feel like doing so would hurt her by opening old wounds. Meeting Naomi is not going to change how I feel about the only woman I've ever known as my mother."

Jess gave me a smile. "I would hope not. Regardless of how others may feel about it, you're doing what's best for you. "

I truly appreciated my sister for her understanding and willingness to help me. One thing I could be thankful for was that Jess had always been supportive of my every effort, even when I felt it wasn't deserved. I'd watched her go through situations in her own life and I didn't always give her the support she needed.

We pulled up to her house and I was instantly excited about seeing my niece. We walked in to Tianna's cries from the den as Jess rushed in to see what was going on. Darnell was rocking her in the rocking chair with a look of defeat and exhaustion.

"Perfect timing," he said as he stood to hand off Tianna to Jess. "I've fed and changed her and she just continues to be a fuss box."

Jess winked at him. "You don't have that motherly touch," she said as she bounced Tianna.

Darnell came over to give me a hug. "Hey, J. How are you doing?"

"I'm doing good compared to you," I said with a chuckle.

He shook his head. "These two ladies definitely keep me on my toes. How's Tony holding up down there?"

"He's doing great. He'll be up here next month and told me to tell you to have your golf clubs ready."

"Oh definitely. He loves getting beat and I don't mind doing it." He grinned. "Excuse me, ladies, I have a few business matters to take care of."

Darnell left the room. Tianna was settled down and looking around the room.

"OK, you've calmed her down. My turn," I said, extending my hands.

Jess brought her over to me. Tianna instantly smiled at me, which warmed my heart. She was such a doll with her head full of jet-black curls. She reminded me of Jess when she was a baby.

I sat on the couch and Jess sat across from me.

"What leads are you checking on first?" she asked.

"I'm going to see if I can look up the address for their old neighbor. Dad said she knew everybody's business, so she might be resourceful."

"Are you looking into the siblings as well?"

"Yes, but he couldn't recall their names."

"I was going to say social media is big, so we could start there."

"Trust me, I've already been on Facebook, Myspace, Instagram—you name it, I've been there. I even Googled her name and found out she'd been arrested twice, once for prostitution and the other for possession."

"What's her name? Maybe I can tap into some of my sources and see what they can come up with."

"Her name is Naomi Lorita Carver. I'm guessing she should be in her early to mid-sixties."

I looked down to see Tianna's eyes slowly closing. I motioned my head for Jess to come take her. After she left the room, I called Tony.

"Hey, how's it going?" I asked.

"Trying to work on this new campaign and it's driving me nuts. How's the fam?"

"Everyone is good. I so love the baby; she's a doll."

"Well, get all the practice you can, that's next on our agenda." He chuckled.

I smiled. "I like the bedroom practice better."

"Awww, see, that's not fair. Six days is a long time for a man to be horny."

"OK, switching topics," I said. "What's your plan for the weekend?"

"This was going to be a conversation for when you got back, but I might as well give you a heads-up. Carrie is moving here."

I deeply exhaled. Just to hear her name pissed me off, but knowing she was going to be residing in the same city as us sent me over the edge.

"What?" I said loudly. "Does she have a job offer or something?"

"The guy she came down with a few weeks ago is part owner of a transportation company and they're doing some reorganization, so he wants her to be a part of that. I know you're not jumping for joy, but I would hope that you two can find a way to get to know each other better."

My mind wasn't set on dealing with Carrie or this news right now. It seemed as if everywhere Tony went she followed suit. Her behavior was so unnerving to me, at one point I'd asked Tony if she'd ever come on to him. He denied it, but it was not a farfetched thought considering they were not biologically related. Tony had another call coming through he needed to answer and we ended our conversation.

Jess came back in the den. "Are you going to Mom's today or tomorrow?"

I looked at my watch. "It's only 4:30. I might as well go ahead and get this discussion over with, so I guess I'll head on over there."

"Well I was over there yesterday, so I'll let you have your time with her. Here are the keys to the car. "

We walked outside and transferred my luggage to the car. On the way to Mom's house, I thought about my plan of action. I didn't know how much I could accomplish within the few days I was here, but I was hoping it would be worthwhile.

I wondered if looking at her I would see myself. I'd always thought I looked more like my dad, but without knowing the other side, it was hard to say for sure. I wanted to know her story—beyond why she abandoned me, but what her younger life was like. Initially when I was told about my birth mother, I hated her. I think the hatred I felt for her was what I inflicted on Mom; I needed an outlet and she fit the description. In meeting her, I prayed that I could suppress those feelings because, as I got older, I realized I did well with my life without her. If she couldn't afford to take care of me, who knew the hardships I would've endured.

I pulled up to the house. Mom and Mr. Frank had purchased the house two months after they'd married. It was newly built with a brick front and gray siding. Mom had put her flower touches to the front yard, giving it a homey appeal. She was always into her gardening and making sure the house was spic and span. As I gathered my purse and exited the car, I could see Diva barking through the glass front door. Mom appeared at the door to let me in. Diva bombarded me before I could step foot inside.

I rubbed her head as she jumped on my legs. "OK, calm down; nice to see you too," I said as I finally made my way into the house.

I hugged my mom, who smelled of Dolce & Gabbana, her favorite fragrance. I looked at her hair and gasped.

"You've finally done the unthinkable and cut it."

She closed the front door. "When you get up in age, you'll understand." She smiled. "How was your flight and why didn't my son-in-law come with you?"

"My flight was good and Tony is busy with work amongst other things," I said, rolling my eyes.

"Oh lawd—that don't sound good," she said as we entered the kitchen.

"Carrie is moving down there. You know I'm not a fan."

"Just when you thought you'd gotten rid of her," she said with a smile.

As I sat at the kitchen island watching my mom cut up greens, I start fidgeting with my fingers. She caught me doing so and put down the knife.

"OK, so what's going on with you?" she said with her hands on her hips.

I pulled out the bar stool next to me and tapped the seat. She dried her hands and sat on the stool.

I exhaled as I looked off in the opposite direction. I turned towards her as she gave me a comforting smile.

"I've been doing a lot of thinking lately and I realize that I need closure in a part of my life that's unfinished," I said, taking a deep breath. "I need to find my biological mother."

Her smiling eyes faded slowly into a blank stare.

I grabbed her hand. "This is not meant to hurt you or Dad, but I need to do this for me. I wanted to talk this over with you beforehand."

She looked away. "If it's what you need to do, I won't stand in your way, but I don't see any good in doing so."

"She can't cause me any more pain than what I've already felt. I want to meet her and ask her questions that only she can answer. I don't know how willing she's going to be to even talk to me, but I want to at least try."

She turned back towards me with tears in her eyes and nodded her head. "Do what's best for you, baby. I appreciate you letting me know, but just know that the Rita I knew back then is totally different than today."

"What does that mean? Have you seen her?"

She nodded. "I was volunteering at the shelter about a month ago and I saw her in the serving line. When she saw me approaching her, she quickly got out of line and left. I searched for her and couldn't find her after that."

"Why didn't you mention that to me?" I said with a frown.

"Why would I? If I'd held a conversation with her, then maybe, but I didn't see the need. I didn't know what your feelings were about her until now."

"I don't hate her anymore. Do you think she goes to that shelter often?"

She shook her head. "I really don't know. I'd only volunteered twice and that was the first time I saw her. I'm sure after she saw me she probably didn't go back in fear she'd see me again."

"I don't understand the reason for running."

"It's a lot of people that run all their lives out of guilt. At some point you got to stop running and face the truth."

We talked more about my plans and Mom offered to come along with me to find her. I declined the offer as I didn't think it would help if Rita had already run away from seeing her. I'd mentally mapped out my plans and hoped things would go accordingly. With Jessica and her resources, I felt confident that I would make a connection. What all this would mean once the pieces of the puzzle were put together was unknown, but I could only hope for the best.

CHAPTER 8
DEREK

Two weeks ago Kelly took the initiative of finding homes for us to look at. Since then, she'd not mentioned it and I could tell she tried her best to avoid the topic. I didn't want to be pushy about it, but it bothered me. I knew what she wanted and, unfortunately for her, I was not caving in to her demands. With or without her, I would move forward in buying a home because my kids deserved it and they'd grown excited over us moving somewhere new.

This week I had relied on my sister, Denise, to pick up the kids and keep them until Kelly or I got off work, due to my annual audit at work. I hated this time of year and didn't enjoy not being able to pick up my kids. I'd finished my last report and leaned back in my chair to relax my mind. There was a knock on the door. I looked up and it was Lacey.

"Mind if I come in? You look like you could use a break," she said with a smile.

I didn't bother with an excuse to blow her off, so I extended my hand for her to enter.

She sat in the chair in front of my desk. "The audit has you stressed out, huh."

I looked around at all the papers and binders on my desk. "Yeah, looks that way," I said, interlocking my fingers. "Lacey, what's up? Why are you here so late?"

She shrugged. "The life of a single girl—nobody to go home to so why not stay and get in some overtime."

"What brings you by?"

She smirked. "I miss you and wanted to see your handsome face."

I sighed and shook my head. "I prefer we keep things strictly professional here at work."

"It's after hours and there's only a handful of us here. I want you, Derek," she said seductively.

As her tongue glazed over her freshly applied lip gloss, I could feel my penis doing a happy dance. Her aggression turned me on considering I'd always been the aggressor in past relationships and even now with Kelly. However, we were both in the workplace and I'd already complicated things and didn't want to make things worse.

"Lacey, please stop making things complicated. This isn't the place for all of that."

"My apologies and you're right, this isn't the place. How about my place?"

While Lacey lived close by the office, I had to pick up the kids. I glanced at the clock, 7:30.

I fidgeted with paperwork on my desk. "Lacey, no, I can't do this."

There was a knock on the partially closed door. I looked up and it was Carlton.

"Hey, Carl. Didn't think you would still be here at this hour."

Carlton glanced from Lacey to me. "Yeah, had some last minute things to wrap up before heading out and I saw your light was still on. Hi, Lacey," he said with a smile.

Lacey got up and smiled at Carlton as she excused herself but not without first winking her eye at me. Carlton slowly closed the door as he watched her walk down the hall.

"I see she has teeth sunk into you," he said, sitting in the chair.

I palmed the sides of my head. "Man, she's so damn persistent."

Carlton shook his head. "Something about these young ladies today that keeps us old men on our toes."

I shook my head. "You can keep that 'old' word to yourself. I'm still young and vibrant, my man."

"Look, if you need me to have a talk with her, I will. I brought her in this company and I have no qualms about getting rid of her if need be."

"I'm not trying to make the girl jobless; I need to be more focused. I love Kelly and I don't need this shit biting me in the ass."

"I'm so glad Maria and I don't have these issues."

"Women like Maria are few and far. I could never see Kelly being the compromiser Maria is."

"Well you don't have the amount of time invested in the relationship like we do. Never say never," he said and winked.

"Any weekend plans?" I said, changing the subject.

"Let's see, golf tomorrow morning, lunch with Maria, and the evening all to myself. Why, you feel like getting out?"

"As much as I could use a 'man day out,' I've been neglecting my kids and woman all week, so I'll take a rain check."

Carlton and I gave each other a fist bump as he got up to leave. I packed up my things and headed for the parking lot. I called Kelly and she was heading from the gym to get Kimora. I let her know I was leaving work and would stop by Denise's to get Kaylee and Kayden.

My other line beeped and I ended the call with Kelly. I clicked over.

"Have you left the office?" she said.

"Yes. Why what's up?" I asked as if I didn't already know.

"Stop by my place for a minute."

"Lacey, I need to get my kids."

"Trust me, it won't take long. I'll even come out front," she said then quickly hung up the phone.

I banged my head on the seat rest as I fought with my lower region on whether I should go or not. As I pulled out the parking lot, I thought of all the reasons why I shouldn't, but as I got closer to her apartment complex, temptation got the best of me.

I pulled into her gated complex and parked at the clubhouse. I could see her walking toward my car.

She climbed in. "Park over there," she said, pointing to a dark area on the opposite side of the lot.

I obliged as she sat in silence. By the time I put the car in park, she was all over me, passionately kissing me. As she straddled me I could feel that she didn't have on any underwear under her dress. She unzipped my pants and tried to put my penis inside her.

Sexually, I was turned on but not enough to go unprotected. I pushed her hands forcefully.

"No, I'm not doing this without a condom."

She sat over on the passenger side and looked at me angrily. She reached over and continued her quest as she stroked my penis.

She opened her mouth and wrapped her tongue around it. I moaned as she bobbed her head. This girl had killer skills with her mouth. She sucked and gripped it tightly with her hand, causing me to moan even louder. I ran my fingers through her short-cropped hair and palmed her head. She massaged my balls and moaned as she looked at me while she suckled on the head. I could feel the pre-cum as it slowly flowed out. The way she worked her hands up and down my shaft; feeling her tongue creating a sensation inside of me, and the suction of her mouth; I could no longer stop the inevitable. I closed my eyes tightly as I applied pressure on her head and grinded until I exploded in pleasure. The release was so powerful it felt like electrical shocks were passing through my body. Every ounce of energy I once had left with my release.

I waited to see if she would take it like a champ and swallow. That thought was quickly eliminated as she opened the passenger side door to spit.

"We can't always have the fireworks we want, now can we," she said as she wiped her mouth.

I grabbed a Wet Ones from my glove compartment and cleaned myself up before zipping my pants. She sat and stared at me as if there was something further to discuss. All I wanted her to do was exit my vehicle.

"Is there a reason you're staring at me like that?" I asked.

"It's not worth discussing," she said, exiting the car. "Have a good night, Derek."

I watched her walk back through the gate as I put my truck in reverse to head home.

I met Lacey through Carlton after he'd hired her at the company. I never knew their connection and didn't bother to ask until one day we went to lunch and he brought it up.

"You must think I'm banging Lacey," he said with a grin.

I threw up my hands. "It's not my business; I'm not questioning it."

"I know there's some gossip going around about us being more than acquaintances, but it's not true. Lacey used to be Maria's assistant."

Even though I'd known Carlton for years as a family friend, he was somewhat of a mystery to me. He was closer to Darnell's age, but since he'd started with the company, he and I hung out more. I didn't like to pry if information wasn't freely given and he never gave up too much initially.

Maria and Carlton dated for nearly ten years and married five years ago. Maria, a Columbiana bombshell, didn't seem to age even though she was six years older than Carlton. They didn't have children, and I'd always wondered if it was by choice until Carlton revealed Maria had reproductive issues.

As we hung out more, he began to open up more about his relationship. She'd gone through several health challenges and even went for treatment for two months overseas. I never inquired on what her ailments were nor did he elaborate. I figured it had to be rather serious for her to leave the country.

Their marriage wasn't normal by far, but Carlton said it was what made their marriage work so well. We'd gone out a few times and seeing him in action was always a bit surreal. While he did his thing, his wife was his number one and he made sure above all to take care of home.

I pulled up to Denise's house to get the kids. Kaylee was already asleep, meaning she would be grumpy when she got home to prepare for bed. Kayden and I talked on the way home about his excitement in moving and asked when we were going house hunting again. While I'd seen a few houses I wanted to check out, work totally consumed me so that I couldn't, but Sunday I would take the kids and we would go. I needed to get some clarification from Kelly on her intentions and decided to call her once I got home.

After getting the kids and me prepared for bed, we all gathered for our nightly prayer. Being able to do this at night with them made me feel as though Karen was right in our circle holding our hands.

I put them to bed and slightly closed my door to call Kelly.

She answered on the first ring. "Hey, I was just about to call you."

"So you were thinking about me as much as I was you," I said, blushing.

"Always. I know this week is busy for you at work, but I miss you. I hope you don't have to work tomorrow."

"Nope. Tomorrow is my family day, so I'll pick you and Kimora up and we'll all hang out. Listen, the kids have been on me about this house. You've not mentioned anything about house hunting since we visited that property two weeks ago. What's the deal?"

She sighed. "I told you we can move forward. I'm working some things out on my end. I don't want to sell my townhouse because I know I'm not going to get nearly the return as what I've invested in it."

"So we're going to have three properties to maintain, huh?" I hoped my voice didn't give away my disappointment.

"It looks that way unless you have a better option."

Yeah, just sell it, I thought to myself. "Why don't you try getting it appraised and putting it on the market just to see if it stirs any interest?"

She smacked her lips. "Derek, I'm not trying to pay two mortgages until I get a buyer. Now, if I get a flexible tenant then maybe I can see that happening."

My idea of a conversation was to ensure she was still onboard and not cause an argument. I decided to not further question the situation.

"OK, well Sunday I'm taking the kids to check out two properties I've found. I would definitely like for you to go."

"Not a problem."

We talked more before ending our conversation. I cut out the lamp on my nightstand and tried to get some sleep. My mind was in motion, which meant sleep wouldn't be coming easily. I thought back to my evening with Lacey; I needed to kill that situation quickly. Initially I didn't see her as a threat, but her last few tactics had been rather bold. I couldn't risk Darnell finding out I was still involved with her nor did I need for it to affect my relationship with Kelly. I rubbed my head in frustration. Trouble was so easy to get into, yet so hard to get out of.

CHAPTER 9
LA'TIA

Since returning to Atlanta, I'd experienced mixed emotions about the city from which I'd escaped. It was a blessing to have people like Rachelle and now Sharon in my corner helping me get back on my feet. However, when you're used to being independent, being dependent on someone else is an undesirable feeling.

Marcus's funeral last week turned out to be a beautiful service of family and friends that spoke of fond memories of him. Despite his faults, he indeed was a good person. Everyone that took notice of Noah commented on how much he looked like Marcus.

Through the ordeal of funeral planning, Sharon proved to be a source of strength to everyone. In meeting Marcus's siblings, Kima and Hunter, it became evident why Marcus felt like the outcast. They were both biracial, with piercing gray eyes. Their father was attended the funeral, but I couldn't make out his ethnicity other than him being white. Everyone that I came in contact with had a friendly demeanor and welcomed Noah and me with open arms.

At the burial, Sharon broke down and once again there wasn't a dry eye in sight. She screamed for her son and begged for his forgiveness. Noah looked around in a state of confusion as tears fell from his eyes and all I could do was comfort him and rock him in my arms. He was too young to understand now, but I vowed to always make sure he knew his father loved him.

After the funeral, Kima and I exchanged numbers. She seemed eager to build a relationship with her nephew. While she was friendly, it wasn't hard to tell she could be quite a handful.

Now with the funeral over, it was time for me to make a decision on the job Rachelle proposed. I needed something fast; moving totally depleted my funds. Sharon promised me that she would look out for Noah and planned on setting up an account for him with a portion of the remaining insurance money. While I could use that money now, I appreciated her looking out for his future. She even volunteered to keep Noah if I decided to take the job working nights.

I'd managed to get some free time since Kima asked to keep Noah. The chaos of my bedroom, from bags to boxes, needed to be organized and I planned on spending the day bringing order to my space. Rachelle knocked on the door.

"Come in."

"OK, it's a beautiful Saturday afternoon and we're both without kids, so let's make the most of the day," she said with her hands on her hips.

"Do you not see how messy this room is?" I said, giving my best Vanna White impersonation. "I have to get more organized before Noah comes back tomorrow."

"Look, you've been dealing with the funeral and getting settled here for the past two weeks. You need a break to relax and enjoy yourself. Now one of my customers blessed me with two vouchers for exclusive spa services at Chateau Elan and we are going," she said, pointing her finger between herself and me.

Just the thought of getting away for a few hours, especially getting pampered for free, sounded like music to my ears.

"I'm game for that," I said and smiled. "How did you manage to pull that off?"

"I have my ways." She winked. "I asked my boss if you can come get a sneak peek of the club tonight. You down?"

"I'm cool with that. I think it'll help me make a decision."

"OK. They'll have you sign a confidentiality agreement. They want to make sure you don't go running your mouth about who's there and what goes on. Very standard practice, even our customers have to sign one."

Geez, that's interesting, I thought to myself. I never even knew such clubs existed and couldn't deny my eagerness in checking it out.

I proceeded to find something to wear for our spa day. If I took the job at the club, it would only be until I could find something better. As grown women with kids, we definitely needed our own space and I didn't want a few months to turn into a year.

I slept most of the way and when I woke up, I smiled at the scenery of beautiful trees and vineyards. As we pulled into valet parking and the attendants opened our doors, we were greeted with smiles and pleasantries. Being able to walk into such an upscale place and be treated with the utmost customer service made me wish I had the money to experience this regularly. As we walked into the lobby, I looked around and took note of the people moving throughout. We were greeted by a waiter with a flute of champagne. Now, this is the good life, I thought to myself.

We spent over two hours getting pampered and thereafter wound down in the Jacuzzi. I needed this newness in my life; something out of the ordinary and finally the opportunity to relax and unwind. As I reclined back on the foam pillow provided on the edge of the Jacuzzi, I could see Rachelle smiling towards the window behind me.

"Who are you flirting with now?" I asked.

"I'm sure he's one of the attendants, but, hell, he kept looking at me so I'm giving him that 'you ain't ready' look." She laughed.

I chuckled. "Oh gosh, you are too much. If he got any sense, he will run while he can."

"Let me just say this. This smile and personality is what got us this five-star treatment we getting right now. The handful of people who know about me working at the club think it's all about sex and it's not. There are some power players that come to the club looking for someone to blow money on with a little conversation. I can do that all day and enjoy this lifestyle, which I can't afford on my own."

It all seemed so fascinating, but taking from different men was something I'd never done. After a while I felt like with all the giving, evidently they'd want more. I sure hoped Rachelle knew what she was doing.

We showered and got dressed so we could head back to the city to rest up before going to the club tonight. I grew nervous with the thought of such a mysterious place. My day was going well so far and I hoped that this night adventure wouldn't ruin it.

Once home, I immediately crashed, feeling much more relaxed than I did earlier. I thought I'd set my alarm before going to sleep, but was awakened by Rachelle.

"Here I am halfway dressed and you still asleep."

I rubbed my eyes. "I set my alarm and either I didn't hear it or it didn't go off. I'm getting up and I don't take nearly as long as you do anyway."

"Whatever." She grinned. "Remember to wear something sexy to show off that nice shape of yours."

Rachelle left the room as I sat on the edge of the bed mentally mapping out what to wear and in which box I could find it. Since giving birth to Noah, I'd fought hard to lose the baby weight by exercising at home. However, that wasn't going as planned since I still had a small kangaroo pouch. I hadn't been shopping in I don't know how long, so finding something sexy that I could actually fit was going to be a challenge.

I went through the unpacked boxes and found some shiny leggings and a long off-the-shoulder, half-sheer shirt. I didn't know if my fashions were up to date with the latest trends, but they would have to do. I put some mousse on my wet and wavy weave and a cute headband to push my hair back from my face. I wasn't into makeup, but decided to step outside the box by putting on some eyeliner and some red lip gloss. I put on my black and gold stilettos and gold jewelry. I gave myself a look over in the mirror, not bad. I changed out my purse and headed out the bedroom door, and met Rachelle in the hallway.

"Well damn," she said, looking me over. "You look sexy as hell. Damn, I might need to go change my outfit."

I flipped my hair and did a brief runway walk. It felt good to be complimented, even if it was an attempt to make me feel better about myself.

Rachelle burst into laughter. "Give a bitch a compliment and she thinks she's runway ready. But really, you look good; I feel underdressed."

"Thanks. There's nothing wrong with what you have on. I honestly didn't think my clothes would fit or be in style. You know I haven't been out in nearly two years."

She shooed me with her hand. "Trust me, your outfit is fitting in all the right places and you'll find that out tonight." She winked.

All of a sudden, nerves rushed to my stomach, making me feel as if I needed to go to the bathroom. It had been so long since I'd been in the nightlife. Hopefully I wouldn't come off as being too uptight and ruin an opportunity.

We left the house and, without asking too many questions, I painted a visual picture of the location and ambiance of the place. I couldn't help but picture a small hole-in-the-wall, tucked back in some industrial park with no windows, and smoke-filled air. Even though I hoped that wasn't the case, I had to lower my expectations so I wouldn't be upset if it were anything less.

We rose through the outskirts of Atlanta in rural areas still under development. We went from well-lit streets to streets lined with nothing but trees and not a streetlight in sight. We encountered a car coming from the opposite direction every few minutes and the darkness of the road gave me an eerie feeling.

We finally pulled into a driveway lit by solar lights illuminating the path. We reached a security gate where Rachelle beamed a smile at the lanky security guard before proceeding to the location. We continued down the driveway, passing nothing but trees and land until we reached the gray stucco mansion. My mouth dropped as I scanned the place; it was far from what I'd imagined.

The driveway turned into a circular formation with a fountain in the middle. Valet attendants rushed to our doors to open and welcome us. There were cars neatly lined up front, from Bentleys to Jaguars. I was sure Rachelle's Honda Accord was going to be parked somewhere in the back as well as any other cars that didn't match the luxury vehicles on display.

I stood shell-shocked by my surroundings as Rachelle grabbed my hand and guided me up the four cobblestone stairs that led to the main doors. We walked in the foyer area, which included marble flooring and cathedral ceilings with a cherry blossom scent floating in the air. There was a concierge's desk to the right in which we stopped so I could sign the agreement. Rachelle picked up her name tag with the alias name, Rain, and I was given a green band. There was a small locker under the desk area where we stored our purses. We walked down the hallway lined with all kinds of erotic photos until we reached another office.

A husky Armenian man walked out and greeted Rachelle with a peck on the cheek then looked me up and down with a smile.

"Well, well, well, this must be the fine friend you were telling me about," he said with a thick accent.

Rachelle smiled as she looked at me. "You know I rolls with the best of them," she said. "Arbi, this is Tia."

He walked over to me and I awkwardly extended my hand for introductions.

"Nice to meet you," I shyly responded.

He looked at my hand as if it were plagued with germs.

"I only shake hands with my patrons," he said as he grabbed me in for a hug. "Nice to meet you too, Tia. Hopefully my hug isn't offensive, but I treat my employees and soon-to-be employees like family."

I blushed. "No problem."

"So Rain brought you in so you can get a view of how things run here, but if you have any questions, please don't hesitate to find me. I hope you'll join us," he said with a smile.

"I appreciate the opportunity," I said.

Arbi had sexiness about him even though he wasn't all that physically attractive. From his smell to his attire, he looked like money.

We proceeded to the bar area, which was illuminated by blue lighting and had plush blue velvet couches. One wall of the lounge had a cascading waterfall with an array of tropical plants. We approached the bar and Rachelle directed me to sit at an end seat as she went behind the bar and chatted with her male co-worker.

Rachelle walked back over to me as she put on her apron.

"If anyone approaches you, be cordial and give them an alias. There are many different rooms here for different activities, so if someone asks you to go to a room, just check with me first."

The whole "different rooms for different activities" made me nervous, yet curious at the same time.

"OK, for all this I'm going to need a drink. Patron margarita on the rocks, please," I said, looking around.

"You got it," she said with a devious smirk.

There were a few people trickling in. I wanted to get up and walk around, but I didn't want to be hounded in the process.

Rachelle walked back over with my drink. "Here you go. Girl, please stop looking so scared; nobody here is going to bite you." She laughed.

I tried to relax my face with a nervous grin. I took a gulp of my drink as I stood to go look around. With my drink in hand, I slowly made my way out the lounge area and back into the foyer. I could see a line of patrons, from couples to well-dressed men, at the concierge desk. I continued down the hall and entered another lounge area with white leather couches. The lighting was red, and there were cabana areas draped in sheers with marble coffee tables adorned with candles and a hookah.

There were a few men walking around as I approached the bar area for another drink. Damn it! I forgot I didn't have a purse as I laid my empty glass on the countertop and started making my way back to the blue lounge. I passed a nice-looking guy and he lightly grazed my hand. I turned towards him and tried to relax my face, which had been frowning.

"Sorry, I didn't want you to get away and I don't like whistling or whatever folks do to get someone's attention," he said with a smile. "My name is Carlton."

His teeth were so well aligned I wondered if they were actually his or veneers. You would think I'd already picked a name since Rachelle told me, but I couldn't think of anything more suited me than the common name most people use in the strip club.

"Hi, I'm Diamond," I said.

He grinned. "There's about three other Diamonds in here as well."

I blushed in embarrassment, but I needed a comeback for his smart remark. "Well hopefully this Diamond is one that stands out over the rest."

"And that you do." He grinned. "Can I offer you a drink?"

I didn't want to spend the whole night under Rachelle and figured I might as well get a free drink and engage in conversation.

"Sure," I said. I sat on the bar stool next to him.

"Let's move over to the cabana in the corner so we can chat," he said.

He instructed the bartender to bring our drinks over as we walked to the isolated area.

"This is much better. Well, judging from your wristband I see this is your first time here."

Great! Now I get to walk around being identified as a newbie.

"Yes, first time here; didn't know clubs like this exist."

The bartender delivered our drinks as Carlton held up his glass for a toast.

"Let's toast to broadening your horizons," he said as we clinked our glasses.

I looked around and noticed the room getting crowded.

"See, it's a good thing we moved when we did." He nodded towards the entrance. "So, Diamond, are you in a relationship?"

"No, I'm not. I actually just moved back to the city."

"Oh really," he said with raised eyebrows. "Where were you before?"

"Charlotte, North Carolina," I said.

"That's interesting. Well, welcome back. You're beautiful; I would think you'd have men lined up."

"Flattering, but no, I don't," I said, glancing at his loaded diamond wedding band. "Does your wife know you're here?" I boldly asked.

He leaned his head back in laughter. "Actually she does. She is good friends with the owner. I've been a regular here for the past year."

Interesting! Why would any wife want her husband to visit such a place where temptation lurked at every corner? Were most of the men here married and looking for a fling?

"What keeps you coming back?" I eagerly asked.

He sipped his drink and stared at me. "It's a private getaway where I can let the worries of my day go and freely enjoy myself. I'm an executive at a prestigious company that keeps me stressed out; this place is an outlet. May I ask why you're here?"

His stare made me feel uneasy as I looked away and fidgeted with my fingers.

"I came to check out the place. My friend Rach...I mean Rain bartends here in the blue lounge."

He chuckles. "Yes, I know Rain. She's good people."

I wondered if he'd tried to get with Rachelle too.

"Yes, she is. We've been friends for over ten years."

He sat down his drink and extended his arms around the edge of the L-shaped couch.

He looked around the room. "So do you like what you see thus far?"

"Considering I've only been here and in the blue lounge, I can't make a fair assessment."

He grabbed my hand and picked up his drink.

"Let me give you a mini-tour. This place is a secret for a reason, but you'll see what keeps folks like me coming back." He winked.

I downed the last of my drink before standing up. I didn't consider myself a lightweight when it came to drinking, but after two drinks, I felt a bit tipsy. As we headed out the lounge, more people had arrived so there were crowds of people mingling and having a good time. I hoped I wouldn't see anyone I knew.

Carlton gripped my hand and placed it closely under his arm. There was something mystic about him that sparked my interest. While I wasn't sure of his age, I guessed he was in his early fifties. He had a gray streak right in the front of his hairline, which consisted of naturally curly hair with tapered sides. He had a killer smile with a nicely trimmed goatee and mustache. Because of his dress shirt and casual slacks, I couldn't see any muscle definition, but he was tall. I imagined he'd played basketball in his younger years.

We walked upstairs to one big room with a disco light where there was a DJ booth playing old school songs. A few people were on the dance floor and the room was lined with tall circular tables and bar stools. In the hallway, there was a minibar set up. Carlton placed his empty glass down and ordered another round for us both. I didn't need another drink, but I didn't want to refuse the offer. He handed me my drink as we proceeded down the hallway.

As I went to open a door on my right side, he quickly grabbed my hand. He grinned and shook his head as he pointed towards a sliding cutout on the side of the door. Sliding back the tinted glass, I looked into a room that was dimly lit, with the smell of vanilla candles burning. I could make out couples on cabana-style beds kissing and groping each other. A lump formed in my throat and I could feel the heat rising from my head down to the spot between my thighs. I quickly closed the glass as I turned to face him.

He whispered. "Are you OK?"

I nodded as we headed down to the next room with yet another sliding glass panel. I was almost afraid to glance in, not knowing what to expect at this point. Carlton did the honors of opening the glass as I glanced in to see a center stage with a dance pole. There were a few men sitting around the stage as if they were anticipating the start of a show. Carlton gripped my hand and turned the knob for us to enter the room. There was a huge security guard with a buzz cut posted by the door. I avoided eye contact with anyone, as my only thought was to about-face and head back to the blue lounge.

We were seated in an area near the end of the stage. As if he sensed my nervousness, he grabbed my hand and lightly kissed it.

"Listen, relax. None of these people are here to judge you; we are all looking to have a good time and unwind. I'll protect you," he said with a concerned look.

I could feel a tingling sensation between my thighs as I crossed my legs. This man was tempting me and I was already hot and horny. Sex had been obsolete for weeks and I'd been too occupied with my own situation to really think about it. But now being in this environment with this sexy, attentive man had my hormones on fire. I sipped my drink as the music changed and the lights dimmed.

The stripper came out in full costume as a gladiator. I couldn't help but admire the build of her body. That used to be me back in the day before I got pregnant. The men and few women that were in the room had their eyes glued on the way she swayed methodically to the music. While I was enthralled by the performance, out of the corner of my eye I could see Carlton looking at me. I purposely avoided his gaze and continued to watch the show.

The DJ did commentary of every seductive move Vanity made as she climbed, slid, flipped, and straddled the pole. I made a mental note to get in a pole-dancing class at the gym ASAP. Carlton placed his hand on my thigh and slowly moved his hand closer to my "burning inferno." I didn't know whether to enjoy the moment by opening my legs wider or slap his hand away. I stared straight ahead trying to look unfazed by his uninvited yet welcomed gesture.

After minutes of watching Vanity dance and having Carlton kissing me on my neck, it was time for me to go. I'd enjoyed my moment with him, but I couldn't let myself fall in the trap of sexing him. As we left the room, he pulled me in close where I could smell the cognac on his breath.

"Can I have some alone time with you?"

Feeling hot and flirty, I smiled. "Is this what you do every night you're here?"

"Not at all. I'm more of the observant type, but when I see something I like, I don't play shy." He grinned.

I slowly exhaled as a few people walked casually by us as if we weren't there. Was that also a requirement of a member? No staring. If so, I liked that exclusion.

"Listen, as enticing as you are right now, Carlton—this isn't how I get down," I said, stepping back from his embrace.

He nodded his head. "I respect that. So will I see you again?"

"Maybe." I smirked. "Well I'll leave you to carry on with your personal pleasures. I need to check in with Rain so she doesn't think I've been kidnapped."

He laughed. "Trust me, she knows you're in good hands. Good night, Diamond," he said, kissing my hand.

I strutted away with an extra twist in my step knowing he was watching. I turned the corner and picked up my step as I made my way down the stairs back to the blue lounge. The bar was packed, but my seat on the edge remained open. I sat down as I looked around for Rachelle. The bartender came over to let me know she'd stepped away for a minute.

As I sipped from my bottle of water, I wondered if working here would be a good thing or a formula for disaster. I didn't want to end up in a mess with Carlton as I'd been in with Darnell. As a mother, I wanted to change my life for the better without taking steps backwards; I owed that to my son. In thinking about my current predicament, I needed money and this job was readily available. While working here would be far from anything to boast about—I had to suck up my pride and make it work in the meantime.

CHAPTER 10
KELLY

To keep my mind at ease, I'd enrolled in kickboxing at the gym to help blow off steam. I enjoyed the release, but it was only a temporary fix. As I sat on my mat for a cool down, I thought back on my night out with Gigi.

After running nearly an hour late after dealing with Kimora and her unexpected tantrum, I needed a drink. When I walked into Dugan's, it was crowded as usual, but I spotted Gigi waving at me from the corner booth she'd secured.

I walked over, instantly noticing her drastic change. She'd colored her hair honey blonde and wore lighter makeup, which was more natural. She looked great. We exchanged hugs then I slid in the booth seat opposite her.

"Well, damn, could this extreme makeover be inspired by a certain someone?" I asked, smiling.

She blushed as she tossed her hair. "I think you can vouch for this upgrade being long overdue."

The waitress came over and we ordered our drinks. One thing about Gigi was when she'd had a drink, her lips got loose, which was exactly what I wanted.

"So what's been going on with you?" I asked with a curious look.

She sighed. "I've been working a lot, that's the main thing. They transferred me temporarily to the Buckhead location and it's been hell the past two weeks."

While Gigi and I worked together, we worked in two separate departments so it wasn't uncommon for me not to notice when she wasn't in the office. Even in not seeing each other, she always called me to stay in touch, which wasn't the case as of late.

"I figured you must've gotten a new boo thang or something, considering I hadn't even heard from you."

She smiled nervously. "Well I did meet someone, but we're taking things slow."

The waitress came over with our drinks. I took a sip of my drink while not taking my eyes off her.

"Are you going to tell me about this guy?" I asked.

She looked away as if my stare made her uncomfortable. "When the time is right I will. I feel like I jinx myself when I talk about things without giving it some time to see if it's even worth talking about. Trust me, if our dating goes beyond a month you'll be the first to know," she said and winked.

I mustered up a fake smile. I couldn't believe that she would sit here and be so secretive. If I didn't know, I wouldn't take it so personally. I could feel myself boiling on the inside.

Gigi got up and waved at someone coming in the entrance. I looked around to see a young lady with a model-like figure walking towards us. They hugged each other as if they'd not seen each other in years. After minutes of them complimenting each other, Gigi turned to me for introductions.

"Kelly, this is my friend's sister, Renae. Renae, this is one of my good friends, Kelly."

Renae gave me a half smile as she extended her hand toward me. Her look was very piercing with her big almond-shaped eyes.

"It's nice to meet you, Kelly," she said with a more welcoming smile.

"Nice to meet you as well."

Gigi slid over in her booth seat for Renae to sit down. An uncomfortable feeling came over me as she continued to stare. I wished Gigi had told me beforehand we were expecting someone else to join us.

To break up the discomfort, I decided to be cordial and strike up a conversation.

"So, Renae, are you new to the area?" I asked.

"I've been here for a little over a year now. I've been working a lot, so I didn't have time until now to hook up with Gigi. How do you two know each other?" she said, looking between us.

"We work together," Gigi and I said in unison.

We all laughed at how rehearsed we sounded. Our waitress came over and we ordered another round of drinks. When the waitress came back over, she pointed out a gentleman at the bar and mentioned that he'd footed the bill for our drinks. We gave him a wave of thanks.

"He's a rather good-looking man, Renae, maybe you want to go check that out." Gigi beamed.

She rolled her eyes. "He's all right, but he's not my type."

"Are you dating right now?" said Gigi.

"It's a rather complicated situation," Renae said.

"When you're dating, everything is complicated," said Gigi as she took a sip of her drink. "Kelly, what's been going on with you and Derek? Are wedding bells in the near future?"

I leaned my head back on the booth seat. "Things are cool, but as far as those wedding bells—I don't know if and when that'll happen."

I didn't want to our conversation to turn into a venting session, especially since at this point my trust of Gigi was in question.

"Men have such a problem committing. It's like they want all the goodies that come with it, but don't want to put a ring on it," said Renae with a smirk.

"The ring isn't the problem; I need a wedding date."

Renae leaned forward and laid her hand over mine. "Trust me, things always reveal themselves in due time."

I didn't know if that served as encouragement or a line from a woman scorned. From her eerie stares to her responses, she made it difficult to decipher if she was being genuine or sarcastic.

Since that evening, I hadn't seen Gigi, but we'd briefly talked a few times. She always steered clear of conversation about her dating life. As my mom always taught me, keep your friends close and your enemies closer.

I took off my gloves and headed to the treadmill to finish my workout for the day.

Derek, the kids, and I went house hunting yesterday and found two houses of interest. The kids were running all over the place claiming their rooms and enjoying the open space. Seeing them run around in excitement made me realize how much they deserved better. While I was torn on the terms of us moving in unmarried, I couldn't deny my own interest about moving into someplace new.

After we'd viewed the properties, we went back to my place. The kids were in Kimora's room watching TV as Derek and I were sprawled across my bed. I sat up and grabbed my notebook and pen off my nightstand. Being raised in a financially stable household, I always strived to be self-sufficient so that I wouldn't have to depend on my parents. Even though I grew up a spoiled child, my house and everything in it was self-funded. With everything that Derek revealed about his current house situation, I needed to feel comfortable that he could sustain financially.

"OK, we need a financial plan," I said, drawing a line down the sheet of paper.

Derek took the pillow from behind his head and placed it over his face.

"After such a great family day, do we have to discuss this right now?" he said in a muffled tone.

I snatched the pillow from his grip and threw it on the floor. "Derek, seriously we need to know what we each bring to the table as far as debt and income."

He placed his hands behind his head as he turned to face me. "And we will do that as part of the house-buying process. Besides, I would never take us into anything I personally couldn't afford. Did you forget I'm a CFO?"

I frowned. "What's the problem with knowing that beforehand? We need to come up with the down payment and how we plan on handling the household expenses. Why wouldn't this be relevant now? You're a CFO so I would think you'll understand the need for financial planning and analysis."

I've never once had to question anything financially with Derek because from what I saw with us individually running our households, he maintained just fine. However, I needed to make sure we were on the same page.

He sat up and grabbed my hands. "Babe, everything doesn't require a strategic plan. I have nearly ten thousand alone set aside for the down payment."

"OK, but what does your savings account look like once we move in? I need to be confident about this and right now, you're not giving me that."

He shook his head. "That's the problem, Kells, you feel like you need to be in control of everything. I would never jeopardize my own financial stability to live beyond my means nor would I impose that burden upon you. So why don't you relax and trust me on this."

I threw the notebook and pen back on the nightstand and directed my attention towards the TV.

I snapped back to reality when I felt someone tap me on the shoulder. I turned around in shock to see Renae. I stepped on the side bars and cut off the machine.

"Hey, girl. How are you?"

"I'm doing good," she said, smiling. "Nice to see you again."

"Do you come here from time to time?" I asked, looking around.

"No, actually today is my first visit. I figured there's no time like the present to get in shape." She smirked.

I stepped off the treadmill as I wiped my face.

"That's true. Are you here alone?"

She looked around. "Yeah, I'm a solo kinda girl. I enjoyed you guys so much the other night. I would love to do that more often."

"Well we haven't been hanging out much lately, but sure, I'm down."

"I can tell by your physique you're a regular in the gym," she said, looking me up and down.

Considering the way she looked at me when we initially met and now, made me question if she was bisexual.

I awkwardly smiled. "After a kid it's a necessity."

"Maybe we can be workout partners. I could sure use the motivation."

"Ummm, sure," I said uncomfortably. "Well, it was nice seeing you, but I have to pick up my daughter."

"OK, have a good night," she said.

I grabbed my bag and headed out the door as John walked in.

"It's interesting how we keep meeting like this," he said.

I walked right past him without responding. He followed behind me.

"Did I do something wrong other than existing?" he asked as he tried to step in front of me.

I stopped within inches of crashing into him as I stood in place.

"What do you want from me, John? Let's not act as if we're friends."

"I don't understand the hostility. I'm being cordial and you're giving me attitude. As two adults that have clearly moved on, I don't understand your behavior."

I looked away as I wanted to boldly ask him what the hell was going on between him and Gigi. It wasn't my place to question it and I knew in doing so it would only make me look jealous.

"I'm sorry for coming off so rude. I feel like any time you say something, it's filled with sarcasm with the intent to taunt me."

"Taunt you? Hell, this is the second time in a year I've seen you. If I wanted to taunt you, don't you think I wouldn't miss a moment to meet you here at the gym?" He chuckled. "You're fine and all, but it's not that serious, Kelly. I'm not sweating you like that and you've made it more than obvious the feeling is mutual. But you have a nice night."

He walked away without even looking back as I proceeded to my car. I felt embarrassed because he was right; there was no excuse to my being cold to him. If anything, Gigi deserved it more. My phone rang—low and behold it was Gigi.

"Hey, what's up," I answered.

"I was trying to catch you before you left the gym, I need some motivation today."

I looked at the clock and rolled my eyes. "Gigi, you know damn well by seven o'clock I'm out."

"Yeah, but I thought since we hadn't caught up with each other in a while you would make an exception. "

"And you wait until now to let me know? Sorry, not today. Which gym location you going to?"

She paused as if she had to think of a location. "Northlake. I figured I might as well go close to home since I can't meet up with you."

I had a feeling that Gigi was seriously playing me. She knew what time I left the gym and purposely called me to see if I'd left. I sent Denise a quick text letting her know I would be a few minutes late picking up Kimora. I continued to talk to Gigi as I found a conspicuous spot in the parking lot to camp out.

Even though I wanted to clear my suspicions without further communication with her, I decided to ask questions about Renae.

"Oh, I saw your friend Renae at the gym today."

"Really? I know she'd asked where I work out and I told her you and I hit up two locations regularly."

"No offense, but is she a lesbian?"

She chuckled. "From what I know of her, no, but I don't know that for sure. She's always been a hard one to read. Why would you ask that?"

"Just a vibe I get," I asked, scanning the parking lot.

"Nowadays, chicks are real bold, so I don't think it would take too long to figure out if she is. I only know what her sister tells me and lately it's not much when it comes to her. In fact they don't even get along."

From a distance I could see Gigi pulling into the driveway of the parking lot. I leaned back my seat in case she could see me from the opposite side of the lot.

"Well I'm pulling up at Denise's now, so we'll chat later. Enjoy your workout."

"Oh I will," she said.

I hit the end button and watched her as she parked her car. She headed to her trunk as she dialed someone on her cell phone. She grabbed her bag from her trunk and proceeded to the door. That's when I caught John standing outside waiting for her to approach. They embraced as she walked up to him and together they entered the gym.

My heart beat rapidly; I felt betrayed. My mind told me to go back in and act as if I'd left something. But in me seeing them, I knew I would react and I wasn't looking to make a fool of myself.

My phone rang as I pressed my Bluetooth to answer.

"Hello," I answered.

"Is everything OK?" It was Derek.

"Yeah, I just lost track of time at the gym. I'm on the way to pick up Kimora now."

"Don't worry, I'll drop her off. The kids are out of school due to a doctor's appointment tomorrow, so I figured we would come to spend the night since the office is over your way. Oh and I also put an offer on the house and need you to sign off on the paperwork."

I hit my head against the seat. I didn't want any company; all I wanted was a hot shower and my bed. Secondly, why the hell would he put in an offer without consulting with me first? I wasn't in the mood to deal with this tonight, but for the sake of argument I'd let him take the lead.

"OK, I'll be pulling up soon."

"You don't sound like your usual self. What's wrong?"

He must've figured something was off when I didn't question him putting an offer on the house.

"I had a pretty hard workout, so I'm a little tired."

"You and Gigi still working out? Haven't heard you mention her in a while."

"She's got a man now, so our schedules don't coincide."

He chuckled. "After all her tireless efforts, she finally got a man. Good for her. Has she introduced him to you yet?"

I wanted to say yeah, he's one of my exes, but figured the whole mention of who he was would only open up a wound I wasn't prepared to deal with.

"No, not yet. Are you almost at the house?"

"Yep, just pulling up now. See you when you get here."

Talking to my parents about Derek and me buying a house together got them all excited. They loved Derek and the kids and were more than ready for us to take that next step in our relationship. When Derek and I broke up after Kimora was born, I told my parents we were taking some time apart to figure things out. I didn't let them in on my mistake nor did they question what the issues were. When we finally got back together, my mom thought we were going to the altar the next day. I didn't understand why Derek hadn't re-proposed, but I had to step outside of my brat stage and learn to let things flow.

Pulling in my driveway, I thought of Gigi and how I had thought she was my friend. With Jessica wrapped up in her new role as a mother, her non-profit organization, and rebuilding her marriage, it left little time for us. I missed Casey; our single-life adventures helped solidify our friendship. I could always count on her to tell me about myself even when I didn't want to hear it and her being there when I needed her the most. Now she was miles away building a life of her own.

Gigi and I had fun together, but she was no replacement for what I missed in Jessica and Casey. Nevertheless, I trusted her, and now her sneaky behavior had made me question her definition of friendship.

CHAPTER 11
JANEN

The day of the photo shoot went rather smoothly. The selection choices I picked out were great and they had some good shots. I was happy for Jessica; she was fulfilling her dreams and having the family she'd always wanted. I could see the love present in each shot taken. I was proud of my baby sister.

As my stay in Atlanta wound down, I thought about my visit to my parent's old neighbor's house. I thought I wanted to handle this alone, but I was so nervous that I invited Jessica along.

The house Mrs. Clara lived in was in need of serious repair from the looks of its outer appearance. As the stairs to the porch creaked with each step, all I could think of was if my weight would make me fall clean through the boards. Jessica stood at the bottom of the stairs and waited until I'd reached the door before she started her climb. I knocked on the door, realizing after two pushes that the doorbell didn't work.

I could see the window curtains move to my left, which indicated someone was home.

The voice of a woman spoke through the door. "Who is it?"

"Hi, I'm Janen Adams. I'm looking for Mrs. Clara."

The door cracked open and a young girl who looked to be no more than fifteen appeared with a frown.

"If you trying to sell us something, we not buying," she said with attitude.

I shook my head. "No, I'm not here to sell anything. My parents used to be neighbors of Mrs. Clara. Is she available?"

She closed the door abruptly. I turned towards Jessica, who shrugged her shoulders. I didn't know if that meant wait a minute or get the hell off my porch. Jessica started down the stairs as the door cracked open again.

A woman with her hair wrapped in a scarf, and wearing thick glasses, came to the door.

"I'm Clara. Who are you again?"

"I'm Janen Adams. My parents use to live in the apartments on Bankhead with you years ago."

Her eyes lit up as a smile came across her face, revealing her dentures with an open face gold tooth. "You Michael and Jo's daughter?"

"Yes, ma'am," I said, returning the smile.

She opened the door wider and stepped outside to give me a hug.

"It's nice to meet you, young lady," she said. "How are your parents doing?"

"They're doing well. My dad is in Florida now with his wife, and my mom still lives here; she got married about a year ago."

"That is so good to hear," she said. She looked around and pointed at Jessica at the bottom of the stairs. "Is that a friend?"

"No, that's my baby sister, Jessica," I said, motioning for her to come closer.

Mrs. Clara put her hands over her mouth. "Oh my, she looks just like Jo."

Jessica walked up to give Mrs. Clara a hug.

"Excuse my granddaughter's manners earlier. She's worse than a pit bull when it comes to strangers coming to the house," she said with a chuckle. "Come on in."

Walking in her house, I was glad the inside had more appeal than the outside. We walked past the living room to a den area where the granddaughter was propped up on the couch with her iPad.

"Kesha, this is my old neighbor's daughters," she said as she touched our hands.

"Hey," Kesha said dryly. She grabbed her iPad and walked past us. All we heard next was a door slam.

Mrs. Clara shook her head. "Teenagers! You ladies have a seat."

We sat on the covered couch across from the rocking chair she sat in.

"Well, first I want to apologize for stopping by without calling first. If I had a number for you, I would've at least called," I said.

She waved her hand at me. "It's OK. I welcome your kind of company. So, what brings you by?"

I rubbed my hands together as I let out a deep sigh. "Well I was told that you may have information about my birth mother, Naomi, or should I say Rita."

Mrs. Clara leaned her head back and closed her eyes. "Honey, what do you want to know about her?"

I shrugged my shoulders. "I don't know much about her other than she's my biological mother. I mean I know the story of Rita and my dad, so it's not like I grew up with my parents singing her praises. I'm actually just trying to find her."

Mrs. Clara leaned forward. "You're a beautiful young lady and I can only imagine the hurt you've gone through with this situation, but it looks like Michael and Jo did a good job raising you. Sometimes things are better left in the past. Times change, but some people don't."

I nodded my head. "I clearly understand that, Mrs. Clara. Years ago, I didn't want to meet this woman out of my own bitterness. But I'm older now, so I'm ready to face whatever it may bring."

Mrs. Clara smiled. "Baby, I'll help you out in any way I can."

"I appreciate that. Do you know where she lives?"

She chuckled. "Rita is quite the rolling stone. She borrowed twenty dollars from me nearly a year ago and I haven't seen or heard from her since. Last I heard she was staying down on Warren Street with her brother. The big rumor has been that her oldest son is by her brother."

I shook my head in disgust and hoped that was strictly a rumor.

"Do you know her son's name?" Jessica said.

"Honey, I'm the worst when it comes to names so I can't recall. I think something is wrong with him though, mentally handicapped. When they lived in the apartments, her brother lived with them to help take care of the boy since Rita couldn't sit still to give him the attention he needed."

"Outside of her disappearing act with not paying you back your money, what can you tell me about her?" I asked.

Mrs. Clara shook her head. "I don't want to paint a bad picture of Rita because I think deep inside there's some good somewhere."

"With all due respect, Mrs. Clara, I just need to know who she is as a woman so I can know what to expect."

She sighed. "Rita for years has been on drugs. She pulled herself together nicely to make me believe she'd gotten herself together when she borrowed that money. But I heard that's the game she runs on anybody she can. Back in the day, Rita was all about herself even though she had them two kids. Her daughter is about three years younger than the son and cute as a button. I think Jo took a liking to Rita because she thought she could help her. When I heard Rita was pregnant with Michael's baby, I was so disappointed. I felt bad for Jo cause she didn't deserve that, not with all she'd done for Rita. To make it worse, Rita walked around as if she'd done something good and it was quite disgusting to witness."

To hear Mrs. Clara talk about Rita made me cringe inside to know this heartless person was actually my birth mother. I hated that my whole existence came from a loveless fling, but deep down I knew I was given the best life by the only woman I would forever call Mom.

The conversation with Mrs. Clara went from my mom to my parents to her own life. I could see Jessica glancing casually at her watch. I knew she was more than ready to go. While it was intriguing listening to Mrs. Clara's stories, I felt as if I didn't know much more than I did when I walked in the door. True enough she gave me a lead on where her brother lived, but still I thought she could provide me with something more resourceful.

I thanked Mrs. Clara for her time, and as we got in the truck, Jessica and I rode in silence.

I reached over and touched her hand. "Thanks so much for coming with me. I had no idea it would take as long as it did."

She shook her head. "I see why that woman doesn't get visitors; she can talk a mile a minute."

I chuckled. "You got that right. So many times I wanted to end the conversation, get up, and leave."

While I felt some ground was covered, I guess I expected more. I figured before my departure, I would visit the brother's house and see if I could make some waves there.

The next day, we had a family dinner at my mom's house and it was nice to have us all gathered together, including my brother, Mikey, and his wife. We talked, laughed, and played games like old times; I truly loved my family. After everyone left for the evening, I decided to stay behind and help Mom clean up. I was thankful that Mr. Frank took it upon himself to retreat to their room so Mom and I could have a private moment.

"I had a great time, Mom," I said and smiled at her.

"I'm glad you did, baby. At least you ate like it." She chuckled.

I playfully slapped her arm. "Yes, and thanks to you I'll have to work extra hard at the gym when I return to Miami."

There was a silence between us as we dried the dishes to be placed in the cabinets.

"Mom, I went to see Mrs. Clara yesterday. She said hello," I said as I eyed her.

She avoided eye contact as she put the dishes away. "Oh did she? I haven't seen that heffa in years."

I chuckled. "She seemed like a nice, talkative woman."

She cut her eyes at me. "I will agree on the talkative part. She was always in other folks' business, so if you didn't find what you were looking for from her then I'd be rather shocked."

"She said she hadn't seen Rita in a while and thinks her brother lives on Warren Street. She then went on to tell me about Rita's other two children, a boy rumored to be by her brother, and a daughter. Do you remember them?"

She threw down her towel. "While even I questioned paternity of her son, I have to give credit to her brother Robbie for being a role model to those kids. Her son was mentally challenged and she didn't have the patience to deal with him; it was rather sad."

"Do you remember her children's name? Maybe I can try to search for them on social sites."

She looked up as if she were trying to recall their names. "The boy's name is David and the daughter, they call her Sunshine but I can't recall her real name. "

I talked to Mom about my time with Mrs. Clara, and thereafter, went back to my hotel to plan my last day in Atlanta.

The next morning, I got up and ordered room service. I called to check on Tony and filled him in on my findings. He listened to me without interruption or questioning, which led me to believe he didn't think too much of the situation. He filled me in on Carrie's transition in, which, likewise, I didn't bother to question. I would have to deal with her once I got back and didn't care to do so any earlier.

I showered and got dressed and grabbed the directions. I didn't quite know what to expect, but only hoped that I wouldn't end up regretting my decision to go alone. As I travelled on I-20 West, I thought about whether I would be able to even recognize Rita if I saw her. I'd never seen a picture of her and hoped that by visiting my uncle, I would at least be able to see some family portraits.

I turned on the street and was overwhelmed with nerves. I slowed down as I looked for the house number. There was a man working on a car in the yard of the house as I put the car in park and said a silent prayer.

The house wasn't nearly as bad as Mrs. Clara's, but the front yard needed some sod. There was an old model Monte Carlo jacked up in the yard with the hood opened. I didn't want to startle the man under the car as I hit the remote to activate the alarm as a way of getting his attention. He slowly rolled from under the car and stood up as he dusted himself off.

He was wearing a mechanics uniform, covered in grease and specks of dirt, and had a bald head and an unkempt beard. As I slowly approached, he put down his tool and walked towards me.

"You looking for somebody?" he asked.

"Yes, sir. I'm Janen Adams. Is Naomi here?"

He crossed his arms as he stood with his feet apart. "You must work for the government or something."

"No, I don't," I said with a perturbed look.

"Well nobody that personally knows her would address her by that name."

I was relieved that I at least had the right house.

"OK, is Rita here?" I asked with a smile.

He looked me up and down. "You look rather young to be friends with her. What do you want?"

I stepped closer towards him in hopes that he would at least see something in me familiar to her. He shifted his position by relaxing his arms to his side.

"Rita used to be my parents' neighbor back on Bankhead."

As if a light went off in his head, his eyes lit up and he walked back over to the car.

"She's not here; haven't seen her in weeks. I'll let her know you stopped by."

I walked closer to the car. "May I ask you your name? Are you her brother?"

He looked at me with a frown. "Is this some kind of interrogation? You asked for Rita, why are you concerned about me?"

As badly as I wanted to get smart with him, I figured I wouldn't get anywhere by doing so. I decided it was time to cut to the chase. Before I could open my mouth, the front door of the house opened and out walked a man.

He was tall and lanky, with a bad case of acne and disheveled hair that needed a barber's touch. He had a black fist hair pick resting in his head as he chewed wildly on a piece of gum. He looked me up and down.

"Who is this, Rob?" he asked, pointing in my direction.

"Go back in the house. I'll be inside in a minute."

He stared at me before giving in to Rob's directions.

"Now, Mrs. Adams, I'm quite busy, so either you can tell me why you are here or you can see yourself back to your vehicle."

"Rita is my biological mother," I said without hesitation.

He was totally speechless as he stared at me in shock.

"And that would make you my uncle. My dad is Michael Adams and I was told you lived with Rita, so I'm sure you know the story."

He removed a handkerchief from his back pocket as he wiped the beads of sweat surrounding the crown of his head.

"So after all these years you emerge," he said with a frown.

I walked closer to him with a frown of my own.

"You have no idea what I've been through to even get to the point where I'm standing here. This was not easy and, if anything, I would think my mother would've tried to find me."

He turned and sat on the porch steps. "I'm not making any excuses for Rita, but giving you up was for the best—trust me."

I rolled my eyes. "Maybe so, but that still doesn't negate the fact that she's my mother."

He looked around and sighed. "Rita isn't here and, trust me, if she knew you were looking for her, she probably would do what she's used to doing—running away," he said, shaking his head.

"Do you know where I can find her?" I asked.

"I can give you a few locations, but she never sits somewhere too long. She comes back here when her spots get hot and she needs to cool out for a minute."

I pointed at the front door. "Was that guy Rita's son?"

He held his head down and nodded. "Yes, that's her oldest, David. He's a little slow but I've been with him since he was a baby; the only male figure he's had in his life. He's come a long way and I'm proud of him."

"Can I at least introduce myself?"

He shook his head. "I don't think that's a good idea right now. He has a hard enough time understanding why Rita acts the way she does. I think announcing you as his sister would only complicate matters."

Did my whole appearance of showing up at his house complicate things? I don't know why I had set my hopes up on this being some happy reunion.

I looked around searching for the right words to say. "Well, the last thing I want to do is make things harder for anybody. Sorry I bothered you," I said as I turned and walked away.

I was halfway to my car when he called out my name. I stopped and turned around as he walked to meet me.

He smiled. "It was nice meeting you; sorry if I gave any other impression. I'm just very guarded when it comes to my family."

I nodded my head. "Understandable. It's hard for me too. I don't know why I set myself up as if coming here today was going to be the 'be all' to my burning questions. I thank you for your time."

"You know I can say that Rita's decision to give you up wasn't easy. She dealt with a lot of ridicule for even being pregnant in the first place. Personally, I wanted her to abort the pregnancy since Michael was married and the fact she wasn't doing a good job caring for David."

I forced a smile. "People make mistakes, I do realize that. However, at some point in your life, you've got to face the truth and I'm offering that to Rita." I reached in my pocket and handed him my business card. "If Rita or you care to get to know me as a person, here's my card."

As he looked down to read it, I turned and walked away. I got in my car with a heavy heart, feeling broken and emotional. I drove off without even looking in the direction of the house. I didn't know what else to expect at this point, if anything, but I realized I should've followed my husband's advice and left this situation alone.

CHAPTER 12
DEREK

Once the offer on the house was accepted, the craziness of packing and finding a suitable tenant became the next big task. Kelly and I were bumping heads on what furniture from each of our houses would make it to the new one. I felt as if she were trying to make all my furnishings part of the yard sale I planned on having. I'd let her have that for now; seeing the excitement on my kids face made it all worthwhile.

Since our last encounter, I hadn't seen or heard from Lacey. I was hoping she'd finally moved on with someone else even though I found myself fantasizing on how she turned me on sexually. She was totally uninhibited, which is what intrigued me most about her. Outside of that, there was no other attraction.

Kelly had evening plans with a friend, which gave me the time to get a great deal of packing done since the kids were with Denise. My phone rang—it was Carlton.

"What's up, C-Money," I answered.

"What's up for the night? You chilling with the lady?" he asked.

"No, sir. I'm free as a bird. Let me guess, you want me to roll to the spot with you." I chuckled.

"I think you're due for some fun after the last few weeks. How bout it?"

"Well, you know, since you put it like that, yes, sir—I'm down."

Carlton stated that he'd send his driver over to pick me up. Rolling with a dude like Carlton always made me feel like I was living the celebrity life. I didn't know much about his finances, but from what I'd experienced—he was rolling in dough. He earned a nice salary with Walker & Co., but from the house he lived in to his luxury vehicles, it always made me wonder just what else he was doing.

I went through my closet and sifted through my shirts to find the perfect outfit. Going to the "spot" was a special treat and if I was rolling with money, I at least needed to look the part.

My phone rang—it was Darnell. I wished I could invite him out, but knowing him he wouldn't go anyway.

"What's up, bruh," I answered.

"At home playing catch-up on some work," he said.

I hissed. "Man, you've got to get back to having an outside life. All work and no play—"

He cuts me off. "Keeps my ass out of trouble," he said. "I've got two businesses I'm managing: a wife and a baby. I'm not missing a damn thing in them streets."

I shook my head. "So you stay locked away cause you can't handle temptation? Dude, that's not living, but OK, whatever works for you."

"Yep and it does. Anyway, I called because I was looking over the latest report from HR and noticed your girl resigned two weeks ago. Did you by chance have anything to do with that?"

This was as much news to me as it was to him. "I hadn't seen or heard from her, so I didn't know."

"Well she stated her reason for resigning was 'personal,' so I was hoping that had nothing to do with you."

"Man, whatever personal issues she got going on don't have anything to do with me. Like I said, I hadn't heard or seen her in weeks. Maybe she just needed to move on or found a better job."

"I'm not blaming you, bruh, I just don't want anything coming back and biting us in the ass later. Why don't you reach out to her and see what's up?"

I shook my head. "For what? I really don't care why she left and I don't want to talk to her. If you want to know, why don't you call her yourself?"

"I'm not calling her, but I'll check with Tina to see if she's conducted an exit interview. Well you have a nice night, bruh; didn't mean to spoil your night over this."

I grinned. "Oh you didn't. You do the same."

I hung up and got back to piecing my outfit together. While I was curious as to why Lacey left the company, in no way did I want to call her and make her think I was the least bit concerned.

I set my clothes out and took my shower. I pressed the icon for Pandora on my iPod to help get me in the mood for the night.

The first time Carlton invited me to the club with him, I didn't think anything more of it than it being the regular club scene. Kelly and I were still in the early part of our rebuilding stage and I hadn't been to a club in quite a while. Carlton didn't give me a heads-up about the type of place it was until we pulled into this driveway that was unlike any nightspot I'd been to. Gated, with a security guard post; I felt like we were going to some celebrity's house versus a club. As we pulled in, he told me exactly what it was and that I would need to sign a confidentiality agreement. I'm thinking, damn, what am I getting myself into if I got to sign such an agreement. I didn't question it further because I didn't want him to think I was being uptight. I figured, with him as a prominent businessman, he wouldn't do anything damaging to his reputation, so I shouldn't be too worried.

Walking in the huge mansion, I had to remind myself not to have my mouth open. I couldn't help but marvel over the décor, the overall ambiance of this prestigious, secret club. Who would've guessed nestled back in the woods that such a place existed?

Carlton received the VIP treatment and I enjoyed receiving it myself; this didn't happen too often in my world. From the entertainment to the patrons of the club, the spot had a carefree atmosphere where people let down their guard and enjoyed themselves. Seeing Carlton in such an environment was so different than the personal side I'd witnessed before. It seemed as if he was very comfortable and the ladies loved him. I tried to play cool, but in the back of my mind all I kept thinking about was what if I saw someone I knew or better yet, with all the flirting Carlton did, what if it got back to his wife.

As I sprayed my body down with Axe Dark Temptation, I slipped on my clothes and gave myself a look in the mirror and smiled. Yep, I'm still sexy and my smile is killer; thanks, daddy, for them braces. I brushed my hair, making sure my waves were intact. While some brothers my age were at the point of losing their hair, mine was still as thick as in my younger years.

The doorbell rang as I looked at the clock—it must be the driver. I looked outside and saw the Silver Maybach with tinted windows in my front yard. Damn, now this was first-class service.

As I threw on my Versace glasses and gave myself a final look over in the mirror, I exited the house and climbed into the backseat as the driver closed the door behind me. I didn't know how Carlton pulled this off, but, damn, I needed to find out his secret.

Minutes later we pulled into Hawthorne Estates, the gated community where Carlton and his wife resided. Carlton's house was off the chain, with a guesthouse in the back as well as a pool. Normally in the summer he would host an annual event but hadn't done so in the past year.

We pulled into the driveway and Carlton immediately came out before the driver could put the car in park. Carlton opened the door and hopped inside. He gave a special knock on the glass for the driver, who proceeded out the driveway without further question.

"Man, you looking like you going to a photo shoot for GQ or something," Carlton said with a laugh.

I popped my collar. "Hey, you never know when an opportunity may present itself. Hell, I'm rolling with C-Money, I gotta look like I got money too." I chuckled.

"I heard that. So what's been going on?"

"Just packing, getting ready for this move. Oh, Darnell called me today questioning me on why Lacey resigned. Did you know about that?"

"I didn't know until she came by the house today to see Maria. I think she's working with Maria on something. I would assume that's better for you. Right?" he said with a raised eyebrow.

I frowned. "I don't care what she does. She hasn't been bothering me and I made sure to steer clear of her. But, yeah, it's a sigh of relief."

I didn't understand why he and Darnell seemed to feel as if I was emotionally attached to Lacey. It was never about trying to make her anything more than a booty call.

"So what's the wifey up to?" I asked.

He shook his head. "With Maria, you never know. Until she has a clear plan, she normally doesn't discuss her ventures with me."

Carlton shared with me before that Maria operated an elite escort service years ago and helped Arbi with the concept for the club. Maria's health made her abruptly exit the business, but she served as a "consultant" in her spare time.

"How's Maria been doing lately?"

He smiled. "From the looks of my bank account, she's doing real good spending money. I swear, that woman and her high-end taste is making me glad she's trying to get back out there and work."

"Is she still taking care of her family in Columbia?"

He nodded. "I think she's going to do that until the day she dies. I don't intervene in it because family means everything to her."

We pulled up to the security gate. Carlton pressed the button to let down the window as he exchanged words with the security guard. We then proceeded through the gate and Carlton had a smile on his face.

"Man, you cheesing like you excited. What you got waiting on you?"

"She's a new host here and I've been hollering at her for the past few weeks, but she is stuck on my marital status. Trying to see how I'm going to win her over tonight," he said.

I shook my head. "Man, I don't know how you do it, but you got balls of steel."

We got out of the car and headed in. The place was packed and I didn't know whether to be excited or spend my time checking my surroundings. If Kelly knew about this place, she would be all but pleased.

We headed to the Blue Lounge and were greeted by one of the hosts, Diamond. I had not seen her before, but by the look on Carlton's face, I could tell she had to be the one. She was thick in all the right places, but I wouldn't have guessed she'd be of interest to Carlton. He normally went for the mellow type that didn't draw too much attention; she was definitely not in that category. I excused myself and headed to the bar.

I took a seat at the bar and checked my cell phone.

"Hello. What can I get you to drink?" a woman said.

I looked up and smiled. "Rain, we meet again. Let me have a Cîroc and pineapple."

She snapped her fingers. "Oh hey, you're Carlton's friend. Where've you been hiding?" she said as she fixed my drink.

"Handling business, you know the life of a hustler. I can't afford this luxury life up in here." I grinned.

"Don't worry, I'll make sure you have a good night," she said and winked.

On my first initial visit, Rain was the first person to make me feel truly comfortable. She was so down-to-earth and humorous. Carlton thought I was trying to push up on her and offered to set me up, but she wasn't my type. I liked her personality and her ability to call it like it was.

She brought back my drink. "Here ya go. You might want to sip slow on that or you'll end up in one of them rooms real quick," she said with a smile.

I smiled back. "Thanks for the word of caution. It's pretty busy here tonight," I said, surveying the area.

"It's a typical Friday night to me. So have you joined the club?"

I gave her a stern look. "This is a nice getaway, but in no way am I trying to spend that type of money to be a certified member. Not trying to knock your hustle, babe, but I got a family and a new home I'm financially responsible for."

She nodded her head. "That's what's up. Don't blame you—take care of what matters most. Some of these dudes have nothing but money to blow. I don't understand it myself, but to each its own."

Carlton came up and leaned over the bar to give Rain a kiss on the cheek.

"Hey, beautiful. Let me get a Hennessey on the rocks."

"You got it," she said as she walked to the other side of the bar.

"So is Rain on your list of conquests?" I asked.

He waved me off. "Rain is the coolest chick ever; she's homegirl material."

I looked over at Diamond greeting other guests. "Man, I must say I was taken aback by Diamond. She's a straight ten."

He ran his hand over his head. "Yeah, she's definitely different than the norm, but it's something about her I'm feeling."

I grinned. "Could it be her boobs or her ass?"

He laughed. "Shit, both to be honest. But she's cool people, she's Rain's best friend."

Diamond came back over to the bar and Carlton focused his attention on her. I couldn't spend my time being around Carlton while he got his mack game on, so I decided to roam around and see which room was popping.

Someone tapped me on the shoulder. I turned around to one of the hostesses.

"Hi. You have someone requesting your presence in the Passion Room," she said with a smile.

I was sure she could tell by my shocked look that I was trying to figure out who the hell would be requesting me. Before I could question her, she was off assisting someone else.

I was curious as to who would be requesting me since I was not a regular here. Who would feel that comfortable inviting me to a room?

I walked up the stairs leading to the room, and downed the rest of my drink. I stopped by the bar to order another one. As I proceeded to the Passion Room, I could feel my heart rapidly beating. Was this some sort of setup by Carlton? I was a mere observer and had never partaken of anything beyond that.

I reached the door and looked in through the sliding glass panel. The room had dim red lighting, making it difficult for me to make out anyone there. I turned the handle and walked in, and was met by the room attendant in her lace bodysuit and red high heels. It wasn't hard to tell she had some work done as she sashayed in front of me.

"Can I have your name, please?" she asked.

"Derek," I answered.

She smiled. "Right this way," she said seductively.

The room had four beds draped in red sheers. I could make out two couples that were engaging in sexual acts. What the hell am I doing here? She led me to a door and opened it.

"Enjoy," she said as she closed the door after I entered.

Unlike the room I'd initially entered, this room was dark, with lit red candles lining the wall. The bed was round, and while I could see a figure behind the sheer white drapery, I couldn't make out a face. I slowly moved closer as the figure stood from the bed. Once I got close and the light shined on her face, I gasped.

"Lacey, what the hell are you doing here?"

She grinned. "The question is, what are you doing here? Obviously you were curious or else you wouldn't have stepped foot in this room. And if you saw what was going on when you initially walked in, then you would've turned around if you weren't interested. So let's stop with the games."

"Games? I haven't heard or seen you in weeks and the one night I'm here you just so happen to slide through and set this up."

She giggled. "Awww, you've missed me after all. But just to ease your mind, no, I'm not stalking you. I came here to handle some business for Maria, saw you off in the distance here with Carlton, and thought to take full advantage of the situation."

I shook my head. "So you resigned from the company to work for Maria?"

"I did, amongst other things. Working at the company wasn't a lucrative gig anyway, so I was never looking to stay too long. But that's not why I summoned you here," she said as she wrapped her arm around my neck.

I could feel the closeness of her body against mine sparking an erection.

"Aww, I see someone's happy to see me," she said and smiled.

She grabbed my hand and led me closer to the bed. Being in a different zone, feeling comfortable and relaxed, I obliged without saying a word as she helped me out of my blazer. As each article of clothing was taken off, I felt like I was being snatched from reality. As if the world paused just so I could have this uncensored, unjudged moment.

As I lay back on the bed, I could feel her positioning herself between my legs. She was in a league of her own when it came to oral sex. As she pleasured me with her mouth and tongue, I moaned in delight. When she stopped, I wanted to throw a tantrum and beg for her to continue. I refrained, knowing that with Lacey, she always came back stronger and better than before.

I made a move to sit up and she pushed me back down as she climbed on top of me.

"Come on, Lacey, you know that's not how we roll," I muttered.

She got up and walked over to her purse. I was thinking to myself, damn, did I just kill the moment or what. As she walked back to the bed with a folded-up piece of paper, she threw it at me.

"You're in luck. I came equipped today with my freedom papers." She grinned.

As I unfolded the paperwork, it showed her results from STD testing she'd had done last week. I shook my head.

"That's good to know, but still, you can get pregnant," I said.

She took her other hand from behind her back and showed me a birth control pill case.

"I've been a faithful user for the last month, so trust me—all bases are covered. Now, are you going to give me the dick or do I need to put on my clothes and walk out of here?"

That was another thing I liked about Lacey, her "I don't give a fuck" attitude and aggressiveness. Her look was stern as she stood between my legs naked with her hand on her hip.

I reached up and pulled her towards me as she assumed her position. Our encounters were never on an intimate level where there was caressing, kissing, or pillow talk. It was straight-up uninhibited sex.

As she rode me, I could feel her walls closing in on me, creating a tighter suction with each up and down motion. Her pace went from slow to rapid as I tried to contain myself from ejaculating too soon. She pinched my nipples, one of my sensitive spots, and I moaned. Lacey's petite body made it easy to maneuver her as I saw fit, but I allowed her to take charge—it was her show.

Just when I thought she was done, she reversed, giving me a direct view of her ample ass and butterfly-tatted back. The more she leaned over, grabbing my legs and moaning, the more turned on I became. I didn't know if I could tolerate anymore without exploding. Massaging my balls, she picked up the pace, and I knew I was at the point of no return as I moaned. She felt the goose bumps, which signaled I was at the point of arrival, so she jumped off me and gave me a rapid hand job as I released myself. Every muscle within me tightened with intensity. Afterwards, I felt paralyzed and exhausted as my eyes grew heavy and I slipped into the abyss of sleep.

I was awakened by a knock at the door and felt as if I'd been asleep for hours. As I fought to open my eyes, with my vision still blurry, I felt the other side of the bed to find that Lacey wasn't there. I sat up and looked around the room; no sign of her clothes,

She'd left. The door opened and the attendant from earlier popped her head in.

"I'm sorry to awaken you, but housekeeping will be in soon."

"Thank you," I said.

After she closed the door, I managed to gain my bearing and get out of bed. I was in need of a shower as I looked down at my stomach and inner thigh, noticing the dried-up semen. I went to the sink to do a quick wash up and slipped my clothes back on. I didn't bother giving myself a look over in the mirror; all I wanted to do was go home.

As I exited the room, I looked straight ahead, avoiding eye contact with anyone. Once I made it to the hallway, I checked my phone and noticed I had a missed call from Kelly and two text messages. Damn it! I knew Kelly was probably wondering what the hell was going on. Normally if I missed her call, I'd call her back minutes later; it'd been over an hour since she called.

One text message was from Lacey: *"That was wild and adventurous. We need to do that again at some point. Sorry to have left you so abruptly, but you were sleeping so well, I didn't want to interrupt. Ciao."*

The next message was from Carlton: *"Sorry, bruh, I ended up leaving considering u were busy...lol. My driver should be outside waiting for u when ur ready to go. TTYL."*

I walked down the stairs and headed out the front door. Sure enough, the driver was waiting as he hopped out of the car to greet me and opened the door.

I got in the backseat and stretched out. I looked at my watch; it was 2:30 a.m. I thought to call Kelly but figured I would hold off until the morning; at least it would give me time to get my lie together.

The more progress I felt I was making, the more steps I took back. Temptation was a hard thing to contend with. I hit my head against the window for stupidly walking into the web Lacey had spun. How was I ever to shake her if I couldn't resist her advances? I only hoped my moments of weakness wouldn't hinder me from the life I was ready to create with Kelly.

CHAPTER 13
LA'TIA

After working nearly two months, I'd managed to eliminate most of my debt and get my bank account in a stable position. Now I was focused on moving into my own place.

Sharon was such a blessing to me, and Noah absolutely loved her. With her keeping him nights while I worked, I always felt bad about not being able to read him a bedtime story and tuck him in. Recently she'd asked if she could take Noah to Disney World with his cousins for a week's stay. I knew Noah would enjoy the experience and I could use the time to look for a job and a place, so I agreed.

There were times I got off work and wished Marcus was here to cuddle with me. The past few months without him had been tough, but seeing my child in a happy state of being gave me the comfort I needed to push through. It was moments when I was alone that I missed him the most.

Carlton had been pushing up on me in a major way. I felt flattered in a sense, but I didn't want a repeat of my relationship with Darnell. To think a married man is going to leave his wife was an asinine thought, so I didn't want to get further involved with him to the point of catching feelings.

One day Rachelle and I went to Pappadeaux for dinner before our shift to have some girl talk.

"So what do you think of the gig so far?" she asked.

"It's bringing in the income I need, that's for sure. I mean it's not as bad as I thought, but honestly I can't see myself doing it long term."

"Well, to each its own. I'll do it until something else lucrative comes along. But anyway, what's up with you and Carlton?" she asked with a smile.

I blushed. "Chelle, he's married; I can't take him serious."

"OK, so he's married, but at least you know who his main chick is. When you're dealing with these single dudes, you got to figure out if you or the next chick is the main one. Hell, everybody out here playing games. Get in where you fit in and let the chips fall where they may."

From her response I assumed I wasn't the only one with experience dealing with a married man. My mentality was different than Rachelle's. She was all about the money. For me, I wanted to regain my independence and settle down in a relationship. I owed it to Noah to provide a stable household with a positive male figure in his life.

"I'm interested in Carlton and he's definitely flattering me with all the gifts, but I'm still uncomfortable with the situation."

She took a sip of her drink. "He's a cool dude though. I've known him for a while and he makes it no secret that he's married; hell, he even talks about his wife."

"Well he never talks about her to me; not that I've ever questioned it."

She waved at me. "I'll tell you this much, his wife has money that she made prior to them even marrying. I think she once operated an exclusive escort service and she helped Arbi get his business off the ground."

I shrugged. "I'm not interested in her finances. I just don't want to get caught up in no love triangle."

"It's all about playing your position. When he's with you, that's your man, and when he's with her, that's her husband. I know it comes off heartless, but shit, that's the reality we live in now and days. My mom and dad been married over twenty-five years and you think my mom don't know my dad has a side piece. I'm not saying it's right, but if everybody is happy and no one brings drama to each other's doorstep—I don't see the issue. When you sneak around doing shit, that's when you get caught up."

I couldn't say I agreed with Rachelle's logic, but there seemed to be a bit of truth within her words. However, when I make the decision to marry, I want my relationship to be exclusive, no side piece, no others in the equation. I didn't believe all men cheated, but from what I'd seen it was quite discouraging.

As Carlton and I began to see each other more, I felt comfortable and there was no pressure from him when it came to sex. Sex further complicated things and, honestly, as horny as I was, I felt like rushing into that wouldn't do me any good. Our conversations were thought-provoking and interesting; he kept me engaged.

Seeing him at the club last night with his friend, I didn't know whether he would treat me as like a regular hostess or what. However, Carlton didn't treat me indifferently and his friend greeted me with a smile.

I went on break and Carlton met me in the employee lounge area.

"I hope Arbi doesn't have a fit about you being back here," I said.

"Please, Arbi will be all right," he said, smiling at me. "I want to take you somewhere after you get off."

I gave him a side-eye look and a crooked smile. "At 3:00 a.m., you want to take me somewhere. As my grandma would say, the only thing open that time of morning is legs."

He chuckled. "Wise woman. I'm not trying to make the situation awkward, but I want some time with you outside of our public places and your place of employment. You should know me well enough to know I'm not going to attack you."

I folded my arms and gave him a stern look. "I've never asked, but I'm rather interested. What's the deal with you and your wife?"

"Our relationship isn't the average one. She understands me; we have a partnership; and bottom line, neither of us is going anywhere."

A lump formed in my throat as he emphasized his final point. "So she knows you come here to satisfy whatever itch you crave and she's OK with that?"

"First of all, I'm a friend supporting a friend's project. I've been around this shit for years, it doesn't faze me anymore. I come here as an observer, I don't indulge in anything more than that. Secondly, my wife is a secure woman and she trusts me enough to know I'm in no way trying to find a replacement for her. Now, does that answer your question?" he asked with raised eyebrows.

I exhaled and gave a half smile. "Well I guess it does. Thanks for being honest."

We sat awkwardly for a moment as I glanced at my watch.

"I really hope that doesn't change anything between us. I like you and I think you like me," he said as he reached to lift my chin.

"That's just it, Carlton. I like you indeed, but I don't know how long liking will stay around without feelings getting in the way."

He rubbed my hand. "Let's talk more once you get off work. I'm about to leave now and go head there. My driver will be outside when you get off and bring you to me."

I nodded my head as we got up to leave. As he went off in the opposite direction, I went over to find Rachelle in the lounge. She threw up her finger to let me know she'd be with me in a minute as she assisted a customer. I sat on the corner seat of the bar as if I was still on break.

She walked over with a smile. "What's going on, girl?"

"I'm going with Carlton after I get off, so just letting you know you don't have to wait for me."

She gave me a playful punch. "Finally going to give him some," she said and smiled. "Girl, you deserve it. Don't know how you've gone this long without having sex."

I rolled my eyes. "It's easier than you think," I said as I got up and walked away.

I loved Rachelle, but sometimes she irritated me with her way of thinking. Whether she knew it or not, I was still mourning the loss of Marcus. I missed him more than I could ever admit. Even though I liked Carlton, I guess sex was my way of preserving myself as if Marcus were away doing a bid and I was awaiting his return home.

When I got off from work, the driver was out front. He stepped out of the car to open my door, but I opened it before he had a chance. All I wanted to do was get in the backseat and have a drink. Maybe that would help calm my nerves.

As we drove to the undisclosed destination, I thought about my plan to move out. I'd found an apartment I liked, but the rent was a little out of my range. I refused to put myself back in a position where I was unable to maintain it; I needed stability.

I poured myself a drink—straight Patron. I knew I had to be pretty bold to drink liquor straight up with no chaser. I needed to relax as I rubbed my neck to relieve the tension I felt building up. I downed my drink and frowned as I sucked on a lime. Whew!

My eyes grew heavy as we hit I-85 North. I wanted to stay awake to see exactly where I was going, but sleep got the best of me.

I was awakened by a tap on my shoulder.

"Tia, baby, you're here," said a familiar voice.

My vision was blurry as I looked into the face of Carlton.

"Come on, I'll help you out," he said.

I wiped my eyes to get better focused. Even though it was still dark outside, my mouth dropped seeing the beautifully lit log cabin.

"Where am I?" I asked as we walked up the walkway.

He grabbed my hand. "This is my secret getaway. We're in Helen."

I'd never stayed in a cabin before because I wasn't a wilderness kind of girl, but it was beautiful. We entered the house and it smelled like fresh fruit. I walked around, taking in the décor and design of the place.

"Do you own this?" I asked.

"Yes, it belonged to my grandfather. I remodeled it about two years ago."

"This is really nice."

He grabbed my hand to walk upstairs. "Well, if you think that's nice, wait until you see the loft."

We walked up into the loft area and I was floored. The bed was on a raised platform with a canopy. And there was a bear rug in front of it. To the right of the bed was a sunken Jacuzzi overlooking the backyard. The ceiling over the bed had a nice-size skylight.

"Don't worry, that skylight is well tinted. We see out, but no one sees in."

I smiled as he read the thought going through my mind. I headed towards the screened-in balcony that had a porch swing and a round outdoor firepit overlooking the woods that encompassed the backyard.

"This is absolutely beautiful."

He walked up behind me. "Yes, I take great pride in this place. My grandfather spent a lot of time here and I would come to stay with him during the summer months. There's a lake through those woods. In the daylight, you can see the path and even the glistening of the water through the trees."

I turned towards him. "How often do you come here?"

"Once a month, at least; it's my serenity." He smiled.

I walked past him and sat on the nearby rocking chair. "Does your wife come here often?"

I had to ask because honestly I didn't want her to come barraging in on us.

"You're in luck because my wife hates this place. I brought her up here right after the renovations were done thinking she would like it, but she didn't. So no worries, she hasn't even spent one night here in all the years we've been together."

"So what's the plan? It's 4:15 a.m. and I'm super tired. Surely you didn't bring me miles outside the city to talk." I smirked.

"Like I said before, I'm not trying to attack you. I wanted to bring you to a place where we could be free with each other. When we're out in public, it's like you keep at a distance from me and I understand why. But here there's no need for that. Look, why don't you get comfortable. There's a change of clothes waiting for you in the bathroom."

I bucked my eyes in amazement. He'd actually taken the time to get me a change of clothes. Wow—this is definitely something new. I didn't bother to give a response as I headed for the spacious bathroom. When I walked in and closed the door, I leaned against it to take in the beautiful space. To the left was a garden tub; in front was a vanity area with a double sink; to the right was a unique-looking shower. I opened the door and it looked big enough for two people. There was a double showerhead as well as jets that lined the two walls. I'd never seen anything like it before, but it looked interesting. To the right of the shower stall was a glass door. I opened the door and inside was the toilet and bidet; opposite was a wall-mounted TV.

After taking it all in, I undressed and headed to the shower. The water felt good as it cascaded over my body. While sleep initially consumed me, the shower generated energy within me. I loved the ambiance of the place and appreciated the fact that Carlton would let me enter his private haven.

I felt like I could stay in the shower forever, but decided to step out. I dried off and went to the bag laid on the counter. Inside there was a black, short slip. I pulled it out and laid it on the counter as I oiled my body. The lingerie fit me well as I gave myself a look over in the mirror. I folded my clothes and put them in the bag, then cut off the light and opened the door.

The lights were out in the bedroom with only the moonlight illuminating the room from all the windows. I could make out Carlton as he sat up in the bed shirtless. This was the first time I'd seen him without a shirt and I must say he looked great. He wasn't built, but for a man in his mid-forties, he had definition.

"I thought you'd fallen asleep in there," he said with a grin.

I joined him in bed. "Sorry to keep you waiting, but that shower is absolutely amazing."

He moved in closer. "Well, lie down and let me relax you with a massage."

I obliged and turned over on my stomach. Even though the lingerie came with panties, I opted to go without. He rubbed my feet as I closed my eyes and took in the pleasure of being pampered.

His hands were soft as he massaged my body. He didn't speak; all that could be heard was the sound of steady breathing. My eyes grew heavy as my body relaxed more and I ended up falling asleep.

I could feel my legs being shifted apart as I awoke. I didn't bother to make a sound or create movement. I could feel the air of his breath inching closer between my thighs. I exhaled deeply, anticipating his next move. His tongue grazed the sides of my inner thighs before kissing the entry point to what lay beneath. As he parted my lips, I could feel my clit pulsating; I hadn't been sexually active in months. My body urged for the touch of a man, but instead of thinking about the person actually doing it, I closed my eyes and imagined he was Marcus.

He kissed, suckled, and flicked his tongue back and forth over my clit. His tongue movement was delicate and steady paced. His circular motions made me shiver as I fought back the urge to moan. As he pushed my legs up to where my knees bent, I was now in a frog-like position. He grabbed my ass as he continued to partake of my nectar. With each stroke, the intensity increased as I could no longer suppress my moans. When his tongue traveled further up, I flinched. I didn't do anal sex and wasn't about to make an exception. I managed to turn over and face him.

"Are you not enjoying yourself?" he asked.

"Yes, I am," I said through heavy breathing. "But I'm not into that and felt uncomfortable."

He smiled. "You have no idea what I was about to do. Just relax; I'm not going to hurt you. Trust me on this."

I gave him a stern stare as I gave in and flipped back over. I exhaled and resumed the position. He went back to my clit and continued to tantalize me as I could feel the flow of my juices escape me. He once again started to trail his tongue up between my butt cheeks. I heard the rip of the condom wrapper as he continued to fancy me with his tongue.

Once he placed the condom on, he slowly moved inside of me. I moaned as his rhythms reached depths I never thought he could go. I tried to keep my legs steady in the position, but his thrusts were slowly breaking me down. I could feel his finger moving to my anus. I fought the urge to flinch as I took deep breaths, not knowing what to expect. He lightly pushed against it and I collapsed like a burning building. Being the perfect gentleman, he made sure I was OK and I could only nod my head. I got on all fours again as he reclaimed his position. He stroked and moaned. If there's one thing I learned in that moment, it was don't count a man out sexually due to his age. His motions increased as he took me by surprise by slowing inserting his finger in my anus. My breathing increased, my nipples hardened, and my moans grew louder. I closed my eyes as I neared the point of orgasm. I screamed out his name, then shivered and collapsed. I felt relieved, pleasured, and exhausted. I couldn't move or utter a word as I saw him get up from the bed and enter the bathroom. I positioned myself underneath the covers, yawned, and drifted to sleep.

I awakened to the sun beaming on my face and the smell of bacon. I wiped my eyes and jumped up as I made out the time on the wall clock—11:30 a.m. I hopped out of bed to find my purse and realized I'd left it downstairs. Oh shit!! I normally picked up Noah by at least ten o'clock. I rushed down the stairs as Carlton stepped out of the kitchen wiping his hands on a cloth.

"Don't worry, it's taken care of," he said with a smile.

I retrieved my phone from my purse and gave him with a puzzled look.

"What's taken care of?"

"I called Rain and told her we wouldn't be back in the city until around two o'clock. She's picked up your son, so no worries."

I leaned my head back and gave a sigh of relief. "Thank you so much. I don't know why I didn't think to tell her that last night before I left."

He smirked. "It's OK. I'm always one step ahead."

I walked towards him and wrapped my arm around his waist as we embraced.

"Thanks," I said while resting my head on his chest.

He kissed the top of my head. "Are you thanking me for last night or this morning?"

I chuckled. "Cute, but since you put it like that, both. I feel like I should be the one down here cooking you breakfast."

"Don't worry; you'll have your chance. Now go get washed up, breakfast will be served shortly."

He playfully tapped me on the behind as I walked back up the stairs. I walked in the bathroom and there was a robe laid out on the counter. I smiled as I retrieved my washcloth from the rack to wash my face.

My phone vibrated and I answered.

"Hello."

"Hey, girl. Just calling to check on you," she said.

"Chelle, girl, I can't wait to talk to you later. This dude is blowing me away. But more importantly, thanks for picking up Noah."

She chuckled. "No problem at all. You deserve that and much more. He was walking around looking for you, but he's good. The girls are outside playing with him so don't worry, take your time. I'm in for the day."

"Thank you so much. I'm enjoying myself, but I'll spare you the details until later."

I hung up the phone as I continued with my morning routine. I slipped on the robe and headed downstairs. The table in the kitchen was set and he motioned for me to have a seat. As I waited for him to join me, all I could think about was the mind-blowing early morning session I'd experienced with him. What struck me even more was the fact that he did all that to please me without intercourse. That was definitely a first for me.

He brought over our plates and walked back to the counter to bring over a pitcher of orange juice.

He sat down at the table. "Freshly squeezed orange juice," he said as he filled our glasses.

Admiring my plate full of eggs, sausage, bacon, grits, and a side of pancakes, I smiled. "You sure know your way around a kitchen, I see."

"Being raised mainly by my grandparents, I had no choice."

I picked up my fork to eat as he slapped my hand.

"I do believe in blessing the food before eating," he said, grabbing my hand.

I felt embarrassed by his gesture; normally I would pray over my food, but I guess hunger got the best of me.

As he said grace, it reminded me of my younger years at my grandparents' house. My grandfather would lead us in prayer and we wouldn't eat until he took the first bite. It was apparent Carlton was raised with those same Southern values.

After grace, we started to eat and initially all you heard was the fork hitting the plate. Considering I didn't eat last night, I was hoping I didn't finish my food too fast.

"Must be good cause you haven't looked up from that plate yet." He chuckled.

I rolled my eyes. "It's all right."

"What are you doing the remainder of the day?"

I shrugged my shoulders as I chewed. Once I cleared my mouth, I responded.

"Maybe take my son to the park. He's missing me right now. I'm the only person who picks him up from his nana's house."

He stared at me as I spoke. I picked up my napkin to wipe my mouth, thinking it was something there he was staring at.

"Do you want more kids?" he asked with a stern look.

"Maybe someday, but Noah's enough for me right now. Do you want kids?"

He laid down his fork and wiped his mouth with a napkin. "I was hoping it would happen sooner than now, but, yes, I still want kids or at least a kid."

"Hopefully I'm not prying, but what's the holdup?"

He cleared his throat. "We were both too focused on our careers initially. When we were in the trying stage, she had several complications and after three miscarriages, we stopped. It was too mentally draining for us both. She's been through a lot medically and the pressure of childbirth is something I don't want to put her through."

I finished my meal and leaned back in my chair. "So even with all she's been through, it still doesn't take away from you wanting a kid."

He shook his head. "No, it doesn't. Thank goodness for other options," he said with a smirk. "So how did you enjoy our early morning session?" he said, getting off topic.

I blushed. "Honestly, I was blown away. I don't think I've slept that good in quite a while."

He chuckled. "Your light snores indicated that."

Again, I blushed in embarrassment.

"What are we doing, Carlton?"

"Seizing the moment; enjoying each other's company. Why? Is that too much?" he asked with raised eyebrows.

"Not at all, but I find it awkward. I like you; I enjoy your company, but I don't understand why."

He shrugged his shoulders. "Why what?"

"Why are we engaging in this affair?"

He gave me a serious look. "Well, why are you taking part in it?"

Good comeback, I thought to myself.

I sighed. "I'm not going to lie. I'm lonely and it's nice to be in the company of a mature man. I have very little patience for the dating life. Besides that, I live with my best friend and her two kids; I'm not looking for anything steady with anyone because I'm focused on creating a better life for my son and me."

"I like you a lot, Tia. I'm attracted to you and it's not just physical. As you saw last night, it's not all about me; I'm a cheerful giver," he said with a smirk.

I wanted to change the subject, better yet change my clothes and head home. Us talking about how much we liked each other didn't change the fact that he was married and would never fully be mine.

I checked my watch. "It's getting late and I need to get back to the city."

He stood up and gathered our plates. "Go ahead and get dressed. I'll call my driver to take you home."

I couldn't decipher if his tone conveyed disappointment or eagerness for me to leave. Either way, I had to get going. Before long it would be time for me to take Noah back to Sharon and I wanted to spend time with him before then.

I got back upstairs to shower and put on the stretch pants and t-shirt he had laid out on the counter. Once I was dressed, I grabbed the bag with my clothes from last night and headed downstairs.

He was sitting on the couch with his feet propped up on the coffee table, flipping through channels with the remote.

"He should be here in about thirty minutes," he said without looking at me.

I sat down in a chair near the sofa. I didn't know whether to strike up a conversation or see if he would.

"Are you going to be here all day?" I decided to ask.

"Yes, I'm heading back tomorrow. I have some things I need to work on. Why, you want to come back?" he asked.

While I would love to come back for his form of pampering, I couldn't have Rachelle picking up Noah for a second day in a row.

"I'll take a rain check," I said and smiled.

He nodded his head and diverted his attention back to the TV screen.

"How long do you plan on working at the club?" he asked out of the blue.

"I don't know, but it's definitely not something I plan on doing long term. Why?"

He turned off the TV and faced me. "I have a business proposal of sorts that I'd like to discuss with you."

While he didn't talk about his business much to me, I was hoping this was an opportunity to work with him outside of the club.

"I'm all ears."

He looked towards the door at the sound of the car pulling into the driveway.

"I'll save this for when we have more time."

I was pissed that the driver showed up, as I wanted to find out more about this proposal.

"Why can't you tell me? I'm all anxious about what you have to say; now I have to wait to who knows when for us to talk about it," I said with a frown.

"Trust me, it's something that will require deep conversation."

I didn't bother to question further since it was evident he didn't want to discuss it as he got up from the couch. We headed out the door and he threw his hand up at the driver as he opened my car door.

He twirled me around and gave me a kiss on the lips. "We will talk soon, no worries."

I smiled as I got in the car, but as he closed the door and walked away, my mind started running rampant. What kind of business opportunity did he want to discuss with me? How could this affect our relationship? Damn, I wanted to know now and not later.

CHAPTER 14
KELLY

I stood with my wine glass in hand surveying all the boxes that filled my living room. Each week, Derek and I grew closer to closing on our new home. It felt surreal to be leaving my townhome. I'd worked so hard to make it my home and now after four years, I was moving on to something greater.

I'd taken my parents to look at the house and they absolutely loved it. My mom even went in the backyard and visualized how nice it would be to have our wedding at the house. She'd stated before that with us buying a house, we needed to start preparing for our wedding. Right now, my focus had little to do with getting to the altar and more about getting settled in the house. More importantly I still needed to find a dependable tenant. Derek didn't understand why I wasn't ready to sell, but I felt it would make for a good investment so why rush.

My phone rang as I struggled to follow the sound, realizing it wasn't on the receiver.

I found it and answered quickly. "Hello."

"You know I'm running late right," she said, chuckling.

"Jess, ever since you've become a mother, it's only right to expect you to be late." I smiled.

"I know; sad, but so true. I'm not that far away. Do you need anything?" she asked.

"Nope. I have snacks and wine. Just bring your ass on, so we can get through a few bottles."

I hung up the phone. Even though we were only packing up boxes, I couldn't hide my excitement about my evening with Jessica. I only wished Casey were here to join in. I missed our gatherings, which consisted of drinks, cussing each other out, and reminiscing.

I'd been over Derek's house last week helping him sort through household appliances and furniture, but tried to refrain from being too pushy about what he should keep or get rid of. I knew a lot of his things had sentimental value and I didn't want to come off insensitive. However, I'd already envisioned how I wanted things set up at the house and it didn't include much of anything he had.

Two weeks prior, Renae invited me out for drinks and since I'd blown her off times before, I agreed to meet her. I needed a night out to relax without the packing debacle I'd been consumed with. She'd invited Gigi as well, whom I hadn't seen in a few weeks.

After going back and forth about our meet-up location, we decided on Barnacle's. I walked in and looked around until I found Renae at the bar, flirting with a man. I approached without her even noticing and tapped her on the shoulder. She turned around with a big smile.

"Hey, girl," she said, extending her arms for a hug. "Here I am running my mouth and not paying attention."

"It's all good. Are we sitting at the bar or getting a table?"

"A table is fine. There's nothing but distractions at this bar," she said flirtatiously as she eyed the man she'd been talking to.

We grabbed a table near the entrance to keep watch for Gigi as the crowd started to thicken.

"So what's been up?" she said, smiling.

"Working and packing."

"Packing? What, is your office moving?" she asked.

"No, Derek and I just bought a house. We should be closing in the next two weeks."

Her eyes bucked in amazement. "That's great news. Congratulations!"

"Thank you. I'll be glad when it's all over. This has been such a nerve-wracking process."

"I'm sure of that. What are you going to do about your place?"

"I'm meeting with a property management company next week. I'm not ready to sell it, so I'll rent it for at least a year."

"Girl, I know somebody looking for a place."

"Are they employed? Single? No children? And have good credit?" I asked.

"Yes. Yes. Yes. And Yes."

"Well I'm open to checking them out. Who is it?"

She smiled. "Me."

I raised my eyebrow. "Really? I didn't know you were looking for a place."

She sighed. "My lease has been up for the past two months, so I'm doing month-to-month. I was going to be my friend's roommate, but I'm too old to be sharing a space with another grown woman."

While I didn't know Renae all that well, she seemed like a cool person. Nevertheless, I would send her through the same protocol I would a stranger. Furthermore, I didn't even know what she did for a living.

"I've never asked, but what exactly do you do for a living?"

"I'm a personal assistant. Trust me, I'm financially stable. I can provide references, pay stubs, and bank statements."

I wasn't sold just yet. I didn't want to make it seem as if I didn't trust her, but I wanted to review my options first. I never liked mixing business with pleasure; it always turned out disastrous.

"I will consider you as a viable candidate, but I would also like to view my options as well. I hope you understand."

"Oh definitely. Just know I'm a sure thing." She winked.

Gigi walked in and spotted us at the table. She slid in next to me and leaned over to give me a hug.

"Hey, ladies. Sorry I'm late," she said, grabbing a menu.

"I guess it's hard managing the life you lead," said Renae with a grin.

"You damn right it is, but somebody gotta do it," she said as she high-fived Renae.

I stirred in my seat and fought the urge to come out and ask her what her life consisted of other than lying. Being fake had never been a preference to me, but every time I was around Gigi, I felt like that was exactly what I'd become.

The waitress came over right on time for me to order another drink. Once she'd taken our orders, I turned towards Gigi.

"OK, so what's been going on with you," I said, smiling.

She sighed. "Besides work, I've been working on a side venture with my cousin."

"Like what?" I asked with raised eyebrows.

"We've been working on a clothing boutique that caters to plus-size women with a local designer on-site to help customers. We meet with a realtor tomorrow to check out storefront locations in the midtown area."

"That's great, Gigi," said Renae. "I'm always looking for opportunities. Let me know if you're looking for a silent partner."

Gigi nodded as she sipped her drink. "We have so many ideas, but we're going to start out small so as not to get ahead of ourselves. That's what's been consuming much of my time; not a man."

"Well you're keeping this man such a secret that I'm starting to think he doesn't exist," said Renae.

"He does exist, but even he hasn't seen much of me these days. Renae, do you mind if I talk to Kelly privately?"

"Sure," she said as she eyed me.

Renae went back over to the bar as Gigi moved to the opposite side of the table.

"I wanted to talk to you because I know I've been a lousy friend lately."

Oh, is that what she prefers to call it.

"Hey, we both have individual lives and things we're focusing on, so I get it."

She looked around the room. "You're right, but still I could be a better communicator with you."

I was starting to feel as though Gigi wanted to say more but couldn't seem to get it out. She avoided eye contact by continuing to scan the room as if she were looking for someone.

"Why the nervous look? You sent Renae away from the table, so I assume this is a serious conversation," I said with a stern look.

She sighed. "I want to be honest with you and out of respect I didn't want to involve Renae."

I leaned back and crossed my arms. I guessed the moment had finally arrived for her to fess up. I refrained from speaking as I waited for her to continue.

"Kelly, I've been dating John," she said quickly. "I felt like you should know that because we're exclusively dating at this point."

Even though this information wasn't new to me, to hear her finally admit it made me want to jump over the table and slap her.

I rubbed my temples. What else could I do besides make a fool of myself in front of all these people? I started to open my mouth, but fought back the words to say.

"Listen," Gigi said, "I understand this is awkward, but initially when John and I first went out, he said that you two were never serious."

My jaw clenched as she fought to defend herself.

I spoke with squinted eyes. "Any woman that's a so-called friend to another woman knows the code of conduct when it comes to exes, one-night stands, or occasional booty calls. No, John and I were not in a serious relationship, but we were intimate."

She nodded her head. "I can't help who I'm attracted to. Now you did say you were involved with him, but when I spoke with him he made it seem like it was nothing. You've moved on, so why are you making such a big deal over someone you never had feelings for?"

Was this bitch serious? The only feeling I felt right now was jumping across this table and wrapping my hands around her throat. I tried my best to keep my composure.

"What we shared was sex and, no, there were no feelings, but still it's the principle. If you can't understand that, then I misjudged your loyalty as a friend as well as your character."

She frowned. "Are you serious right now? I am a loyal friend and if I didn't have character, I wouldn't be discussing this with you. Is this seriously a deal-breaker in our friendship?"

I rolled my eyes in disbelief. "Bitch, are you crazy or just stupid? Without trust, what is a friendship? I feel betrayed. You've been dating him for months and now you feel the need to tell me."

"Like I said, we were getting to know each other; it was nothing serious."

"Point is, you were seeing him and didn't think it was important to let me know then, so why are you now?" Then I chuckled. "You know, I've known for months. I saw you guys months ago having lunch at Maggiano's. Then the night you called me claiming you wanted to meet up at the gym was only a ploy to make sure I was gone before you showed up. I waited in the parking lot just to verify as I continued to talk to you on the phone. I'm not as dumb as you think I am."

Gigi leaned back, looking unsettled. "This was not some spiteful attempt to hurt you, Kelly. You've moved on with your life and I didn't think things would be so touch and go after all this time. He said so himself that he didn't think you would make a big deal out of it."

I threw my hands up in disbelief. "I wonder why. This was a perfect setup that you fell for. What a real friend would've done is just asked me straight up. You chose not to do that, so I don't know what you're expecting from me right now."

"I'm not expecting you to do anything, but I certainly didn't think you would react this way. To me, sex is just sex. It's not like this happened weeks ago or even months. How can you be so territorial over something that wasn't yours to begin with and you've got a man now?"

I didn't appreciate her tone or how she was coming at me with her slick remarks. I nodded my head to try to calm myself, but before I knew it, I picked up my drink and threw it right in her face. I grabbed my purse, but paused as she reached for a napkin to wipe herself.

"Enjoy your life and, oh, that drink was on me," I said with a wink and slapped twenty dollars on the table before exiting.

Before I could reach my car, I heard Renae calling after me. I turned around as she jogged over to me.

"What the hell is going on?" she asked with a puzzled look.

I opened my car door. "Why don't you ask your so-called friend in there?"

She held her chest to catch her breath. "I think she's in shock as well as embarrassed. I surely didn't see this coming."

I got in the car and started up my vehicle. "I really don't want to talk about it, but I'm sure she'll give you her version. Thanks for the invite out; I'll see you around."

I didn't bother waiting for a response as I closed my door and put my car in drive, leaving Renae standing with a dumbfounded look.

Since that time, I'd received two calls from Gigi, which I refused to answer. When Renae did call, she managed to avoid any conversation about what happened with Gigi or bring her up. As far as I was concerned, Gigi was just a stranger on the street.

My doorbell rang and I hopped down the stairs to the door. I peeped out and saw that it was Jess. We exchanged a hug as she walked in.

"Damn, you've been doing some serious packing," Jess said, looking at the bare walls.

"If I wasn't so particular, I would've gotten a moving company to handle all this shit. I'm so over this," I said, throwing my hands up.

We walked upstairs to the kitchen where I poured Jess a glass of wine and refilled my own.

"Have you decided what you're taking and what you'll sell?"

I gave her a side-eye stare as I sipped my wine. "I'm having a hard time with that. Girl, my stuff is top of the line and nobody is going to pay me a third of what I've spent on it. I'm taking about ninety-five percent of my stuff with me even if it means storing it in the basement."

Jess shook her head as she chuckled. "Poor Derek is stressing over what he's willing to give up, and, between you and I, you guys are neck and neck. This is about to be pure comedy."

"Come on, Jess, I'm not trying to knock his style or his ex-wife's, but it's not contemporary. My stuff is more trendy, elegant…"

"More prone to get broken or messed up, since you have kids in the household. I can see you panicking at their every move, cause you're like that now with them being here. The house needs to be kid-friendly, my dear."

I downed the glass of wine. "Maybe I'll put some shock wire around the formal living and dining room area," I said.

Jess laughed as we moved to the living room area.

She clapped her hands. "So what do you need me to do?"

"Those crystal pieces over there need to be wiped down and wrapped."

She walked over and sat on the floor. "Have you heard from Casey?"

"Actually two days ago she called. She's planning on visiting soon, maybe next weekend."

"Yeah, she left me a message and I haven't gotten around to calling her back. Is Josie coming with her?"

"No, she'll be working; she finally got a job."

"Oh that's good. So what's been going on with you?"

I poured another glass of wine. "Well, besides throwing a drink in Gigi's face, nothing much."

Jess stopped wrapping as she looked at me with a shocked expression. "What the hell! Why?"

I waved my hand. "Being a trifling, desperate bitch is why."

"It takes a lot for you to get out of character, so it must've been severe."

I filled her in on the situation with John, minus the fact he'd been the culprit of the paternity petition, and how Gigi had been going behind my back dating him.

Jess shook her head. "I don't know why she hid it from you, but I give her credit for at least telling you."

I frowned. "Credit for telling me? Jess, I already knew what was up. I'd witnessed them having lunch and meeting up at the gym. She's lied for months; that heifer gets no gold star from me."

"I mean she did violate the code and she should've been honest from the start, but come on now, you know she's a desperate woman. I told you from day one meeting her that she was a 'by-any-means-necessary' chick; not someone I would trust around my man."

"Jess, you look at every woman as a threat, considering what you've gone through with Darnell."

Jessica threw up her finger. "Now wait, you're making me sound like an insecure woman and that's definitely not the case. I know a thirsty chick when I see one and she definitely fits the description. I'm not saying she was right for what she did, but honestly it shouldn't have surprised you. Your life is good, don't sweat that."

One thing I could say about Jess and Casey was they didn't bite their tongue with their opinions. Honestly it made me feel as if the situation was petty and I was making it bigger than it was. I valued friendships and didn't appreciate being made to feel taken. Jess was right on one thing, Gigi had always been hell-bent on getting a man.

We continued talking as we packed. It felt good to catch up with Jess. I could see the happiness she had in her life now with the baby and rebuilding her marriage with Darnell. They went through such a turbulent period, but I was glad they'd fought through those rough times and were dedicated to making it work.

My cell phone rang as I looked around to find where I'd last laid it. I rushed into the kitchen and answered.

"Hello," I asked through heavy breaths.

"I hope I didn't interrupt your moment," she said.

I chuckled. "Girl, please, if that were the case I wouldn't have even answered."

I looked at the caller ID to confirm it was Renae.

"What's up?" I asked.

"I wanted to know if I could come by and take a look at your place," she asked.

I avoided the topic at all costs, but Renae was relentless about being my tenant. After the whole incident with Gigi, I didn't want to make anything personal with anyone she was connected to. Even though I had no intentions of making her my tenant, I told her to come on by. Hell, maybe with her here, I could put her to work as well.

I gave her the address and walked back in the living room.

"This chick I met through Gigi is coming by to look at my place."

"You cool with her like that?" she asked.

"I've known her for a few months now and she seems OK, but there's some mystery about her, I must admit. She's the sister of one of Gigi's friends."

Jessica tilted her head. "I always say never mix business with pleasure. I know you want a reliable tenant, but I suggest letting property management handle the screening and selecting."

"I plan to. She's been rather pushy about renting it, so I'm only letting her view it as a courtesy."

"It's a good thing I'm here. You know I have a good eye for judging folks' character. You see I was dead on about Gigi." She winked.

I threw a bundle of bubble wrap at her as she laughed and ducked. The doorbell rang and I took another sip of wine and went to the door.

Renae walked in with a bottle of wine. We exchanged hugs.

"Your hair looks nice," I said as I admired her freshly chopped hairstyle.

"Thanks. Every time I tell myself I'm going to let it grow out, I end up cutting it."

"It fits you. Listen, my best friend, Jessica, is here. I want you to meet her before I give you the tour," I said, walking up the stairs.

When we reached the living room, Jessica stood up from the floor and walked toward us with a perturbed look. Her reaction caught me off guard, but she quickly smiled as she extended her hand.

"Nice to meet you. I'm Jessica."

"I'm Renae. Pleasure to meet you as well." She smiled.

There was an awkward pause as they both stared at each other.

"Gosh, forgive me but you look so familiar," said Jessica as she frowned to remember.

"I get that a lot," said Renae with a nervous smile.

To break up the strange encounter, I proceeded to show Renae around. I could tell even though she showed interest that something definitely had changed from her initial arrival.

"Are you OK?" I asked.

"Oh yeah, I'm cool. Your friend kind of threw me off with her look."

I waved her off. "It's nothing like that. She works with a lot of people and thinks she knows everybody."

After I finished showing her around, I offered her a glass of wine. I went to the kitchen, leaving her alone with Jessica.

"Are you originally from Atlanta?" Jessica asked.

"No, I've been here for about a year. I'm from Savannah."

"Oh, OK. Do you like it here?"

"It's OK, but I'm looking to move within the year."

I returned back to the living room and overheard Renae's statement. With her mentioning she was looking to move away, why would she even think I would consider her as a tenant?

"Really. Why?" I asked, handing her the wine glass.

She smiled. "I'm young, single, no kids. I stick and move; no sense of staying somewhere too long when you got nothing holding you back."

Jessica chimed in. "What exactly do you do to afford the luxury of moving around like that?"

While Jessica's question came off strong, I knew Renae would handle it accordingly.

"I'm a personal assistant, so I spend a lot of time travelling anyway." She smirked. "If I didn't know any better I would think Mrs. Jessica is property management."

I tried to chuckle to downplay the comment, but from the look on Jessica's face I could tell she was thinking of a comeback. To break up the tension in the air I decided to change the topic.

"Are you going out tonight?" I asked Renae.

"I thought about it, but no. I'll be at the crib, curled up on my couch, watching Netflix. Why, you care to stop by? You can even bring Jessica," she said, winking towards Jessica.

Jessica's cell phone rang with perfect timing. She stepped into the dining room to take the call.

"Well, I'm going to get back to the crib since your friend doesn't seem too pleased by my presence."

"Thanks for stopping by with the wine," I said as we walked to the door.

She smiled. "No problem. Maybe we can do dinner one day next week," she said, handing me back the wine glass.

As we exchanged good nights, I made sure she got in her car before closing the door. I turned as Jessica stood at the top of the stairs with her hand on her hips.

"You know that chick was a few seconds away from getting cursed out," Jessica said with a straight face.

I chuckled. "Well you started it."

"I know her from somewhere and from her reaction she's seen me too. When I don't get a good vibe from a person, it's hard for me to fake it."

"Jess, relax. She's gone and you don't have to be in her presence. I don't know Renae all that well, but she seems like cool people."

Jessica rolled her eyes. "Just keep a watchful eye out for her cause I can tell there's something to her. Well, my husband has summoned me home, so it's been real but I'm out of here."

"Go on home and make that baby number two," I said.

She blushed. "Girl, please, I love the act of baby making, but I can't see having another until Tianna's at least four. Have you and Derek discussed more kids?"

I held up a hand to stop. "Pump your brakes. I love my baby, but no, ma'am; I don't want any more kids. Collectively we have three; that's more than enough. Planning on getting my tubes tied immediately after we get settled in this house."

"Does Derek know?" Jessica asked with surprise.

"No, we haven't discussed it, but hell I would tell him the same thing."

"I hope you don't go through this without first discussing it."

"I'm tired of giving in to what he wants. This is my body."

Jessica folded her arms. "So you're going to do this and tell him afterwards?"

I turned my head without a response.

"Kells, I love you to life, but you're wrong as hell if you do that. Derek wants a future with you and you don't think this is important enough to discuss with him first? Trust me when I tell you, you doing that could ruin your relationship for good."

"I appreciate your concern, Jess, but I got this."

Jessica shrugged her shoulders then reached in for a hug. I watched her as she walked to her car and closed the door.

What a night! After three bottles of wine, all I wanted to do was go to sleep. I couldn't help but think about the awkward moment between Jessica and Renae. Jessica could be a bit overbearing, but her intuition was normally dead on. It left me thinking what was it that Renae could be potentially hiding? We all had hidden secrets, but I only hoped whatever she harbored wouldn't come back to bite me in the judgment department.

CHAPTER 15
JANEN

It had been a month since my visit to Atlanta and I'd yet to hear from Rita or Robbie. I didn't want to express my disappointment, so I put on a smile like everything was OK and didn't bring up the matter.

My schedule was rather busy, as I'd accepted a two-week project in New York. It felt good to be back and it gave me time to catch up with my best friend, Sharee. She insisted that I stay with her versus getting a hotel.

It was Friday night and after a long week, we both decide to spend the evening with a good bottle of wine and sit out on the terrace of her condo.

"Girl, I sure miss you being here. Hanging out isn't the same without you," said Sharee.

"I know exactly what you mean. I miss having your crazy butt around, too."

"Maybe I need to pull a Carrie and find me a Miami man, so I can be closer to you." She smirked.

I pretended to shiver. The thought of Carrie made my blood boil.

"You know I decided to be nice by inviting her out to lunch for some girl talk before I left. This heifer was nearly an hour late and had the nerve to get there and tell me she only had thirty minutes to meet. You know at that point, I let her ass have it."

Sharee laughed. "Damn, she played you like that."

"After I let her have it and left her ass sitting right in her seat at the restaurant, before I could get to my car she'd already called Tony. I'm totally convinced that bitch got a problem."

"Well, you know what I think," said Sharee, eyeing me as she took a sip from her glass.

"And that is?"

"What woman makes it a point to be where another man is with total disregard for the woman he's with?"

I chuckled. "A stalker."

"Come on, J, you know what I'm getting at. I honestly think Carrie is whipped and can't let go. Somewhere in this brotherly-sisterly image they portray, they've crossed the line. And while it's evident that Tony has moved on, she's still holding on to hope that she can get that old thing back."

I totally understood where Sharee was coming from as I'd thought of that myself. When I'd asked Tony about them, he'd always been adamant that there was nothing between them sexually.

"I've had my suspicions as well, but Tony won't admit it. He said he's never been intimate with her."

She smacked her lips. "The hell he say; she gave his ass some head or something. No woman acts like that without cause; it's beyond emotional attachment. Why the hell else would she act like such a bitch towards you? Easy, you're black and you've managed to get what she wants."

I nodded as I sipped my wine. "Well, hating and being a stalker ain't exactly helping her cause. As long as she stays in her place when in my presence I'm good."

"So how are things with Tony? No little mixed babies in the near future." She winked.

"We are doing OK and it's way too soon for kids."

"I'm still looking for a white man to sweep me off my feet," she said, chuckling. "I love my brothers, but something has got to give."

"I hope you don't think me being with Tony was my way of saying I'm sick of my black brothers. It's all about chemistry and that transcends color lines."

Sharee rolled her neck as she spoke. "I wasn't insinuating that either, honey. I'm just saying, for me, I've never been interested in white men nor been approached by one. I'm interested in seeing what that interracial love is like. But moving right along, have you heard anything from your biological side?"

"I'm done with that situation. I don't know why I even extended that olive branch to begin with."

"Well, friend, I think you did the right thing. When you're trying to make peace with a situation, regardless of how painful it may be you have to handle it dead on. You did your part and that's all you can do."

My phone rang and I looked down at the screen indicating a caller from a private number. I stepped inside and closed the door before answering, thinking it could potentially be my client.

"Janen speaking," I answered.

There was silence on the other end even though I could hear the person breathing.

"Hello."

"Oh sorry, Janen, it's me, Robbie," he said nervously.

I felt my heart beating rapidly as I took a seat on the couch.

"This is certainly a surprise. How are you?"

"I'm doing OK. Sorry it's taken me so long to call you."

"Yeah, I was starting to think I wouldn't hear from you. But I'm glad you called."

Once again there was silence.

"Hello. You still there?" I asked.

He cleared his throat. "Yeah, I'm here. Well I called because I wanted to let you know Rita is in a rehabilitation center now. When you were here, honestly I hadn't seen her in weeks. I got a call about a week thereafter from her saying she'd signed herself into rehab. I went to visit her for the first time last week and I tell you, I haven't seen my sister look that good in a long time. I had a conversation with her about your visit."

My heart pounded and my hands started to shake as I waited for him to continue. Once again he grew silent. I could hear sniffles on the other end and allowed him to collect himself.

"She cried when I mentioned you, but she was so happy that you wanted to meet her."

I couldn't contain my tears as they slid down my face. I didn't even know what to say. I had to take it all in.

"I think it would be good for her if she saw you, Janen. She has visitation once a week and I wanted to know if you could come and see her."

"Yes, yes, I'll be there. Just tell me when."

He gave me dates as I stood to find a pen and paper to write them down. I let him know I'd get back with him to confirm when I'd be able to come.

As I put my phone on the counter, Sharee came back in.

"Are you OK?" she asked with a concerned look.

I smiled as tears continued to run down my face. "Just when you think all hope is lost, I get that call. That was my biological mother's brother, Robbie. She's in rehab and he asked to come down and visit. She wants to see me."

Sharee came over and gave me a hug. "What a blessing! See, you thought everything you did was in vain. It's true, girl—it's never about our timing, it's all in His timing."

I was so happy to have received such a call while I was here with Sharee. With Tony, he never asked if anyone had contacted me and therefore, I kept my feelings locked up. With Sharee, I could always be myself and even if I pretended, she knew me well enough to know when something wasn't right.

I immediately started looking for flights, and, considering my assignment would be over next Sunday, I decided to fly directly into Atlanta. I wanted this trip to be strictly about Rita and decided not to let my mom or Jessica know I would be in town.

Sharee brought the bottle and our wine glasses in from the terrace.

"I think this occasion deserves a toast," she said, filling our glasses.

She handed me mine. "To closure," I responded.

We toasted as my cell phone rang. I looked at the caller ID—it was Tony.

"Hey, babe," I answered.

"Hey. Why haven't I heard from you all day?"

"I called you and when I didn't get an answer on your cell, I called your office. I figured you would see my missed call and get back to me when you were free. Why do you sound so edgy?"

He sighed. "It's been a long week and I miss my wife."

I blushed. "Awww…I miss you too, babe. What's going on at work?"

"I'm working on this new project for a hotel down in the Bahamas. I might need to spend a few days down there and was thinking when you come back you could join me."

I didn't want to further put a damper on his mood with my news of going to Atlanta to see Rita.

"Let's play it by ear; I'll need to check my schedule."

"Babe, we need to make time for each other. With you being gone for two weeks and me possibly being there a week or longer, that's a whole damn month of us not seeing each other."

Hearing the irritation in his voice, I tried to lighten the situation. "Tony, I know that. Don't you think I miss you too? How about you come to New York on Wednesday for a few days?"

"I can't afford to take any days off; it's busy here. Plus we can use the Bahamas as a mini-vacation. Let's work on making this happen, OK, babe?"

I never wanted to let my husband down, but I really didn't want to miss my visitation with Rita. Visitation was only once a week on Tuesdays and I had other commitments in Miami lined up. For the sake of argument, I told him I would work it out, but I had no idea how I was going to do so.

Sharee gave me a side-eye stare. "Any reason you didn't share with your hubby the news?"

I rubbed my temples. "He's not interested, so why would I share it with him?"

"He's your damn husband and he should be compassionate enough to understand why this is important to you."

I shrugged. "I don't force the issue, Sharee. He's entitled to the way he feels, just like Joann and Dad."

I quickly changed the subject, not wanting the joy of my day to be ruined with the current conversation. Tony was a great husband, but when he felt a certain way about a topic, he wouldn't budge on it.

I'd always wondered what it would be like to meet Rita. I smiled knowing that soon I wouldn't have to wonder—it would be a reality.

CHAPTER 16
DEREK

We'd finally closed on our house, and as soon as those keys were in our hands, it was off to the races with getting things moved. My sister agreed to keep the kids for the next few days so Kelly and I could get settled. While I was eagerly getting things settled to see the look on the kids' faces, I didn't quite understand how Kelly felt. If she was excited, it sure didn't show, as it appeared she had other things on her mind.

After finally setting up the formal living room, which consisted of Kelly's furnishings, I fell on the floor and asked her to join me.

I rubbed her back as she scooted closer to me. "I know you're tired, babe, but it seems like you have something on your mind."

She looked at me with a forced smile. "This whole move has been overwhelming paired with work, so I don't think tired truly describes how I feel. I'm still looking for a tenant and it's frustrating."

I leaned my head back on the couch. "It's only hard because you're making it that way. You're getting yourself overly involved in the process when you should leave it to the property management group you've hired."

"This is my first time doing this, so I feel I need to be hands-on to let these people know I'm serious about my business. My townhome is my first major investment and I want to make sure it stays in the condition it's in."

I nodded. "I understand your logic, but you've got to take a step back and let these people do their job. Otherwise, what you need them for if you're doing it yourself?"

She nodded her head in agreement, but I knew even so, it wouldn't stop her. Kelly felt like she had to be in control of every aspect. I'd seen her progression in trying to relinquish that control aspect in our relationship, but in other areas, she went full throttle.

"We truly have a beautiful home, Derek. I know the kids are going to be so happy when they see their rooms."

He chuckled. "After all the money we've spent, they better. OK, break time is over," I said as I stood up.

"Damn slave driver. That wasn't even a thirty-minute break." She smiled as she stood up.

"I don't plan on using all my days off dealing with unpacking. I'd rather get it done now so we can relax later."

She worked on getting the kitchen set up while I worked on the kids' playroom. We'd decided to have the girls in the same room for now and turn the other room into a play area. I'd painted the room a sky blue, which included clouds and inspirational wording. I stood back to admire my work and had to smile; damn good job.

My cell phone rang as the caller ID showed a private number.

"Hello," I answered.

"Hello, handsome. How's everything going?"

I shook my head. I hadn't heard from her since our encounter at the club several weeks ago.

"I'm good. What's up?" I said dryly.

"Well damn, you don't have to sound so excited. I just wanted to check up on my old friend since you don't call me."

"Listen, I'm kind of busy right now…"

She cut me off. "Yeah, I heard you're moving into your new house with your family. Congratulations."

I wanted to ask how the hell did she find that out, but figured she'd heard it from Maria.

"Thanks. Well, let me get back to unpacking."

"I want to see you."

"I don't think that's a good idea," I said, scanning the hallway.

"Oh, but I think it is," she said provocatively. "I know you want this, Derek. I'm the drug you need; stop fighting it. I'm not trying to break up your happy home."

"I can't talk right now, Lacey. Good-bye," I said as I ended the call.

Her aggression was a gift and a curse. Just when I thought she'd moved on, she popped up like a jack-in-the-box.

Since that night she seduced me at the club, I couldn't shake how that moment turned me on. Lacey was a freak; I enjoyed the way she took control and totally blew my mind sexually.

Things between Kelly and I were fine, but sexually we were at a standstill. Her lack of a sex drive left me unfulfilled; to put it bluntly, it made me want Lacey more. I knew the stress of the move could've been a contributing factor, but I was a man with needs and expected my woman to bend to those needs accordingly. Some nights I would try to set the mood and her lack of enthusiasm would kill the moment. In those moments, it turned from me wanting to make love to my woman and make her climax, to me just getting mine while thinking of somebody else. Cold game, but that was just keeping it real.

The doorbell rang and I looked out the window and saw the delivery truck for our bedroom furniture. Kelly insisted on purchasing a new bedroom suite when I clearly felt her suite was sufficient. Wanting this move to go as peacefully as possible, I gave in. I met the movers by the stairs as they made their way up with the mahogany king-sized sleigh bed. Our bedroom was the size of two master bedrooms with two walk-in closets and a sitting area. I watched as Kelly directed the deliverymen on where to place the furniture.

The doorbell rang again and I rushed down the stairs. I peeped out and saw Darnell.

I opened the door. "Hey, bro. What you doing round these parts?"

We exchanged hugs as he walked in.

"I figured I'd stop by and see if you needed any help. After Carlton said he'd been over to help, I was like, damn, I'm some kind of brother." He chuckled.

"No biggie. I wasn't expecting any help, man, but I appreciate it."

Kelly walked downstairs and gave Darnell a hug.

"Hey, Darnell. Did Derek drag you over here to help?" she asked.

"No, he didn't; just wanted to come by and lend a hand."

"Well, thank you, because I'm tired and about to go on break," she said, grabbing her purse from the counter. "Babe, I'm going to Target."

She kissed me as she left. The deliverymen were done with their setup as I went upstairs to inspect; the furniture definitely complimented the room.

I walked back downstairs and joined Darnell in the family room where he was unpacking boxes.

"This house is beautiful, man. Now Jessica's talking about maybe we should look at a new home," he said, shaking his head.

"So what you going to do?"

"Not a damn thing. We live in a decent neighborhood, we have adequate space for the three of us, so we are good. I know you've spent a shitload of money with all this new furniture up in here."

I sighed. "Man, Kelly got expensive-ass taste. I definitely caught myself blowing the hell up on some of these purchases, but when I look at how well they fit, I can't be mad."

"So, how are things between you two?" Darnell asked with a piercing look.

"Things are good. It's been stressful moving two homes into one, but we've managed to avoid arguments, so that's a plus."

He cut his eyes at me. "Any more encounters with Lacey?"

How did I know this was what he ultimately wanted to discuss? I didn't want to discuss her because in my eyes she was a non-factor. But from Darnell's look, I could tell he was going to push the issue.

"Lacey has been keeping her distance. My focus is on my home and family."

He nodded his head. "As it should be; I just hope this doesn't somehow come back and bite you in the ass."

I loved my brother, but right now I didn't need the negative energy.

"Look, bro, I'm good and this situation is dead. Stop trying to make my situation like yours."

He raised his hands. "I'm not trying to make anything like mine. And, bro, whether you want to admit it or not, it's the same; we've both stepped out on the woman we proclaimed to love. The only difference is I was married and you're not, but no doubt the shit is the same. I'm not saying you don't have matters handled, but you can't control a scorned woman. While you think she's moved on, she may be in the background plotting."

I always valued the advice of my brother; however, on this situation, I didn't feel she was a threat. True enough, Lacey called when I least expected it, but she had not done anything disruptive in regards to making our fling known to Kelly.

Once Darnell left, I looked around at our home and marveled in its beauty. I was so blessed to have this home, my kids, and a wonderful woman by my side. However, I couldn't deny the fact that I was still carrying on a sexual relationship with Lacey. I needed to meet with her one last time, not for sex, but to make it known that I could no longer communicate with her.

I'd made the decision once we were settled that I would propose again to Kelly. She'd given me everything I wanted; now it was time that I gave her what she deserved. I felt ready and confident in my decision and only hoped that my plan would go accordingly.

CHAPTER 17
LA'TIA

After my night with Carlton, I couldn't stop thinking about what it was he wanted to discuss with me. I tried to be patient, considering he would be traveling for the next week on business. The few times he did call, I wanted to ask him about it, but the calls were so brief due to his tight schedule.

When he finally returned back to town, he asked me to come meet him at the cabin. This time I told him I would drive myself there as he gave me directions. I packed an overnight bag and took Noah to his grandmother's for their trip to Disney World. I was going to miss my baby, but hopefully upon their return I'd be in my own place, and next it would be on to a better job.

The hour-long ride gave me time to think things over. The club had been very good to me financially. I normally worked four days a week, but due to my plans of moving, I'd decided to put in as many hours as I possibly could.

I'd visited Marcus's gravesite for the first time last week and sat there for what felt like hours just reminiscing. I missed him greatly, but was thankful for the seed he left behind. I wasn't in love with Carlton, but what he did for me was provide some form of companionship that I missed with Marcus.

Since being back in Atlanta, I'd thought so much about my own family and how I needed to get in contact with them. There was never any real closeness there between us, but despite all the drama in the past, I was willing to put forth an effort. I decided once things were set with me having my own place, I would reach out to my mother.

I turned off the main road and turned onto the dirt driveway towards Carlton's cabin. When I pulled up, he was outside trimming bushes, wearing shorts, a long-sleeved t-shirt, and a Braves hat. It was a rare sight to see, as I'd normally only saw him in semi-casual dress at the least.

He dropped his hedgers as he walked over to open my car door.

"I thought I asked you to call once you were near," he said.

"Sorry. Between the music and getting caught up in my thoughts, I forgot," I said as I kissed him on the cheek.

I grabbed my bag from the backseat as he finished up his outdoor work. I walked in to the smell of apple-scented candles mixed with the aroma of spices from something cooking in the kitchen. I dropped my bag and walked in the kitchen to investigate the smell. The Crockpot was on and I peeped in to see a roast with potatoes, carrots, and onions—my type of meal.

I walked out of the kitchen just as he entered through the front door.

"Couldn't resist seeing what smelled so good, huh?" He smiled.

I blushed. "No I couldn't. I love a man who knows how to cook up a wholesome Southern meal."

"Well you know I can do that and more," he said, winking. "Why don't you come up and shower with me?"

"I showered before I got here."

"What, you're only allowed to take one shower a day?"

"I have a better idea. How about we take a bath together?"

"I'm cool with that, as long as you don't have the water piping hot. A man's balls are sensitive and I know how you women love hot water."

I laughed, as that was the only way I could truly enjoy a bath.

"I promise I'll go easy on the hot water," I said, walking up the stairs.

I ran some bath water and poured in some bath oil that sat on the edge of the tub. The view from the bathroom window showed a deer shyly scavenging through the woods. I loved the scenery this place offered as well as the peace I felt being here.

Carlton walked in the bathroom wearing only his boxer shorts. For a man in his forties, his body was well defined even though he wasn't all that muscular.

I stood up and gave my best Vanna White impersonation. "Would you like to test the water and see if it's to your satisfaction?"

He grinned as he dipped his hand in. "It's tolerable," he said and disrobed.

This was the first time I'd actually seen him completely in the nude in full light. I tried my best not to stare, but he was definitely not lacking in the penis department.

I turned around and took off my clothes as he stared at me.

"If I didn't know any better, I would think you were shy," he said with a smile.

I glanced over my shoulder seductively. "I am."

"OK, well I'll just admire the view from the window. Don't want you to feel uncomfortable," he said, turning his head.

When I undressed, I walked over to the opposite side of the tub and slipped in. I held my knees close to my chest. He reached underwater and grabbed my legs, extending them on top of his.

"This is so relaxing," he said as he leaned back and closed his eyes.

"OK, so now that we finally have the time, I'm interested in what you wanted to discuss with me the last time we were here," I asked.

"Geez, you don't waste any time."

"Time is precious, why would I?" I grinned.

"How comfortable are you with me?" he asked.

I frowned. "What kind of question is that? I'm out here in the boonies with you and have been around you well over ten times; of course I'm comfortable."

"What are your expectations being with me?" he asked.

Was this some sort of trick question? I knew he was married and wasn't going to leave his wife, so what other expectations could I possibly have.

"I'm not sure I understand that. I know your situation, about which, thankfully, you were honest from the start. I'm not expecting you to leave your wife or put a ring on my finger. My expectation is that you continue being honest with me and us enjoying each other's company for however long it lasts."

He smirked. "Could you see yourself being with someone like me?"

It was clear that Carlton wanted to see how emotionally attached I was to him at this point.

"I like you, Carlton, and I enjoy spending time with you. But knowing your situation, my heart is very guarded. In fact, it has an electric fence around it."

He smiled and nodded. "That's fair enough."

I gave him a sideways look. "OK, so now that you've beat around the bush, what's really on your mind?"

"Tia, no doubt I do love my wife and don't plan on changing my marital status. My wife is a different kind of woman and we keep no secrets. She knows where I am now and she knows who I'm with."

My eyes grew big as my heart started to beat rapidly.

"She knows about me?" I asked, staring at him intensely.

He nodded his head. "Our marriage works because we are honest with each other. Yes, she knows about you."

I leaned my head against the wall. What the hell had I gotten myself into?

"I don't even know what to say. Are you going to tell me next she wants to have a sit-down dinner with us?" I asked sarcastically.

He laughed as if what I'd said was funny. Right now, I didn't find a damn thing funny.

I leaned forward with a serious look. "Is this some sort of game to you? What, do you pick girls from the club, wine and dine them, then fuck with their mind like this?"

He gave me a puzzled look. "No, not at all. How can I 'fuck' with a person's mind if I'm being honest and laying everything out upfront? I like you, Tia; if I didn't, I would've screwed you well before now without a second thought of another invite. Pussy comes a dime a dozen and that ain't hard for me to get whatsoever. I see something in you that I actually adore."

I folded my arms across my chest and gave the "yeah right" look. "What is it you adore about me? Or should I say, besides sex, what else do you want from me?"

He stared at me. "From what I've seen of you, you seem like a great mother and I applaud you on filling the gap of his father. I tip my hat to any woman who can do that alone, especially with a son."

It made me feel good to hear someone giving me props for my role as a mother. I didn't get too many pats on the back for it, nor did I expect it. My son was my top priority and everything I did and strove for was for his betterment.

"I appreciate your recognition. All this talk and I'm still puzzled as to how this relates to whatever you wanted to discuss with me. Plus you didn't answer the second part of my question."

He rubbed his hands over his face. "Since you don't have the patience to just let the conversation flow, then I'll just spit it out. I want you to be our surrogate."

I stared at him in shock as I struggled to wrap my brain around what he'd just said.

"Excuse me?" I asked.

"I think you heard me the first time. Yes, I asked you to be our surrogate."

I frowned at him as I forcefully splashed water in his face. I got up abruptly and stepped out of the bathtub, trying my best not to make an ass of myself by falling.

"Come on, Tia. We are two adults having a conversation and you take an immature approach of splashing water in my face," he said as he grabbed a nearby towel.

I wrapped a towel around my body. "Be glad I didn't haul off and slap you. What makes you think I want to be involved with you like that? I can't believe you would ask me something like that."

He slowly got out of the tub and dried himself off. I stood awaiting his response with my hands on my hips.

"Let's calm down and talk about this rationally."

I walked out of the room and slammed the door. My mind told me to throw on my clothes and get the hell on. However, I wanted to fully understand Carlton's logic of proposing something so preposterous. Looking through my bag, I realized I didn't have anything to slip on. I went to the nearby dresser and pulled out one of Carlton's t-shirts. I sat on the bed as I waited for him to exit the bathroom.

He walked out wearing a robe and sat down in the corner chair near the patio.

"Listen, I know in your mind right about now you may think I'm the biggest jerk."

"Finally something we agree on."

He smirked. "OK, I'll take that. This is a business deal, Tia, nothing more, nothing less."

"A deal? Me having your baby comes with a lot of responsibility."

"I only asked you to carry my baby, not care for it."

I squint. "And does Maria know you're asking me to do this?"

He nodded his head. "Yes. Since she is unable to bear children, we've always discussed surrogacy as an option. We already have an egg donor; it's just a matter of finding a surrogate mother. She understands how much I want to have a child."

"So let's get this straight. Your wife is OK with selecting me as a surrogate even though we are intimately involved?"

"Yes."

I busted out laughing as he shook his head with a straight face. I couldn't even believe I was having such a conversation. This shit was something straight from a soap opera.

I folded my arms. "How many women have you propositioned?"

"This isn't some offer you make to any woman with a uterus, Tia. You're the only one I've asked. Maria told me years ago when she first got sick to do so, but I needed to focus on being a supportive husband to her. Now that I'm getting older and thinking of retiring soon, I'm ready and so is she."

"Since this is a business proposal, what do I get?"

He smiled. "A rent-free place, a monthly stipend, free medical insurance, and a signing bonus."

Wow! This sounded like a well-thought-out plan. While the perks were enticing, I would have to do a lot of soul-searching on this one.

"Is this a rent-free place of my choice?"

"No. It's actually my guesthouse."

I shook my head. "Oh wow. Now I've heard it all. You want me to live at your house right under the watchful eye of your wife. Damn, does this include a personal chef and a bodyguard?"

He interlocked his hands as he looked at me sternly. "I understand this isn't something that you've ever dealt with before, but I would hope that you'd give it some thought."

I ran my fingers through my hair. "You do realize this is major, right? I mean I'm giving up nearly ten months of my life for you."

He held up his finger. "But it's not without a price. This is a fee-for-service transaction, sweetheart. Consider it as a temp job and I'm the client."

I smirked at his lame analogy. If I'd ever needed a drink, right now was certainly the time.

"We've discussed this enough. I'm going downstairs to finish up dinner. I'll call you when it's ready."

I nodded as he got up from his seat and headed downstairs. As I lay back on the bed staring out the skylight, all I could think about was the direction of my life. I wanted so desperately to get back to that place of independence. I'd gone from running away to another state and getting on public assistance to coming back to the same place I'd run from to work in a secret club and get caught up with a wealthy married man.

While all the things he offered were the things I needed to help me rebound and get on my feet, was it worth the sacrifice of my body and integrity? While this surrogacy would make me come off as a hero for helping a married couple unable to conceive, the fact remained this was a married man with whom I was having an affair. I closed my eyes as my head started pounding from all the thoughts crowding my mind.

At this moment, as the tears escaped my eyes, I wished even more than ever Marcus was here. If he were, he would never allow me to subject myself to the things I was now doing just to make ends meet. Hustling was all he knew in life and he would do it if it meant providing for his family. I think that same mentality laid in me at this point, but it was far from who I was. I needed to get back to me, because this life I was leading was far from where I'd imagined myself to be.

CHAPTER 18
KELLY

After a month of being in our new home, we were finally settled. From painting to furnishing every room, we'd managed to pull it off. Even though I was on a spending hiatus from all the damage I'd done to credit cards and my savings, it felt good walking into our beautiful home.

Derek and I had discussed having a housewarming in the next few weeks for our family and friends. I loved hosting events, and with a bigger house and huge backyard, now was the perfect time.

I'd finally gotten a tenant for my townhome, a newlywed young couple. They loved the place and I felt they would take good care of it. I let Renae know that I couldn't lease the place to her, mainly due to her finances. While she had sufficient income, property management felt more secure with a two-person income and I couldn't agree more. I could tell she was disappointed, but she said she understood and was thinking of moving out of state sooner anyway.

Since right before we moved, I hadn't been to the gym in weeks. Today would be my first day going back and I was eager to return to my routine. Renae agreed to meet me there.

As I walked in, I spotted Gigi and we locked eyes. I hadn't seen her or spoken to her since that day at the bar. I went to the open area to stretch and noticed her approaching me. Even though I was still salty at her, I had so much goodness in my life that I refused to let her bring negative energy into it. I could be cordial, but that was as good as it would get.

She sat on the mat next to me and just stared at me. I continued with my stretching as if she weren't there.

"Hello, Kelly," she said.

"Hi, Gigi," I said dryly.

"I've missed you. I didn't think I'd see you here anymore since it's been weeks."

I continued to stretch, avoiding eye contact. "Yeah, my schedule has been hectic so I haven't been working out."

Gigi looked around the room and fidgeted with her fingers. "I know that you feel betrayed by me, but I never meant to…"

I held up my hand. "Look, that's over and done with, let's move on."

"No, we can't move on without first discussing this. I've called you several times since then to talk things over and you've never returned my calls."

"I know I didn't and mainly because I needed to get over it in my own time. Yes, I felt like you backstabbed me. I'm over it though."

"Why weren't you honest with me, Kelly?"

I frowned at her. "Honest with you. What the hell are you talking about?"

"Come on, Kelly. About John and the situation between you two," she said.

My heart fluttered realizing that John had told her.

"When John saw how upset I was over the incident between us, he told me about the paternity situation. At first I was angry at him for not telling me, but then I realized that him not telling me was his way of looking out for you. He's never spoken badly about you and even then, he pretty much said he did what he needed to do to protect himself. After that, I couldn't be mad at him because it made me see that he's a responsible man. I wouldn't have judged you, Kelly. Hell, I've done some things in my past I'm not proud of too. I just wish I would've heard this from you."

I ran my hand over my face as I let out a sigh. "Certain things that happen in a person's life are not the easiest to talk about. However, from where I'm from, the code is never to mess with someone that your friend has been with, even if it's a one-night stand. OK, I didn't give you the backstory as to John and my past dealings, but that doesn't negate the fact I was still involved with him."

She shook her head. "When I originally met with John for lunch, it was simply to discuss business."

"We don't need to backpedal, Gigi. It happened, regardless of what it originally started out as. I've had time to think about the situation and I've come to realize that everybody doesn't think the same. You saw an opportunity and you went for it."

She reached out and touched my arm. "There was never any malicious intent. Kelly, you have to believe me on that. I even stepped away from John for a while to think things through, but when it came down to it, I've fallen for the man."

I nodded my head. "If you're happy, that's all that matters. Things happen; I'm ready to move on."

She smiled. "I hope moving on means we can move past this in our friendship. I truly value you as a friend, Kelly, and I mean that."

"It might be a slow process, but we'll see where things go."

"I accept that," she said. There was silence between us, then she picked back up on the conversation. "Renae told me you and Derek just bought a home—congratulations. How's that going?"

"Thank you. We're finally settled, so it's all good."

I could see Renae entering the building and waved her over. She approached us with a shocked look.

"Well, well, nice to see you two being cordial." She smirked.

"And it feels good," said Gigi.

I was proud of myself for clearing the air with Gigi. I came to realize that the friends I have, the close friends within my circle for over ten years, were the friends I most needed.

Gigi got up from the mat. "Well, ladies, I've been here for the past two hours, so I'm going to leave. Hope we can get together sometime soon."

She left as I got up from the mat and walked over to the line for the treadmill; Renae followed.

"How are things with the house?"

I smiled. "I'm loving it, girl. It's been such a blessing how things have come together. Seeing how the kids love their new space is what's most rewarding."

"Aww…Kelly's big happy family." She chuckled. "Next thing you know, you'll be prego since you guys are living together full-time now."

I rolled my eyes. "Not hardly. I'm faithfully popping my birth control pills."

"Damn! Does he want more kids?"

"I really don't know. Believe it or not, it's not something we've discussed. All I want at this point is to make Walker my last name."

"Don't rush it, girl. The grass ain't always greener on the other side."

"Is this advice from a personal experience?" I asked with a perplexed look.

"I've never been married and honestly don't believe in it. Everybody runs game—single or married."

"In that case, you don't believe in relationships at all, huh?"

She shook her head. "I believe in arrangements, but, hey, that's just me."

That was part of the mystery with Renae; she said things that kept you guessing.

A treadmill freed up as I jumped on. I was thankful Renae had to get on one further down; I didn't feel like talking. Now I was tasked with getting things set up for the housewarming. Jessica and Casey insisted on handling things, but with both of their schedules, especially with Casey in a whole other state, I decided it would be best if I handled it.

The nurse at my doctor's office called me to schedule the tubal ligation and I postponed. I wanted to proceed with it, but my conscience wouldn't allow me to proceed without finding out first how Derek felt. I almost lost him with the last fiasco and didn't want to take a chance on doing this without consulting him first.

After working out on the treadmill and taking a Zumba class, I was ready to call it a day. Renae left with me and we stood out front to chat.

"Oh, on Friday, one of my acquaintances is having a party. How about you come with me?"

I sighed. "Girl, I'm in the process of planning my housewarming, so I'm good."

"Oh, OK," she said with a perturbed look. "You need any help with anything?"

"Maybe as the date approaches. You do plan on coming, right?" I asked.

She cleared her throat. "Ummm…just depends on my schedule."

"OK, well I'll let you know. I'm about to head on home. Have a good night."

We headed to our vehicles as my cell phone rang. I look at the caller ID and noticed it was Jessica.

"Hey, what's up, girl?" I asked, hitting the car remote.

"Remember when I told you I knew that girl looked familiar. I've figured out where I know her from," she eagerly responded.

I got in the car and hit the start button. "OK and where is that?"

"You're going to flip out, girl. She used to work at Walker & Co."

Just as I was about to put the car in drive, I continued to sit in park with my mouth open. Renae had not once mentioned she'd worked there, but then again I'd never asked.

"Talk about a small freaking world. How did you figure it out?"

"I went up there today to have lunch with Darnell and ran into Keverly. Seeing her instantly made me think of Renae, because months ago when I was there, she'd walked by and given me a cold stare, which I found to be rather odd. Recalling that, I asked Keverly about the girl who passed by us that time and she said her name was Lacey. I'm a hundred-percent sure it's her, so I asked if she went by another name. She said her name is hyphenated, Lacey-Renae."

I was stunned and confused. Was this all some coincidence? Or was there a motive to all the secrecy?

I closed my eyes. "I'm obviously shocked right now. I knew there was something mysterious about this chick, but damn, never would've thought that. This is crazy."

"So that led me to think did Gigi know?"

"I honestly don't think she did," I said as I rubbed my forehead. "I don't understand the logic here and I don't want to jump to conclusions."

Jessica smacked her lips. "I think she's up to no good. Have you ever mentioned Derek to her?"

"Yeah, I have, but she's never been formally introduced to him."

"No formal introduction needed when she's been to your townhouse where you definitely had pictures around of Derek and the kids. In seeing that, wouldn't that spark some sort of recognition, like 'oh yeah, I use to work with him.' I mean come on, Kells, you gotta see where I'm going with this. Hell, she's even gotta remember seeing me, considering the way she stared at me," she pleaded.

I rested my arm on the windowsill and massage my forehead.

"Jess, it's not that what you're saying doesn't make sense, I'm trying to understand her motive."

"When a woman wants something, trust me, she will go through whatever lengths to get it. All I got to say is be careful because my intuition is flashing all kinds of red signs with her."

I thanked Jessica for the information and hung up the phone. So many thoughts flooded my brain as I tried to gather the pieces together. One thing was certain, she was definitely hiding something and I planned on finding it out sooner than later.

CHAPTER 19
JANEN

"Tony, can we talk about this like adults?" I pleaded.

After weeks of dealing with his mood swings, the issue could no longer be ignored. Since my reconnection with Rita, Tony showed little to no interest in anything related to my excitement in meeting her.

He continued to pack his bag without so much as looking in my direction. As he went to the closet, I threw his bag off the bed and stood in his path.

"What the hell is wrong with you?" he screamed.

I folded my arms. "I should be asking you that. You've been giving me the cold shoulder for weeks now and I'm sick of it. Now you're about to head out of town and it's like you don't even care to resolve whatever issues we have between us."

He threw his clothes on the bed and stepped toward me aggressively, so much so that I stepped back.

"I've been super stressed, working long-ass hours, and feeling neglected when I get home. Do I have a meal awaiting me when I get here? No. Have you taken the time to try to listen to my issues? No. Are we having sex regularly? No. Do you still not understand where my frustration stems from? Since you've had this 'family reunion' with your long-lost mother, you've forgotten your duties as a wife."

"Forgotten my duties? You've been getting in late, and anytime I try to discuss what's going on, you seem to have your ass on your shoulders. What about me? You haven't been the supportive husband I've needed. I've expressed to you how important reconnecting with my biological mother was to me and you've brushed it off like it's nothing."

He grinned. "So because I'm not running behind your ass for updates every time you get a phone call or questioning you about your findings, that makes me non-supportive? Maybe you need to stop reaching and take the blame for your own downfalls as a wife."

If nothing else, that last statement stung me to the point where I hauled off and slapped him. As I watched his face turn beet red, I regretted touching him. He pushed me aside, making me fall on the bed, and moved towards his bag to finish his packing. Disgusted by my own actions, I went to the living room to give us both some space.

When I went to Atlanta to visit Rita, I told Tony that I would meet him in the Bahamas after my visit. I could tell he wasn't thrilled by my last-minute change, but he went along with it.

On the day of the visit with Rita, my nerves were all over the place. I couldn't eat and I had bouts of nausea. Robbie asked if I could stop by to pick up some of her clothes before going to the facility. On the way to the facility, all I could think about was how would our conversation go? What would she think of me? Would she be standoffish? The more I thought of questions, the more nauseous I became. I pulled up to the gates of the rehab center and was met by the guard. I gave him Rita's name and showed him my identification. He returned my card and opened the gate. As I continued down the tree-lined driveway, I could feel my stomach tighten and my mouth grow watery. I instantly pulled over and held my head out the door as I vomited. I grabbed a tissue from my purse and wiped my mouth, and took deep breaths trying to compose myself. After I cleaned up and popped a mint in my mouth, I proceeded to the main entrance.

Once I found a parking spot, I looked myself over in the rearview mirror and applied a fresh coat of lip gloss. I grabbed the bag of clothes and my purse and headed to the entrance.

Thankfully the place was rather clean and smelled of fresh pine. The officer at the front desk buzzed me into another area where I was instructed to leave my purse in one of the lockers. I proceeded to the security desk and gave the officer the bag containing the clothes, which they emptied out onto the conveyor belt for scanning. I walked through the metal detector and awaited the completion of the search.

The officer smiled as she inserted the clothes in the bag and handed it to me, then directed me through another door. The attendant there took the bag and put a tag on it.

"It'll be delivered to her room," she said. "You can either go out to the courtyard to my right or the meeting room to my left."

I peeked in both to see which had fewer people. I decided to go to the meeting room. The room had corner areas with sofas, and in the middle of the room there were regular round tables and chairs. I picked a corner of the room and sat on the sofa. I closed my eyes and took a deep breath as my hands trembled.

When the door opened, I stood and watched the woman I'd never known come closer towards me. She was rather thin, with flawless honey-colored skin. Her hair was combed back in a short wavy style. Even though you could tell she'd been through rough times, she still possessed beauty.

We stood awkwardly, staring at each other with nervous grins. Finally, after not being able to do much other than stare, she spoke.

"I'm Rita," she said, extending her hand.

As she spoke those two words, I could see that she was in serious need of some dental care. I fought back the emotions I felt as I extended my hand with a smile.

"I'm Janen. Nice to meet you," I said, inviting her to have a seat.

She sat on the sofa across from me and fidgeted with the buttons on her cardigan.

"Janen, you're absolutely beautiful," she said and smiled.

"Thank you. How are you?"

She grinned. "It's tough, but I'm hanging in there. Robbie said you live in Miami."

"Yes, I live there with my husband."

An awkward pause followed as she looked at the other families in the room.

I took a deep breath. "I've always wanted to meet you; even when I was fourteen and they told me about you."

She looked at me with a somber look. "Believe it or not, I've always thought of you. But considering my lifestyle, I didn't deserve you."

I scooted closer to the end of the couch where she sat. "Why didn't you make an effort to change that lifestyle if you knew I didn't deserve it?"

She looked away as I could see her nose starting to flare, showing either she was pissed or holding back tears.

"I spent years trying to please my mama," she said. "That woman was the biggest bitch I'd ever encountered. I never could understand how you could birth a life and have so much hatred toward it. She treated me like shit and never let a moment slip by without making me know how unwanted I was. If it weren't for my brother and sister, I probably would've committed suicide. That woman made me feel worthless. Even through that, I gave her respect and tried to do things that would make her proud. She perpetuated in front of everyone else like she was a caring, loving mother, but that was far from the case. As I got older, I realized that I could never please the one person I wanted love from the most. My father wasn't in the picture; only saw him twice before he died when I was ten. I went through so much heartache trying to please others; by the time I had my firstborn, David, I grew selfish."

I looked at her as she spoke with such emotion. I couldn't imagine growing up without my parents loving me as they did; it would've made everything that much harder for me.

She went on to talk about how David and his diagnosis as mentally challenged caused her emotional stress; she felt responsible for his condition. In fact, she denied his condition until he was six; that's when Robbie stepped in to help raise him and made her get him the help he needed.

"Robbie has been my saving grace, because who knows what condition David would be in today if it weren't for him. I have a daughter, Carlita, and everybody used to call her Sunshine. Her father, William, and I were actually in a relationship and for once, I thought life for me and my family would finally change. But when she was only six months, he up and did a disappearing act."

I shook my head. "You never thought to get the courts involved."

She frowned. "If a man doesn't want to step up and handle his responsibility, I'm not forcing him to do shit and I didn't. If I saw their asses on the street, I wouldn't even look their way. I struggled, but I did the best I could."

I pressed my lips together as I looked away. I looked back at her. "Why did you get involved with my dad knowing he was married and living with his wife in the same complex?"

She huffed. "Your dad could charm the pants off any woman." She chuckled. "He helped me out a lot with the kids. I can't pinpoint when it happened, but I fell for him. He did things that my kids' fathers should've been doing and I longed for that. I enjoyed the moments we had, but I knew he wasn't leaving Joann. People thought I got pregnant to trap him, which wasn't true. When I told him about it, he wanted me to get an abortion; hell, even Robbie begged me, but I wouldn't. I'd told Michael we needed to tell Joann, but he insisted on keeping it from her until the time was right. Well, by my fourth month of pregnancy, I became the talk of the neighborhood and Joann found out."

She went on describing how my mom confronted her and the pain and humiliation she felt afterwards. Thereafter, my dad would sneak and call her to check on her, but she turned cold towards him and changed her number.

"I truly felt like your father used my weakness as a way to get closer to what he wanted," she said with a shrug. "But a person can only do what you allow them to do, so I take full responsibility in betraying your mom as I did."

I cleared my throat. "What made you give me up?"

She massaged her neck as she contemplated the right words to say. "First of all, I couldn't afford another mouth and I didn't think it was fair to raise another child in unhealthy circumstances. Secondly, I finally decided that a man should take on the responsibility of caring for his seed. Michael knew my situation, so when I made the decision to go full term with the pregnancy, I told him I planned on setting up an adoption. He didn't believe me until I showed him the paperwork from the agency. He talked things over with Joann and she didn't want that to happen. Joann showed me a lot about her character by doing that, but it also made me feel all the more guilty."

My head started to lightly pound as I looked up at the ceiling, hoping the tears I felt coming on would flow back the other way.

"For years, I gave Joann hell after I found out she wasn't my biological mother. She showed me nothing but love, but I resented the fact that I was an outside child and my brother and sister were a product of their marriage. I felt empty inside, abandoned, not because I wasn't shown love from the only parents I knew of, but because it was hard for me to understand how a woman could hand over her child with no regrets."

She shook her head as tears flowed from her face. "I tried to see you, but Michael threatened that he would file a restraining order if I came anywhere near you. You will never understand how giving you up affected me. No, I wasn't in love with your father, but carrying you for nine months, I cared and loved you enough to realize I wasn't the mother you needed. Joann is a hell of a woman; she took you in and treated you as if you came from her own womb. There's no way I could step in between that bond; she gave you all that I couldn't."

As we sat there in total silence, I thought about all that Rita said and realized I had all the clarification I needed.

I looked at my watch. "Visiting hours is almost over, but thank you for being open to talking to me."

She smiled. "You deserved to know the truth. I've always wondered what kind of woman you'd grow up to be and I'm thankful to God you took the right path in life."

"Thank you," I said.

As Rita stood up to leave, she reached out to me for a hug. I got up to oblige and as we hugged, we both shed tears. In some odd way, I felt sorry for her. I wished her well in her recovery and told her I would keep in touch.

She held my hand. "I don't know if it's possible, but we are having a family day in a few weeks. I'm going to invite my other children and would love for you to meet them."

"Let me know the date and I'll try to make it," I said with a smile.

We hugged once more before she headed back to her confinement. As I headed in the opposite direction, I closed my eyes and thanked God for giving me the inner peace I needed.

When I left Atlanta to head to the Bahamas, I wanted nothing more than to be in the arms of my husband. I'd missed being away from him and couldn't wait to share with him my visit with Rita.

Once I arrived to the Bahamas, I felt good and ready to enjoy our time together. Our schedules were both hectic, so I wanted to make sure we had a great time. One evening during dinner, when I brought up the conversation of Rita and my visit with her, there was minimum reaction. It bothered me, so I decided not to further discuss it with him.

From the moment we came back from the Bahamas, the tension in our household mounted. Rita called me two times a week since my visit and I enjoyed getting to know her more. However, I felt that the tension between Tony and I had little to do with me and more about his demanding job responsibilities. No, I didn't cook and yes, our sex life had taken a backseat, but I didn't feel totally responsible since we'd both been overwhelmed.

As I sat in the living room waiting from him to emerge from the bedroom, I closed my eyes and prayed that I could make right my wrong before he left. I opened my eyes when he walked out of the room.

I stood and walked over to the breakfast bar.

"Baby, I don't want you to leave like this. I apologize for putting my hand on you; I shouldn't have done that."

He looked at me blankly as he took a gulp of water. I waited for him to say something, as his stare started to make me uncomfortable.

"So you're not going to say anything?" I asked, irritated.

"Apology accepted. Maybe this time away will give you time to really think about how you've been over the past few weeks."

Here we go again! He was making it all about me, but to avoid further argument I bit my tongue.

"I'm not trying to argue with you, but I think we both could use the time to reevaluate our priorities. I don't think I'm the shitty wife you make me out to be, but I will make it a point to do better."

He walked over and gave me a kiss on the cheek before picking up his bag to leave. As he opened the door to leave, he stated he would call once he landed in Los Angeles, and immediately he walked out. I stood with a puzzled look as the door closed behind him. Not even a kiss on the lips or a hug? It was obvious he was more pissed than I thought.

He would be gone for a week and I'd made plans to visit with Rita for family day. I hadn't shared with anyone my meeting with Rita, but I planned on spending time with Mom while I was there this time.

With our anniversary approaching, this was not how I wanted things to be in our marriage. While I could admit to not giving him the attention he needed, I wouldn't consider myself the horrible wife. Bottom line, I needed to rectify all this and I planned on doing so sooner than later.

Thinking about the family day with Rita, I wondered how all this would go considering I'd never been a part of their family. I hadn't asked many questions about my siblings because I figured all I needed to know I would find out then. I just hoped that me attending wouldn't add any more pressure to my life than I already felt.

CHAPTER 20
DEREK

After Lacey called me at the house the other day, her calls became frequent. I couldn't ignore the fact that she was becoming a nuisance and I needed to let her know that we were done.

I called her one evening after work to see if she would be available to talk. She excitedly accepted and invited me over to her place. I'd planned on a more mutual place, but she insisted on staying in. I knew going to her apartment was her tactic of getting me into bed. This time I needed my brain to overpower my penis.

Since settling in the house, I felt more confident in my relationship with Kelly and wanted to focus on our life together. Our housewarming next weekend would be the first of many events at our house. While I wasn't enjoying how the cost of this event was stacking up, I had to admit I was excited to see how my family and friends would react to our new home. Kelly did her thing with the décor and the planning of the event.

More so than that, I planned on proposing to Kelly; something I was sure she'd least expect. I still had the first ring I proposed with, but decided to upgrade it. I took Darnell with me to help pick it out, and even though it put a dent in my finances, she deserved it.

I pulled into the gate of Lacey's apartment and hoped that this "meeting" would go amicably. Lacey had never done anything over the top before to create a red flag, so I hoped after our conversation, she wouldn't cause any issues.

I knocked on the door and she immediately opened it wearing a silk robe. Judging by the way it hugged her body, I quickly gathered that she had nothing on underneath. I kept repeating, "down, boy, down, boy" in my head.

I walked in and had a seat on the far end of the couch as she sat on the opposite end with a smile on her face.

"What's up with the somber look?" She frowned.

"We need to have a serious conversation."

"About?" she said.

"The fact that whatever this is we're doing needs to stop."

She scooted down and put her feet in my lap as if I'd not said anything of importance.

"Stop what?" she said, folding her arms.

I picked up her feet and placed them back on the floor.

"Let's not play dumb, Lacey. You calling me, us seeing each other—it needs to end."

She scratched her scalp. "You came over here to have a conversation with me about something you could have mentioned over the phone, or did you come to get one in before you make your final departure?"

This was one time her cockiness wasn't a turn on. She spread her legs, revealing what I'd known since walking in. I turned and shook my head, mainly to clear it and stop the erection I felt coming on.

"I'm not here for sex, Lacey. I came here, or should I say I wanted to meet with you because I thought as two adults it would be better face-to-face."

She shrugged her shoulders. "There's nothing to be handled. You don't want me to call you, fine. You no longer want the good sex I offer, that's your lost."

I nodded my head. "I appreciate you making this easy."

She nodded her head, still giving me an evil smirk. "Are you done?" she asked.

"Yeah," I said as I stood to leave. "Listen, Lacey, I wish you no ill will; I wish you the best. You're a good girl, but…"

She shook her head. "No need for all that. You've made it very clear where I stand."

She extended her hand like she was inviting me to join her outside of the door. As I walked out, she said nothing and neither did I. By the time I crossed the threshold, I could feel the wind of the door as it slammed shut.

I left feeling assured that there would be no issues with Lacey. While our conversation was pretty straightforward, I would be lying if I said she didn't make me a bit uncomfortable. Since I'd known her, she'd always been an unpredictable woman, but I enjoyed that aspect of her. Right now, I didn't know if that mystery about her was such a good thing, but hoped she would back off for good.

My cell phone rang—it was Carlton. "Hey, what's up, my man?"

"Just checking on how things are going since it's been a minute."

"Things are going well. How are things with you?"

"Can't complain and if I could, who would give a damn." He chuckled. "Maria told me about the housewarming next weekend; we'll be there."

"That's great, man. Just to give you a heads-up, I'm proposing to Kelly."

"You're finally ready to make her a happier woman. Congratulations, man. You got more balls than me proposing in front of everybody."

"Yeah, I'm going to be nervous as shit, but I'm going make it happen."

"I ain't mad at that, bruh. Well, on another note, I wanted to invite you to the spot tonight; seems like it's perfect too since we got something to celebrate."

"I'm down, but you know it's a work night, so I'm not trying to be out too late."

He chuckled. "You're definitely sounding like an old family man. I'll have you back by a descent hour."

Kelly never understood the freedom Carlton had and found it rather odd that he could spend so much time away considering he was married. I didn't know if she considered me hanging around him a bad influence, but I avoided such conversations at all costs. Carlton was good people and his outside life had no bearing on my own.

Carlton mentioned the club was celebrating its second year in business, so it would be "quite festive." I didn't even question the festive part, but it definitely sparked my attention as my imagination went wild.

I picked up the kids and pulled in to find Kelly already home. Normally she would go to the gym after work.

As the kids raced through the doors to their room, I took Kimora upstairs to lay her down, then proceeded to our bedroom.

Kelly was on her laptop and immediately closed it as I moved towards her.

"I'm going to assume you were online shopping," I said with a grin.

"Just checking on a few things for the housewarming," she said.

I leaned over to give her a kiss. "Why aren't you at the gym today?"

"Just didn't feel like it," she said as she laid the laptop on the nightstand.

"Do you mind if I hang out with Carlton for a few tonight? He's just getting back in town and invited me out," I said.

"Not a problem," she said nonchalantly.

With her dry response, it only left me wondering if she was OK.

"Are we good?" I asked.

"Yeah," she said, not looking in my direction.

I shook my head as I stepped in our walk-in closet to find something to wear for later. It wasn't unusual for her to be in a funk, especially when she was close to her time of the month, which, judging by the date should be on by now.

When I walked out of the closet, she'd already left the room. I laid out my clothes. I could smell food cooking in the kitchen as I headed downstairs.

"Oh, didn't know you'd started dinner," I said.

"Trying out this place one of my co-workers told me about that makes homemade ready-made meals. Hopefully it doesn't disappoint."

"Smells good," I said as I wrapped my arms around her waist. I kissed her on the neck; I was horny.

As I heard the kids coming down, I stepped away and helped get their plates together for dinner. I headed upstairs to get Kimora so we could all eat together. I loved our family moments like this and never took these times for granted.

After dinner, Kelly tended to the kitchen while I helped the kids with their homework. I made sure their clothes were laid out for school and prepared Kimora for her bath. My kids meant everything to me and no matter what I was dealing with, I knew I had their unconditional love.

I went in the bedroom to find Kelly back in bed flipping through the channels. I closed our bedroom door and walked over to her side of the bed.

"I'm not liking this vibe I'm getting from you. Are you sure you're OK?"

"I'm fine; just tired."

I felt frisky and knew if it was her time of the month I wouldn't be getting any, but that didn't mean she couldn't do anything.

I stood next to the bed. She looked at me as if I were bothering her.

"What's up?" she said with a stern face.

As much as I wanted to give her a smart-ass comment, I knew that wouldn't work in my favor if I expected something from her.

"I was thinking about you giving me a little attention before I go out."

She sighed as she pulled back the covers and threw her legs on the side of the bed. Her whole demeanor instantly turned me off.

"You know what, never mind," I said as I shook my head.

I went in the bathroom and slammed the door and stripped down for my shower. I was horny and pissed at the same damn time. To be turned down in such a way as if I were a bother to her puzzled me. I'd not once hounded her for sex in the past week, so the least she could've done was oblige with a smile.

As I let the heat of the water hit my back, I'd hoped she would walk through the door and follow through with my request. Judging by the time I'd been in the shower, I might as well have hung that thought up. I was better off rubbing one off and getting it over with, but that lacked the intimacy I needed.

I didn't want her to see me upset over her actions nor did I want it to ruin my night. After I dried off and wrapped my towel around my waist, I walked out of the bathroom.

She was back on her laptop and didn't bother to look my way. I felt like snapping, considering she didn't have the decency to even address the way she'd treated me.

I went in the closet and continued to dress. I stepped out and gave myself a look over in the mirror. I knew I had her attention; I was looking rather fly in my blazer and jeans.

I turned towards her and decided to give her a dose of her own medicine as I picked up my wallet.

"All right, babe, I'll see you later," I said, walking out of the room.

I didn't hear a response nor did I bother looking in her direction. I was sure my actions had given her enough to marinate on while I was gone.

As I drove to Carlton's house, I listened to old school rap music on the radio. When Afrika Bambaataa's "Planet Rock" came on, I cut up the music and danced in my seat as if I was already out on the dance floor.

I pulled up at Carlton's and parked my car then headed over to the Lincoln town car. The chauffeur greeted me as I approached. Carlton walked briskly out of the house and walked to car with a perturbed look on his face. He got in and tapped the window for the driver to take off.

"What's up, man?" I asked with concern.

He shook his head. "Out of all nights, Maria is coming to the club a little later."

"Wow." I couldn't think of anything else to say. Out of all the times we'd been to the club, I'd never seen Maria there nor heard Carlton mention she went.

"Didn't you tell me she helped Arbi out with starting the club?"

"Yeah, and she's never come to any events." He sighed.

"Well damn, man. I'm all hyped up to have a good time, but if she's going to be a vibe killer why don't we go somewhere else?"

He shook his head. "If I didn't go, I'll have to hear Arbi's mouth and, even worse, hers. She's not planning on coming until later, so I have a little playtime before I have to be on my best behavior." He grinned. "You ready for some fun?"

I nodded. "Yes, sir. After my evening with Kelly and her stank-ass attitude, I could use a good time."

Carlton patted my shoulder. "Shit, you planning on marrying her, this is only the beginning, bruh." He chuckled.

It seemed as if we got to the club quicker than usual and it was packed as we waited in line to pull up to the valet area. We stepped out of the car and walked the red carpet up the stairs to the door, where two ladies dressed in leotards made like a tuxedo welcomed us.

Walking in, I felt like I had celebrity status. Carlton shook hands with several others there as I took in the ambiance and the beautiful eye candy floating around the room. As Carlton continued to mingle, I made my way to the blue lounge. Luckily I was able to find a seat as the bartender, Rain, came over with a napkin and a shot of Patron.

"Well, well, well…look who's back." She smiled.

I grinned. "Yeah, I make my rounds every once in a while. How's it going?"

"Have you seen the crowd in this place tonight? My night has been crazy, but you know what, that's more money so I can't complain," she said as she winked.

"Well, don't work too hard," I said as I took my shot and headed to see what else was going on.

It was amazing how many men brought their wives or girlfriends to the club with them. I could see Kelly now tooting up her nose at a place like this.

I looked around and didn't see Carlton. As I passed by the entrance, I had to do a double take as I noticed Maria walking in with Lacey. I tried to turn quickly, but Lacey and I caught eyes and she smirked. Lacey was stunning, as her hair was freshly done, unlike earlier, and even though she wore a mini-dress, it gave her a classy, yet sexy look. I figured it would be rude of me to bypass Maria without speaking.

Maria looked like money as she stood in the foyer with her fitted tuxedo slacks and sheer shirt, and her hair pulled neatly into a bun. While she'd definitely aged over the years, she still was undeniably beautiful.

I walked over and gave her a hug. "Nice to see you, lady. You look great."

She smacked my arm. "You've always been quite the charmer. Congratulations on the house."

I nodded. "Thanks. Have you seen Carlton?"

She rolled her eyes. "I'm sure I'm the last person he cares to see here."

Out of the corner of my eye I could see Lacey staring at me as if she wanted me to say something to her. While she looked amazing in her mini-dress, I refused to give her the attention she asked for.

I excused myself and headed upstairs to see what was going on. I stopped off in the club area to the lively sounds of Frankie Beverly and Maze's "Before I Let Go." The dance floor was packed as couples two-stepped to the music.

After standing around people-watching, I made my way to the strip club room. I peeked in the sliding side panel and saw the room was filled. I figured I would check out the other rooms, but not before grabbing a drink from the bar.

As I made my drink order, I felt a tap on my back. I turned around and there was Lacey.

"What a coincidence we see each other tonight."

I didn't want to talk to her; I didn't want to open the door I'd just shut earlier today.

"Yeah," I said and turned back towards the bar.

I grabbed my drink and headed down the hallway to the open patio area. There were a few people out chatting.

I diverted my attention to the outside cabanas on the back lawn. My cell phone vibrated, and I looked down and saw a text message from Kelly.

"I'm sorry for my actions earlier. You didn't deserve my bitchy attitude and I apologize. Love u…have fun…and hurry home."

It gave me great comfort to know she'd thought about how she treated me earlier and was apologetic. This was one of the many ways Kelly had grown within our relationship. Lacey walked out and stood next to me. "So you're really serious about not talking to me?"

I sighed and shook my head. "I don't know what you expect from me at this point. I saw you earlier and we discussed this."

"You discussed, I said nothing but reassure you I wasn't going to call you anymore. We're here, in a public place, and you're treating me as if I've violated the code."

I leaned on the rail and turn towards her. "OK, you have my attention. What is it you want to talk about?"

She walked closer towards me with a grin. "I want one final round with you."

Was she serious? As a horny man, that was definitely not something I needed to hear right now.

I shook my head. "I don't think that's a good idea, Lacey."

"Oh but I do," she said as she gripped the front of my pants.

I was taken by surprise as she massaged my manhood through my pants.

"See, I knew you wanted me just as much as I want you. Why fight the feeling when we have the opportunity to handle it and walk away?"

I removed her hand and stepped back. "Why are you making this difficult?"

"Admit it, you want me. If you didn't, it wouldn't be difficult to walk away from me. Look, meet in the Seduction Room in ten minutes."

She walked away before I could make any protest. While my desire for Lacey hadn't subsided, I knew having sex with her would only make matters worse. I rushed down the hall in search of Carlton. The night was still young, but I couldn't think of a better place I'd rather be than home right now.

I found Carlton in the foyer and pulled him to the side.

"Man, I hate to leave, but I'm finding myself in a heated situation, so I need to get home before I get in trouble," I said.

Carlton chuckled as he patted me on the shoulder. "It happens and I commend you for knowing when to tuck your tail and go home. My driver should still be outside."

I thanked him for understanding then rushed out the doors and down the stairs of the club. Luckily the driver was right out front waiting as I went up to him and knocked on the window.

On the drive home, I anticipated a call from Lacey wondering where I was, but instead I got a text. I dreaded opening it knowing she probably had some choice words for me.

When I opened it, my mouth dropped. It was a picture of her riding another man. Under the caption it read, *"This could've been you."* I shook my head in amazement; it wasn't as if I could be mad about it, but I'd be lying to say it didn't sting me in some way. I immediately deleted the text as the driver pulled up at Carlton's house for me to get my car.

As I made my way home, all I could think about was getting in bed with the woman I loved. There was nobody in that club worth me losing Kelly for.

I pulled up to the house and deactivated the alarm with my remote then pulled into the garage. I tiptoed in and up the stairs. The clock illuminated the time, 1:30, as I stepped in our bedroom and slowly closed the door. I went in the closet to remove my clothes and got in bed naked.

I could hear Kelly lightly snoring, but tonight unlike nights before, she was going to be awakened. I scooted closer to her and rubbed my body against hers. My penis became erect as I stroked her breasts until her nipples hardened.

I positioned myself over her as she rolled over on her back with a smile. I kissed her on her forehead and then her lips and made my way down to her freshly waxed vagina. That was one requirement I had—no hair.

I slowly kissed her outer lips before spreading them apart as my tongue went on a hunt for her pearl. My tongue rapidly glided over her clit as she moaned. The more I sucked, the more intense her moans became. She was nice and wet, as she demanded that I enter her.

As I prepared to enter her, the look on her face from the nightlight beside our bed made me think of Lacey. I thought about the picture Lacey had sent to me before I got home and the feeling her touch created when we were on the patio. Thoughts of her made me think of the times we had sex and how hard I grew with each intense thrust. Before I knew it, I was inside of Kelly giving her hard thrusts as I pinned her legs back towards her head. I made sure every inch of me was inside her as I became enraged like an unleashed beast. I could feel her wiggling under me as if it were too much, but I couldn't resist the feeling of satisfaction I felt. I released her legs and quickly pulled myself out then helped her flip over on her stomach. I gripped her waist and pulled her towards me as I prepared to enter her doggy style. With each thrust I thought about how Lacey use to talk shit to me, which made me even more excited. I started talking dirty to Kelly and all she did was moan, no response. I pushed her back down for deeper penetration and thought about how Lacey would wrap her legs around me and move her hips to my rhythm.

I couldn't contain myself as I cried out, "Baby, I'm coming. La…Kelly."

Oh shit! I caught myself about to call her Lacey. I tried to clean up my word and hope that she didn't catch it as I collapsed on top of her. She kissed me on my forehead as I rolled off her and she got up to go to the bathroom.

As I lay on my back, I couldn't move. All I could think about was the incredible sex we had and how exhausted I felt. I could've royally fucked up the mood by calling her Lacey. I hadn't had sex with Lacey physically, but I sure did mentally. I knew it wasn't right, but the release I got from it was what I needed as I yawned and drifted asleep.

CHAPTER 21
LA'TIA

  Finally the day had come for me to move into my own two-bedroom apartment. I couldn't have been happier as the movers moved in my furniture. I'd taken the night before off so I could be up and ready to go the next day. Rachelle joked about how I seemed happy to be moving out of her house. I thanked her for her hospitality and made sure her daughter had a good welcome back to her room by purchasing the Hello Kitty bed-in-the-bag she'd wanted.
  As the movers brought in the last box, I jumped for joy looking at my beautiful apartment. Luckily I was able to get the floor plan I wanted, as originally it was already taken. The apartments were newly renovated, with stainless steel appliances, marble countertops, and mahogany-colored cabinets. I had a sunken living room with remote blinds and a screened-in patio.
  Ms. Sharon was keeping Noah for the next two days while I got the place organized. The apartment manager agreed to let me paint throughout the apartment as long as I had it professionally done and repainted at the end of my lease. I had a vision of how I wanted each room. While my money was looking right, I'd paid up my rent for the next four months.
  Chelsea, Arbi's assistant, called me this morning to remind me of the anniversary celebration at the club and how he counted on me to be there two hours ahead of time. As I looked at the clock, I realized I hadn't gotten a wink of sleep since five o'clock this morning. Even though I didn't work at the club the night before, I had spent the evening with Carlton at his cabin.
  Since his business proposal, I'd really been in deep thought and refrained from seeing or talking to him. It worked out that he

had to spend a few weeks out of town, so he didn't have time to hound me on my decision.

When we met last night, the conversation flowed without him even mentioning the proposition. I felt it needed to be addressed at some point, so I started off.

"In thinking about your business proposal, I've come to a decision," I said with a confident smile.

He leaned forward in his chair. "I'm listening."

"I have a few conditions of my own, so if you're willing to negotiate, we may be able to seal this deal."

He smirked. "Awww…spoken like a true business woman. OK, you've got my attention."

I ended up telling Ms. Sharon about the proposition, a well-edited version, that is. I told her the wife asked me to be their surrogate due to being unable to carry a child. As expected, Sharon found it to be a blessing that I would even consider giving the married couple a child they couldn't conceive on their own. I didn't like lying to her, but I knew if I said what it really was, I wouldn't have gotten the reception that I did. Now that I had her approval on my "kind-hearted" act, I felt confident I could pull it off while gaining financially.

"For starters, I move into my own apartment of choice. There's no way I can live comfortably under the watchful eye of your wife."

He nodded. "Go on."

"Secondly, my bonus will be in the form of two month's rent and professional movers to unload my furniture. I need health insurance not only for myself but Noah as well."

He took a moment to think about all that I'd said as he leaned back. With his arms propped on each side of the chair and his fingers interlocked, he stared at me.

I looked away as I waited for his response, which wasn't coming as soon as I'd like.

"Is your silence an indication that you're not willing to compromise?" I asked.

"I never want to come out and say yes to something I haven't fully thought about. But no, I don't think it's a hard request, I just need to run it by Maria."

I rolled my eyes. "Well the thing is I've already signed my lease and I'm moving tomorrow."

"So if you've done all this, then it's almost like you have me by the balls then."

"If you want to put it like that, then yes. It's either on my terms or it's not feasible for me. Remember, this isn't all about you two."

He stood up as he grabbed his cell phone. "Excuse me for a second," he said as he went downstairs.

Truth is I wanted him to say the deal was off. While I was confident in doing things my way, the bottom line was that this situation freaked me out a bit. True enough I could use the money while I looked for another job, but if need be I had no qualms with staying at the club for a bit longer until that time.

I didn't need Carlton or his wife thinking they had full control over me. I still needed to feel a sense of independence and that was where having my own place came in.

Carlton came back upstairs. "Maria wants to privately meet with you before we agree on anything."

Here we go again with another meeting with a wife. I could only be grateful that this time it was on my terms and not like the situation with Darnell where I was totally blindsided.

"I hope you plan on being somewhere close by." I grinned. "I do keep my peace maker with me at all times in case situations get out of hand."

"Maria is not that kind of woman. Her mouth can be rather slick, but to lay a hand on you, she wouldn't do that."

"Well good. So do you know what she wants to discuss?"

"The terms of this arrangement, I'm sure; you know that woman-to-woman understanding." He smirked.

"Whatever works," I said with a sigh. "I have an early start tomorrow, so I'm going to go ahead and get up out of here."

He stood up and gave me a concerned look. "It's eleven o'clock and you want to drive on these dark roads this late."

I grabbed my purse. "My car does have headlights and I'm fully aware it's a deer's playground on these dark roads, so I promise to be extra cautious."

He pulled me close to him and looked me in the eyes. "I've missed you and I was hoping you could stay with me tonight."

"As much as I would love your pampering, I have to prepare for my move. Maybe after the club tomorrow you can come by and check out my new spot." I winked.

Now I was in the living room of my apartment, which was once covered with boxes. I nodded at the progress. I unpacked a few more boxes before taking a shower and napping before getting ready for work.

Beep…beep…beep. The sound of the alarm clock made me want to slam it against the wall. I could hit this snooze button and get ten more minutes in, but I would probably feel the same way, so what the hell. I dragged myself out of bed and prepared myself for the night.

I'd been given orders to "look my absolute best" tonight, which generally translated into wearing the most revealing, sexiest outfit in my possession. Hosting at the club gave me the luxury of shopping on a consistent basis for outfits. I never wanted to be the chick caught wearing the same outfit twice, but I had a good eye for switching pieces up, so it worked perfectly.

As I slipped on my curve-hugging miniskirt, a lace black short-sleeve top, and my thigh-high boots, I gave myself a look over in the mirror. I put on my accessories and ran my cotton candy lip gloss over my lips. I wasn't into makeup and definitely didn't need it, so I kept my look simple.

I grabbed my essentials from my purse and transferred it into the mini handbag I carried to work. I sprayed my Daisy perfume by Marc Jacobs and headed out the door.

I walked to my car only to notice something odd about it. I walked on the passenger side and noticed I had a flat tire—shit! I didn't know the first thing about changing a tire and I damn sure didn't want to roll up to the club with the donut on. I reached in my purse to call Rachelle.

"What's up?" she said.

"I have a damn flat. Do you think you could scoop me up?"

She smacked. "Girl, I'm halfway to the club now."

I sighed as I made my way back to my apartment. "All right, let me find a way," I said then hung up the phone.

I texted Carlton as I was more than sure he planned on being at the club tonight. He texted back that he'd send his driver to pick me up and he should be here within fifteen minutes. I sent him my address and gate access code and paced the floor of the living room, hoping I wouldn't be late.

I started thinking about this upcoming meeting with Maria. I'd tried to imagine what she looked like; in my mind I figured she was short, slightly out of shape, but still had some type of appeal to her. I'd looked throughout the cabin and hadn't found one picture of her.

My phone rang. "Hey."

"Just checking to see if you found a ride," said Rachelle.

"Yes, Carlton came to the rescue. He's sending a driver."

"Awww shucks now. That dude is really feeling you, Tia."

"Oh whatever." I chuckled. "I'll see you in a bit," I said, hanging up the phone.

I hadn't told Rachelle about the proposition mainly because she thought she knew so much already. I had to tell Carlton to let our business be just that. Rachelle was my dear friend, but she didn't need to know everything.

I looked out and saw a Lincoln town car approaching. I headed out, locked my door, and walked to the car as the driver got out to greet me by opening the door. Damn, I could really get use to this treatment.

With five minutes to spare, we pulled up at the club. I walked in just in time, as Arbi was meeting with everyone in the foyer, going over the plans of the night. I headed over to where Rachelle was.

"Damn, girl, you trying to shut it down in here tonight I see," she whispered, looking me over.

I blushed. "It's a special occasion, right."

After the meeting, I went to get my instructions for the night. My job wasn't hard at all, but I disliked the horny men who always made it a point to tell me what they would do with me. I let them live the fantasy, but never teased to the point they really thought they could have me.

The night started off busy and the crowd thickened within seconds. I made my way upstairs to check the room levels. As I was coming down the stairs, I spotted Carlton making his way through the door. He looked quite sexy with his blazer, button-down shirt, and denim relaxed straight jeans. It was nice seeing him in something outside of slacks. It gave him a hip look with the swag to match.

He stopped in his tracks when he saw me. I walked over to him for a hug.

"Thanks for the driver. He got me here right on time." I smiled.

"No problem," he said as he checked me out. "Damn, you look amazing. I got a lot of thoughts going through my head right now."

I blushed. "Save them for later," I whispered.

He grinned. "Oh that I shall. Listen, I need to talk to you real quick."

We walked over to a side room.

"What's up?" I said.

"As a heads-up, Maria will be here tonight. She's never come to an anniversary celebration before, so I'm just as shocked as you are."

I could feel a lump form in my throat as I thought about how awkward it would be meeting her in this setting.

I put one hand on my hip and the other on my head as I thought of what to say.

"Ummm, so what do you want me to do? Surely she's not trying to hold a conversation with me here."

"Oh I'm sure she's not. She's coming to support Arbi."

I gave him a sideways look. "Yeah, right. This woman is coming to check me out."

"Well it shouldn't be hard for her to understand why I'm attracted to you then," he said, looking at my butt.

I slapped his shoulder. "Knock it off," I said with a smile. "I'll be cordial because bottom line this is my job, but this is awkward as hell."

"I know it is, but don't let her see you unnerved cause she'll really be a smart ass then."

Obviously he didn't know my mouth could be just as slick. In the words of my grandma, I could be real "nice nasty" when need be.

I headed over to the blue lounge to let Rachelle know. She was busy with a patron as I went back behind the bar.

"Guess what, his wife's going to here tonight."

She gave me a frowned look. "Carlton's wife?"

"Yes," I said.

"Get the hell out of here. Out of all the times he's been coming here, I can only remember once that she's come through. Damn, she must really want to check you out."

"That's exactly what I told him. Thank goodness she caught me on a good night. I'll happily give her a nice view of this ass she can gladly kiss."

The guy at the bar must've overheard that part as he grinned. "Yes, beautiful, and what an ass you do have," he said.

Rachelle and I laughed, and I headed back to my post. The night was going well so far, as smiling faces of men and women came through the door ready for a good time. I went upstairs to check the room levels and all were at a steady capacity. I went downstairs to check off my report when I noticed two ladies standing in the foyer checking out the scene. One of the ladies I recalled seeing once before, but the other one was a new fresh face. Then it hit me—it could be Maria.

I could see Carlton's friend walking over to greet her, which must've meant that it was indeed her. I glanced in her direction, and she was nothing like I'd envisioned. You could tell she was older than Carlton, but she was no doubt beautiful.

I could feel the young lady she was with looking directly at me. When I looked at her, she had a menacing smile on her face. What the hell was her problem?

Carlton came around the corner and made his way over to me.

"As a heads-up, that's Maria," he whispered.

"Oh it didn't take long to figure that out. Who's the pit bull with her and why is she staring at me like she wants to take a bite?"

He chuckled. "Her bark is bigger than her bite; no worries. That's Lacey, Maria's assistant. How about I introduce you?"

I grabbed him by his jacket sleeve. "I don't think this is appropriate," I whispered hastily.

"I think it'll help lighten the mood and even make her leave early." He winked.

"I'm not walking over to her. If she wants to meet me, she needs to come where I am," I said, avoiding eye contact.

He walked away and as I glanced over I could see Lacey make her way up the staircase. I looked toward Carlton to see him walking hand in hand over to me with Maria. My heart started to palpitate rapidly.

"Maria, this is…" he started to say before being cut off.

"I think we can cut the introductions, dear, as we clearly know each other at this point," she said with a fake smile. "Tia, I'm amazed by your beauty. You're not quite what I expected."

I guessed that was the sharp tongue he warned me about.

I chuckled sarcastically. "I'll take that as a compliment."

Carlton cleared his throat. "I'm going to grab some champagne, I'll be right back."

If looks could kill, he would have a red dot pointed on the back of his head. I didn't appreciate being left with the she-wolf, but I was well equipped to handle my own if need be.

"Did Carlton advise you of the meeting tomorrow?"

"He told me about the meeting, but failed to give a date. Tomorrow is fine. Where should we meet?"

She smiled. "How about your place?"

"Considering I'm still unpacking, I'd rather not. How about Starbucks?"

"Oh dear, how tacky is that, meeting at a Starbucks to discuss such business as ours. If you're OK with it, then you can meet me at the cabin. I'm sure you're well aware of where that is."

Her plan of intimidation didn't shake me one bit as I continued to smile.

"That's too far and I have to be able to pick up my son by a certain time. We can meet at the clubhouse at my apartment. They have private rooms there; let's say two o'clock."

She looked directly in my eyes. "I'll be there," she said then walked away.

I could tell by her demeanor that she was looking to play hardball with me. I needed her to understand that I didn't approach him with the proposition; he approached me. I could walk away from it and still be happy. I didn't need her bullshit attitude and her failed attempts at making me feel less worthy. If she thought her intimidation tactic scared me, she surely thought wrong. If anything, it had me fired up and ready to beat her at her own game.

CHAPTER 22
KELLY

As I sat in my office at work, I turned my chair towards the window, which gave a perfect view of the Atlanta downtown area. I thought about my night with Derek and how I'd acted like such a bitch. Lately my sex drive had been at an all-time low due to stress, and I hated having what I referred to as "one-sided" sex. I felt horrible about the way I treated him and couldn't make myself apologize in his presence, so I sent him a text in hopes it would make him come home early. My plan worked and at that time I was ready to give him the blow job he wanted earlier and more.

From the moment he got in the bed, I wanted to dominate and make him forget about what happened earlier. As he caressed my body and stroked my breasts, I was turned on and ready for action. He satisfied me orally and from there, that's when shit went left.

Derek was always such a gentle lover; sex between us was always lovemaking. Last night, I felt like I was fucked, which totally blew me. Now I admit I liked it rough sometimes, but this was far from Derek's style and it was not what I wanted. I knew we hadn't had sex in days and maybe it was penned-up frustration, but as quickly as I was turned on, I was turned off. I didn't even get mine and, by his actions, it didn't seem that he cared. When I got out of the bathroom, he was snoring as if he hadn't slept in days versus the cuddling we normally did.

This morning there wasn't much conversation between us before we left, but I wanted to ask him who was that in my bed last night.

My cell phone rang; it was Gigi. I'd been meaning to call her and when I did, there was never enough time to really talk.

"Hey, girl," I answered.

"I'm so sorry I'm just now getting back to you. With this boutique, and work itself, I'm completely drained. How are you?"

I sighed. "Stressed out. The housewarming is this weekend so I'm trying to pull things together.

"Oh yeah, that's right. I'm going to try to make it, but don't be mad if I can't."

"No problem. Listen, I have a question for you about Renae. Did you know she use to work for Walker & Co.?"

"Walker & Co.? Isn't that Derek's family business?"

"Yes."

"No, I had no idea, but then again I never asked. She said she's been a personal assistant for years, so I never bothered to question it further. That's quite interesting though."

"Yeah, it's rather interesting. I know I've mentioned Derek's name plenty times around her and you would think she'd have said something by now."

"I'm totally shocked myself, Kelly. I mean Renae and I have never been close like that, so there's a lot I don't know about her. But this right here definitely raises an eyebrow."

"Not like it does mine. It leads me to think what else she could be hiding. I don't even feel comfortable around her anymore."

"Well, have you asked Derek about her? It's amazing he hasn't said anything if he knows you two have been hanging out."

"Funny thing is I don't think I've ever mentioned her to him. We don't hang out like that for me to even make mention of her, but I do plan on asking him once all this housewarming stuff is done."

"I really wish I had more insight to give, but I'm stumped. Do you want me to confront her?"

"No, please don't. I prefer to handle this my own way."

I concluded my phone call with Gigi and tried to focus on my work. The day flew by and before I knew it, I was changing my clothes to head to the gym. I hadn't been in nearly a week, mainly because I'd been too tired.

Before heading into the gym, I pulled out my calendar to write down a meeting I had set up next week with my tenants. In reviewing my calendar, I noticed my period was late. What the hell?

How did I miss that? Reviewing the date from last month, I was officially four days late. Shit!

I tried to calm myself as I rubbed my forehead. I refused to jump the gun just yet knowing that I'd been stressed out with the whole move, getting settled in, and the craziness of planning this housewarming. That's it—I'm stressed. I couldn't even fathom the thought of being pregnant and felt nauseous by the thought.

I put away my calendar, grabbed my gym bag, and headed into the gym. Once I put my bag in my locker, I went to the mat to do warm-ups. I spotted Renae walking in. She waved at me as she headed to the locker room. I was hoping I could jump on a treadmill before she came back out. I'd already promised myself that I would put this situation on the back burner until after Saturday.

Luckily a treadmill freed up and I rushed over to hop on. I put in my earbuds and zoned out to the beats coming from my iPod.

Casey, Josie, and Ramon were coming in tomorrow night for the housewarming. I truly missed Casey and was excited to see her. I would even be happy to see Ramon since I hadn't seen him in a few years. There was never a dull moment when he was around. I'd arranged for us to all go out Friday for drinks and thought about asking Renae since she'd already declined my invite to the housewarming. When I asked why she wasn't able to come she stated she had to work.

After thirty minutes on the treadmill, I continued my cardio workout on the Stairmaster. Renae rushed over to the machine next to me.

"Hey, lady. You've been M.I.A. from this place. What's been up?"

I wanted to say, I been finding shit out about your sneaky ass, but thought to go with a safer response.

"Yeah, I've been quite busy," I said, avoiding eye contact.

"How's everything going with the housewarming? You haven't reached out to let me know if my assistance is needed."

"It's going good. I've been handling things on my own; I'm a bit of a control freak."

She nodded. "It's OK. If you want something done right, you gotta do it yourself. So what else is new?"

Did she really want to know that? I gave her a sarcastic grin.

"I should be asking you," I said between breaths.

"Work has me on lock, but other than that life is good. I'm going to be moving soon."

I looked at her. "You found another place."

"I'm moving to Chicago."

I slowed my pace on the machine as I gave her a frown. "Chicago?"

She chuckled. "Yeah, I know. I've lived in a lot of cities and I figured why not try Chi-Town."

"Well, good luck on that," I said.

There was silence between us. My focus was on getting my workout done and heading home as I increased the speed on my machine.

"Some of my out-of-town friends and I plan on going to Twist on Friday. Wanna join us?" I said.

She smiled. "I might stop through for a minute. Just make sure you keep your girl on her leash."

I gave a mischievous grin; whatever Jessica threw her way, I wasn't going to interfere.

"You're a big girl. You can handle yourself."

I completed my workout and headed home. Before I could even step in the door, I heard Kimora crying. I instantly grabbed my bag and rushed through the garage door.

Derek was standing with her in the kitchen rocking her.

"What happened?" I asked with a concerned look.

"Kaylee stepped on her hand by accident."

I reached to grab Kimora from his embrace. Even though I knew it was an accident and eventually she'd be OK, I needed to make sure my baby was fine.

I rubbed and kissed her hand as I cradled her in my arms. She slowly calmed down and reached for her sippy cup on the nearby counter.

"Glad you got her to calm down. She was making me a nervous wreck and poor Kaylee felt horrible."

I nodded. "Things happen, it's OK."

"I ordered pizza for dinner and I made a salad."

I nodded as I headed upstairs. I went to speak to the kids and lay Kimora down on her bed until I could get myself settled.

Derek came in the room and closed the door.

"How was your day?"

"It was cool. And yours?"

"Considering I had a hangover, not too well. I ended up coming home for a few hours to sleep it off."

I shook my head. "Well you brought that on yourself drinking like a fish knowing you have to work the next day."

"Not like that at all. The three drinks I had were stronger than I thought. What's going on with you?" he asked as he leaned over on the bed and rested his head in the palm of his hands.

I continued to undress. "What do you mean?"

"I think you know what I mean, Kelly. You haven't been yourself and I think it's more than just the stress of this housewarming."

I stood in my bra and underwear with my arms folded. "What was that about last night?"

He gave me a puzzled look. "What was what?"

I rolled my eyes. "The fact that you came home and fucked me like some one-night stand. You didn't even care about me getting mine like you normally do. I just found it rather odd."

He walked over to me and kissed me on the lips. "I was a horny, intoxicated man. If my actions made you feel that way, then I'm sorry, but you should know that I would never treat you like anything less than the queen you are. Sometimes men can be selfish and I guess last night was my turn. Please forgive me, love."

Being so close to him and seeing the sincerity in his eyes made me relax a bit. Derek had never given me reason to doubt him. I leaned in for a kiss but he leaned away from me. I frowned at his reaction.

"What's that about?"

"Anything you care to tell me?" he asked with a straight face.

He stepped away from me and sat on the bed, not taking his eyes off me.

I scratched my head as I tried to figure out what the hell he could be talking about.

The seriousness on his face eased as the corners of his mouth curled to form a smirk.

"Any reason you haven't told me your period is late?"

My eyes widened in amazement. Damn, he'd been keeping up with it better than me.

I slapped my forehead. "Funny thing is I didn't even know it until I looked at my calendar today. I've been so consumed with this housewarming that I hadn't even noticed. I don't think I'm pregnant, I think it's stress."

He rubbed his nicely trimmed goatee. "When do you plan on ruling out the possibility of pregnancy?"

I headed to the bathroom, not even wanting to entertain the thought of being pregnant. He followed me in as I went to the Jacuzzi tub to run some bath water.

"If it hasn't come by Saturday, then I'll go buy a test."

"So what if you are pregnant?"

I turned towards him. "Then we will deal with it at that time. For now, I don't want to speculate."

"What's wrong with talking about a possible situation? By your tone of voice, I can already tell you don't want to be pregnant."

I sighed. "If I'm being honest with myself, then no, I don't want to have another baby right now. Kimora isn't even two yet and together we have three active kids."

"I'm not knocking you for feeling that way, but realistically if you are pregnant, then what?" he asked with his arms folded as he leaned against the countertop.

"We deal with it, I guess. What do you want?"

"Of course I would want my child. I agree we have a full plate right now with the three we have and our new home, but if it happens, I would be fine with it."

I sat on the side of the tub. "I honestly think it's stress, so hopefully we have no worries."

As Derek left me alone in the bathroom, it only left me time to think about the big "what if" of being pregnant. I'd worked so hard to get myself back into shape and invested so much in creating this great home we have now; another kid would be a setback.

I cut off my bath water and prayed that my theory of stress was the factor for my missed period. Here I was, unmarried with one child and joint ownership of a house with a man who was not even my husband. I was no longer forcing the issue of marriage, but what I wasn't going to do was create another hindrance for myself.

CHAPTER 23
JANEN

My flight to Atlanta was filled with turbulence from the inclement weather moving along the southeast coast. As the plane rocked and dipped, I prayed that all would go well on my visit unlike the flight experience. When the plane landed, I couldn't move without saying a silent prayer. By the time I got up from my seat, my sweatpants were nearly stuck to my skin as I'd been sweating profusely from nervousness. I couldn't wait to get in my rental and head to my hotel room for a shower.

Tony had been gone for two days and in that time we'd been communicating better. I'd decided that after the family event with Rita tomorrow, I would make a surprise visit out to L.A. the next day since his trip was extended for another week. Our first year anniversary was approaching and I didn't want to go into it with this tension between us.

I breezed through the streets of Atlanta and reached my hotel in record time. I checked in and once in my room, I immediately collapsed on the bed. I didn't know which one I wanted more, sleep or a shower. The shower won as I thought of how I'd been sweating on the flight.

I listened to "Soon As I Get Home" by Faith Evans on Pandora as I showered. I could only smile thinking of the surprise I'd planned for Tony. I'd called his assistant and asked that she make sure an extra key was left at the front desk as well as his Saturday schedule.

Tony was right about my neglect as a wife. I thought I was balancing things, but the realization was I never stopped to ask him how he was doing. Through our conversations I apologized and we were in a much better place than when he'd left. However, I needed to do something over the top to show him that I was committed to make things better within our marriage.

Looking back at my parent's marriage always gave me the motivation to try to do things differently. I never knew why my dad was such the womanizer he was, because from what I saw, Mom was a supportive wife. I never wanted Tony to feel as if I wasn't there for him, which could potentially open the door to him finding comfort in another woman.

I got out of the shower and dressed. I decided to give Robbie a call to let him know of my arrival.

"Hello," he answered.

"Hi, Robbie. It's Janen."

"Hey, Janen. I just got off the phone with Rita. She sounds so excited about seeing you all tomorrow."

I smiled. "I'm excited and nervous at the same time. How's David doing?"

"He's good. He just walked up the street to get his hair cut."

"Is Carlita coming tomorrow?"

"I called her two weeks ago and she said OK, but of course I haven't heard back from her. She lives in Maryland, so hopefully she's able to come down. I'm not sure if her other daughter, T, got the message since we had to go through so many people."

Interesting enough, Rita never mentioned her youngest child. I wanted to ask Robbie what was her situation but figured I'd hold all my questions until tomorrow.

"Make sure you're there a little before noon, so we can all get through security together."

"Do you need a ride?" I asked.

"No, I'll test out my bucket. I've invested enough work in it, so hopefully we'll be OK." He chuckled.

After we hung up, I grabbed my keys and headed out the door. I needed to make it down I-20 to Mom's house before the traffic kicked in. Jessica would be coming over with my niece as well.

I put in my earpiece and called Sharee since it'd been a week since we last talked.

"Oh, now you remember my number," she sarcastically answered.

"Sharee, please knock it off. What you up to?"

"Relaxing right now since Jacob wants to stop by when he gets off."

"Jacob? Is this a new boo?" I asked.

"See what happens when you don't call; you miss out," she said, chuckling. "He works as a courier and he's been trying to get me to go out with him for months. I turned him down because one, all the damn ladies in my department lust over him every time he makes a delivery. And two, he ain't a brother, so you know he didn't grab my attention like that."

"Awww, you got swirl fever. It ain't all bad, Sharee, trust me."

She laughed. "He's a Latino man, so to me I didn't steer too far from my own kind."

"You are nuts. So what made you decide to go out with him?"

"Basically I did it to piss off this bitch in my department who thinks every man that smiles her way wants her. But on the other hand, he is fine, so you know I said why not, can't hurt to see what he's about."

"I'm proud of you, Sharee, for stepping outside your comfort zone. Just give the man a chance and don't run him away."

"Who me?" She chuckled. "I'll give him a chance, I always do. I just hate the fakery of men being all sweet initially and then weeks later, I get the jealous, stalker side. I'm not about that life right there."

"Well, all right, crazy lady. You keep me posted on how things are shaping up between you two."

We exchange good-byes as I turned onto my mother's street. I pulled in the driveway and she was outside with Diva watering her plants. I got out of the car to Diva barking and growling.

I clapped my hands. "Hush that fuss, Diva," I said.

I walked over to Mom and gave her a kiss. "You are looking fabulous, lady."

"I do my best, doll. You have a glow about you. Are you pregnant?"

I rolled my eyes and chuckled. "Not hardly. Where's Mr. Frank?"

"Running some errands, he should be back shortly. He was going to take us to dinner, but I told him I preferred to cook since I know you don't get home-cooked meals often."

"Not unless I cook myself and that ain't often."

I helped reel in the hose as we made our way into the house. I could smell the sweet smell of peaches as I entered.

"Please tell me that's the smell of peach cobbler," I said.

"Yes, ma'am. You and Jessica can fight over it. I thought I had enough ingredients but was only able to make a small pan of it."

"Well I'm the guest and she can get it anytime, so she will lose this fight." I smirked.

I sat at the kitchen island as I watched my mom stir the pots on the stove.

"So, honey, what's new in your world?" she said.

"I'm actually going to Rita's family day tomorrow at the rehab and meeting my other siblings."

She coughed and grabbed her water from the counter to take a sip.

"Are you OK?" I asked with concern.

She shook her head as she continued to gulp down the water.

"You sure you're ready for all that?" she asked.

I shrugged my shoulders. "Hey, it is what it is. I'm not expecting much, so there's no room for disappointment. Robbie didn't even know if her two daughters would actually be there."

"Have you seen Rita?"

I nodded my head. "Yes and we talked about things, mainly why she gave me up. I understand why she did it and I'm grateful that she did considering her circumstances. I just wanted to know how she could've done that to you knowing you were a friend to her."

My mom shook her head as she diverted her attention back to her pots.

"It ain't nothing worse than to be stabbed in the back by someone you consider a friend. But there's a lesson in everything we experience in life. For me, I think if Rita had taken the time to address me woman-to-woman, then maybe I would've forgiven her. But she's dodged me for years and right about now, I don't need her apology. What's done is done and I've moved on with my life while she's still trying to get her life right."

Even though Mom stated she didn't want any apology, the bitterness she felt was still apparent. Rightfully so, she deserved an apology regardless of what she said. I only hoped that with Rita's rehabilitation, she would see the need to right a lot of her wrongs with people she'd screwed over in life.

Jessica, Tianna, and Darnell came over for dinner. I was so happy to see my niece and have some time to spend with her. Even though Tianna cried when I removed her from Jessica's arms, I didn't care and eventually she calmed down.

Once Mr. Frank came back, we all sat down for dinner. All that was missing was Mikey and his wife, but they were out of the country for two weeks. We all had fun laughing and just catching up with each other. While I initially wasn't a fan of Mr. Frank, I could tell he truly loved my mom and she looked happy; that I couldn't argue or be mad at.

After dinner, I helped clean the kitchen before heading back to the hotel. All my traveling of the day along with the food I'd eaten was starting to make me rather sleepy.

The next morning I woke up in a panic thinking I'd overslept as I glanced at the clock on the nightstand. It was only nine o'clock, so I fell back on the pillow and stared at the ceiling. I'd gotten the sleep I needed and now my mind was going full-speed ahead thinking about what meeting my birth family would be like.

I went through my teenage life full of so many emotions, from anger to resentment, that this moment seemed surreal. I did a lot of things I regret now, but I realized it was all out of my own hurt and pain.   Now as a grown woman, I was thankful for all the trials and storms I went through in life because it truly gave me the strength to stand as the woman I was today. I could also thank my mother, Joann, for showing me what a real woman did when faced with adversity.

I got out of bed and prepared for my day. My mind said to call Tony, but judging by the time, he would probably still be asleep. I dressed and headed downstairs for breakfast.

My cell phone rang. It was Robbie.

"Good morning," I answered.

"Good morning, Janen. I wanted to call and see if I could take you up on the offer for us to ride with you."

"Sure, not a problem."

"Thanks. I went to go grab a cup of coffee and a newspaper from the store and the car acted like it didn't want to start back up, so I figured I might not want to trust it going that far."

"It's understandable. I'll be there around eleven o'clock."

I hung up the phone and proceeded back to my room to grab my purse. Leaving the hotel, I decided to stop by Walmart and grab a few things for Rita that she might need. I didn't know why, but I felt sorry for her in a sense. I wasn't ready to call her mom, but I could admire the fact she was making an effort to get her life on track.

Shortly thereafter, I pulled up at Robbie's house. David was already sitting out on the porch. He was nicely groomed, with a plaid button-down shirt, slacks, and some boots. He looked much better than when I initially saw him. He went in the house to tell Robbie I was outside.

They walked to the car and got in. I prayed my allergies wouldn't flare up at the loud mixture of cologne that rushed to my nose. I immediately rolled down the windows to let some air in.

"I'm sorry, guys, but I have allergies," I explained.

"No problem. We both are a bit heavy-handed when it comes to spraying cologne." He grinned.

I glanced back in the rearview mirror at David as he stared out the window.

"How are you, David?"

"I'm good," he said.

The rest of the ride was rather silent as I tried to relax myself by humming along to the music on the radio. Once we arrived at the center, we got out of the car and noticed a young lady sitting in a hunter-green Jaguar XJ with chrome wheels. From the Maryland license plate, I figured it had to be Carlita.

"Oh, that looks like Carlita," said Robbie as he walked over to the car.

David followed as I stood on the curb to wait for them. As she emerged from the car, I gasped at how much she looked like Rita. She was tall, light-skinned, and nicely shaped, with long wavy hair. I couldn't tell if her hair was a weave or not, but if so, she had a good beautician.

Carlita took off her shades as Robbie pointed in my direction. I awkwardly waved, but she quickly turned her head. If I didn't know any better I would assume that was intentional.

As they walked towards me, Carlita ironed out her clothes and held on to her Louis Vuitton purse as if someone was going to run up and snatch it from her.

She gave me a smile as she extended her hand. "Hi, I'm Carlita."

"Nice to meet you, I'm Janen."

We walked in silence as we entered the building and signed in. After going through security, we were directed to the courtyard area where Rita was already sitting with another young lady and little boy.

Carlita and David immediately walked over to the young lady and exchanged hugs while introducing themselves to the little boy. I stood off to the side as Rita turned towards me with a smile and reached out for a hug.

"You look beautiful," she whispered.

I could only smile as I looked at her. She didn't look as vibrant as she did the day I first visited. It almost looked as if she hadn't slept in a few days.

Once everyone took a seat, the young lady stood to introduce herself.

"Hi, I'm La'Tia," she said. "And this is my son, Noah."

I smiled as she took the first step in greeting me with a hug. Unlike Carlita, she seemed more inviting and sincere. I stooped down to greet Noah but he ran and hid behind her leg. I took a seat near Rita.

"It's so nice to see all of you. Glad everybody could make a little time for me." Rita smiled.

"Rita, do you have Medicaid for insurance?" Carlita said out of the blue.

Rita gave a puzzled look. "Yeah. Why?"

"Cause you need to see if they can do something with your teeth. If you trying to get your life right, then you need to start working on getting your appearance right too," she said as she ran her fingers through her hair.

I was shocked by her statement and ill-fitted timing to even mention it.

La'Tia shook her head. "Carlita, let's not start with the nonsense."

Carlita threw up her hands and continued playing with her hair.

David broke the silence. "So, Ma, when you getting out of here?"

"Maybe in another month," she said. "I'm working on a few things and I prefer to stay in until I can get stuff squared away."

"Like what?" Carlita chimed in with a scowl.

Rita slammed her hand down on the edge of the chair. "Did you really come here to get under my skin? Cause if that's what you came for, you're succeeding at it."

Carlita smirked. "No need to get all sensitive, Rita. I'm simply asking what you got in the works just so there are no surprises. I mean, are you waiting to get baptized, for financial aid for school, for a job to come through. I'm just curious and I'm sure everyone else is too."

Carlita was turning out to be quite the bitch I figured she was from the parking lot. Her behavior showed me that Rita wasn't on her favorites list, but to come and bring on such negativity let me know that her purpose for being here was to be dramatic.

La'Tia stood up and grabbed Noah by the hand. "Look, I didn't come here for all this foolishness, so if that's what this reunion is all about, then I'm out of here."

An attendant cautiously walked over to us. "Ma'am, if you like, we have the kids playing over in the play area. I can take your son over there. Trust me, it's gated and fully secured, you can see it from here," she said, pointing at the area.

Rita looked at La'Tia. "Please don't leave. Let Noah go play for a minute."

Noah happily went with the attendant. La'Tia watched them walk over to the area.

"I wanted you all to come so you could meet Janen. I gave Janen up when she was born. She reached out to me a few months ago and we've been in touch ever since."

Carlita started clapping her hands. "Welcome to the dysfunctional family, Janen."

"If you got to act like that, then you can leave," said Robbie in a stern voice.

"I don't understand the problem. We haven't all been together in years and now that we have the opportunity to address certain issues, I'm made to be the villain."

"It's all in your approach, Carlita. I understand you have some hostility, but the way you going about it is all wrong," said La'Tia.

Rita leaned forward in her chair as she spoke. "Look, I know I don't get the damn Mother-of-the-Year award, but I still deserve respect. You're right, we haven't seen each other in years and I blame nobody but myself for that. Nobody deserved to see me back then because I was a complete mess. I can't do nothing about the past but apologize. I'm doing what I need to do to make a better life for myself now. Carlita, I'm glad you were able to run off and marry a wealthy man and live in luxury. I've wanted nothing but the best for all of you since I wasn't able to give you that."

Carlita sighed. "OK, let's not start with the speeches because, like you said, the past is the past and there's nothing that can be done about it. I just want to know after nearly thirty years of living your life under the influence of drugs, how you plan to rebound from this? No disrespect, but it's not like Robbie lives in the finest area of Atlanta. So what's your plan?"

"I don't really know as of yet. I know I want to get out of Atlanta cause I do need a fresh start."

The more they talked, the more I felt like an observer in the room. This conversation was so far beyond me. I didn't have a right to intervene because I didn't know Rita or the circumstances that any of them went through with her. I thought meeting everyone would be more about me getting to know them; not a counseling session.

"So, Janen, what do you do?" La'Tia asked.

I felt as if that was her way of getting off the topic at hand. Now with all eyes on me, I knew it was my turn to be interrogated.

"I'm a fashion stylist and I currently live in Miami with my husband," I answered.

"Any children?"

I smiled. "Not yet, we're still newlyweds"

"Well gosh, if I'm thirty-eight, how old are you?" Carlita asked.

"I'm thirty-seven," I answered. I stared directly at Carlita to let her know I was ready for whatever smart-ass remark she had coming for me.

I guess my stare said enough as she backed off and glanced down at her cell phone. I decided to further question her since she was obviously the opinionated one of the group.

"So, Carlita, tell me a bit about yourself," I asked.

She tilted her head and rolled her eyes. "I've been married for three years and I live in Maryland. I have no kids and don't want any."

"How long have you been in Maryland?"

"Six years. I needed a change of pace, so I moved there with a friend and the rest is history. So what made you decide to meet the family after all this time?"

"I found out I was adopted, so to speak, when I was fourteen. As I got older, I felt the need to find my biological mother as a part of the healing process. Trust me, this was no easy decision and my decision wasn't well supported, but I did what was best for me."

She mumbled, "Sometimes it's better not knowing."

I turned towards La'Tia. "So do you live here?"

"Yes, I just moved back. I was living in Charlotte for a little over a year."

"Oh yeah, I'm sorry about your baby's daddy. It's awful. I had to hear about it months later from someone else," said Carlita.

La'Tia rolled her eyes. "Yeah, quite unfortunate," she said sarcastically. "So, do you have any siblings?"

"Yes, I have a brother and a sister; I'm the oldest."

We continued to talk as the conversation amongst everyone lightened up, even Carlita. David had quite the sense of humor as he became more engaged in the conversation. It felt good just to see everyone laughing and smiling, especially Rita.

After nearly two hours of conversation, it was time for us to leave. I gave Rita a hug and let her know I'd bought her some items. She looked more upbeat than when I'd arrived, which showed she really enjoyed us all being together.

La'Tia and I exchanged numbers. I explained that I was leaving town tomorrow, but if she wanted to hang out later, we could.

The whole ride home Robbie and I talked about how Rita livened up as the day progressed. David even engaged in the conversation and seemed to warm up to me in a sense.

When I pulled up to their house, I got out of the car to give them both a hug. I still had a long way to go in really getting to know them as individuals, but I figured what I'd learned thus far was a good start.

I headed back to my hotel as my cell phone rang.

"Yes, Jessica," I answered.

"Well, hello to you too. How did everything go?"

"It started off rocky, but by the end it was cool."

"Glad to hear that. We are meeting at Halo Lounge in Midtown tonight around 9:30. You want to ride together?"

"No, I'll drive in case I want to break out early, I don't have to ruin your fun. Besides, I have noon flight out to L.A. tomorrow so I can't be out too long."

"I understand that. Well the reservation is under Kelly's name but you can call me when you're on the way and I'll look out for you."

We ended our conversation as I pulled up to the valet area of my hotel. All I wanted was a nap before dealing with the night's festivities.

I hadn't hung out with Jessica in that kind of setting in years, especially with her friends. It would be nice to have someone else with me so I didn't feel like the outcast of the group.

As I reached my room, I called La'Tia to see if she was interested in going out with me tonight.

"Hello," she answered.

"Hi, La'Tia. It's Janen," I responded.

"Oh hey, girl. So what's up?"

"My sister and some of her friends are meeting tonight at Halo. I wanted to see if you were interested in going."

She paused as I anxiously awaited a response.

"I work at a club at night, but I can swing by for a minute before I go in."

"OK, that works, if it doesn't put you out of your way."

"I'll be fine. So what did you think of everything today?"

"Rather interesting, but overall I'm glad I got to meet you all."

La'Tia chuckled. "Girl, the dramatics never cease with us, that's why we can't be around each other more than a few hours. I can't even tell you the last time I'd seen my sister and brother, let alone Rita."

"It's obvious there are some underlining issues there, but I think as adults, we have to find a way to move past all the dissension. Life is too short for all that."

"You're right, but I'm at a point in my life where my responsibility and commitment is to my son. I can't change other people and I can't put my focus on trying to right situations with people who don't want to equally take that step."

"That's true. What's the deal with Carlita?"

"Excuse my French, but she thinks she's the shit. She's a beautiful person in looks and has been told that all her life from what I've heard, but inside she got a lot of ugly that I can't get with. I remember when I lost my job and I called her for help as a last resort and she basically treated me like some stranger begging for change on the street. Our relationship has always been rather distant, but out of all of us, Carlita got the most attention from Rita."

That was interesting, considering how Carlita acted during the visit. I'm sure there was more to their relationship then I'd probably ever know.

"So what's your relationship with Rita like?"

"I moved with my dad's mom when I was eight and stayed with her until I graduated from high school. I went to see Rita every other weekend and mainly that was time spent with Robbie and David while she did her thing in the streets. She was there, but her presence was absent, if you can understand that. Drugs just rip away a person's soul and everything they do is all about them. After a while, I stopped wanting to be around her and eventually once I graduated, I stayed away."

Listening to her made me realize all the more how fortunate I was to be raised by two loving parents even though I didn't appreciate it then.

"I'm sorry to hear that, La'Tia. Even through all you've endured it's good to see that you've turned out to be such a mature young woman."

"I'm still growing and it's not been easy at all. I've had some hard lessons to learn and I'm still learning how to be a better person. Oh and you can call me Tia."

We continued our conversation with talk of Rita and how we hoped this rehabilitation would truly be life-changing for her. I could tell that, unlike Carlita, Tia didn't harbor the same sentiments for Rita.

After grabbing dinner, watching TV, and catching up with Tony, it was near time to get ready to go out. I laid my clothes and accessories out before heading into the shower.

I always loved my shower time; my reflective moment of peace to clear my head. After meeting with Rita and the family today, I couldn't say where things were headed at this point. I could relate to the growing pains of my siblings in a sense, but unlike them, I had positive guidance in my life.

I got dressed and headed over to the lounge. As I drove up to the valet area, I pulled in behind Kelly as she exited her car. She looked fabulous, but with Kelly that was nothing new. I initially didn't care too much for her, but over the past year and a half we'd come in contact, I could see a change within her.

She spotted me as I got out of the car, and walked towards me.

"Hey, lady," she said, smiling.

We embraced and exchanged pleasantries as we made our way to the entrance.

"I'm sure we're the only ones here," Kelly stated as she looked around the lobby area.

"Jess said she was on her way."

Kelly chuckled. "That means she was just putting on her clothes. Jess is the queen of tardiness these days."

We were escorted to our reserved patio area, which included a beautiful white leather U-shaped couch with a coffee table in the middle. The view was very nice as it overlooked a nearby park. The middle panel separating us from the other areas was covered in vine plants cascading over it.

"So how is Miami treating you?" Kelly asked.

"It's going good. Congratulations on the new house."

"Thank you. Indeed a blessing and I absolutely love it. Will you be able to stop by tomorrow for the housewarming?"

I shook my head. "No, I'm heading out to L.A. tomorrow morning to see Tony."

"He's working out there for a while?" she asked.

"Only for another week, but our schedules have been rather full, so I'm going to surprise him for a few days," I said with a smile.

Jessica walked in. "I've arrived," she said as she struck a pose.

"Late as usual." Kelly smirked.

"Oh shut up. From the looks of it, I'm not the only one," she said as she gave us hugs. "OK, where are the drinks?"

"I was waiting until everyone got here before I ordered. Have you heard from Casey?"

Jessica rolled her eyes. "She was waiting on Ramon; you know he's a diva."

"Oh my, I haven't seen him in years," I said.

"He's still a mess," said Kelly.

As we made small talk, I could feel my cell phone vibrating in my purse. I answered as I stood up and moved closer to the patio railing.

"Hey. Are you here?" I asked.

"I'm not that far away. Should be there in ten minutes," she said.

I gave her the location in the lounge in which we were seated and told her to let me know when she was in valet.

Casey, Ramon, and another lady all walked in and exchanged hugs. Casey introduced the young lady as her girlfriend, Josie. We all sat down and Kelly ordered a bottle.

My phone vibrated as I looked down to see a message that Tia was in the valet area. I excused myself to go meet her.

We met in the lobby and exchanged hugs.

"You look great."

"Thanks. So do you." She smiled.

As we made our way back to the patio area, Jessica was heading in our direction.

"I'm on my way…" she said then stopped mid-sentence and stood frozen in place.

Tia took one look at her and mumbled, "Oh my God."

I looked from Tia to Jessica. "What the hell is going on?"

Jessica had an evil look in her eyes as she stormed past me. I turned to follow her when Tia grabbed my arm.

"I know her, or should I say we awkwardly know each other," she said as she looked away.

I shook my head and frowned. "I'm not understanding."

Tia held her head down as she shifted from one foot to another. "I had an affair with her husband."

I gasped as the thoughts of Darnell's infidelity came rushing back to the forefront. I couldn't believe the culprit of my brother-in-law's transgression was none other than my newfound half-sister.

"You've got to be kidding me," I said. My heart was racing and I felt light-headed.

"This isn't the time or place to discuss it, Janen," she said as she turned to walk away.

I called her name and she stopped to turn towards me. "You have to understand how shocking and unreal this is to me. Here I am ready to introduce you to her, my sister, and come to find out you already know each other and not in a good way. Imagine how I feel right now."

Tia looked at me with tears in her eyes. "I can imagine and I know it's not good. I had no idea she was your sister, but even if she wasn't, the situation in itself was wrong and there's nothing I can do about it. Look, I'm going to leave so you can go check on her."

I watched her as she walked away. I rubbed my forehead as I headed to find Jessica. Who knew this night of celebration would turn into such an eventful moment rehashing one of the worst times in Jessica's life? Now I wished I would've followed my gut instinct and stayed my ass at the hotel.

CHAPTER 24
DEREK

I'd been up since six o'clock helping Kelly with some last minute things for the housewarming and, to say the least, I was tired. We set up in the backyard pop-up tents, tables and chairs, buffet tables, and serving trays. I felt like we were preparing more for a wedding reception than a housewarming. While I didn't understand why such an event called for all this stuff, I had to admit once again that Kelly had done a great job.

Our guests were scheduled to start arriving around one o'clock, which hopefully would give me enough time to shower and get in a nap. The kids were not yet up and I hoped they would stay asleep until then.

While Kelly went out with her friends last night, I went to pick up her ring from the jeweler. With our room door slightly closed, I rushed to the closet and opened my sock drawer to marvel once more at the two-carat Asscher-cut diamond platinum engagement ring.

I smiled thinking about how excited Kelly would be about the proposal as well as seeing that the ring had been upgraded. Since she'd made the decision to move forward with the purchase of the house, she never discussed marriage. I was glad of it because for one, I didn't like being pressured, and two, it gave me the opportunity to think about it and do it in my own timing.

I exited the closet and was heading for the bathroom when my cell phone rang. I looked at the caller ID and see it was Darnell.

"What's up, bruh?"

"Maaaann, I need to talk to you."

"Are you OK?" I asked in a concerned tone as I shut the door.

"Yeah, I'm straight, but Jess told me some shit this morning that I really need to talk to you about."

I looked around the room. "OK, so where are you? Do you want me to meet you somewhere?"

"I'm on my way to pick up Tianna from Denise's. I'm not saying we got to meet up but I prefer we not talk about it while you're at the house."

"OK, give me ten minutes. I need to go to Target; I'll call you back."

I hung up my phone and slid it into my pocket, then I picked up my keys and wallet from the nightstand. I met Kelly at the staircase.

"I'm running out to Target. You need anything?" I asked.

"Gosh, you're a mind reader, I was about to ask you to make a run there. Yeah, get some big black trash bags and some foil."

I made a mental note as I continued down the stairs to the garage. Once inside the car, I use my Bluetooth to call Darnell back.

"I'm out now, what's up," I asked.

"So Jessica comes home last night pissed, but she said she didn't want to talk about it so I let her be. This morning I got up, cooked her breakfast in bed, and she started talking about last night. Now let me back up. You remember me telling you Janen found her biological mother."

"Yeah," I said even though I couldn't directly recall.

"Well, she found her and last night Janen invited her half-sister to the lounge."

"OK, so let me make sure I comprehend this correctly. Janen's half-sister who Jessica didn't know showed up last night at the lounge."

"Yes, but the cold part is who her half-sister is."

He paused as if I was to guess the mystery half-sister, but I had no idea.

"Man, just tell me."

"I'll be damn if she didn't say Tia."

I scrambled through my mind to see if the name would ring a bell and I came up clueless.

"Tia who?" I finally responded.

"The chick that tried to say she was pregnant by me."

"What the hell? Bruh, you have got to be kidding me," I said in astonishment.

"Man, when she said that, I swear a chill went all over me. I mean how ironic is it that this chick is Janen's half-sister?"

"Wow. I'm shocked, man. I guess it's safe to say Jessica didn't kick her ass considering Kelly didn't mention it."

"She said it took everything in her not to turn that place out."

"Damn, that's crazy. I'm sure that was awkward as hell for Janen."

"Yeah, she said she felt bad for her cause she was totally oblivious. And now on to even more interesting news."

"Oh damn, I hate to even think where this is going."

"Brace yourself, bruh, cause this one does involve you."

I shook my head as I attempted to figure out what news he could be bringing to my attention that came from Jessica.

"Aww shit, this doesn't sound good."

"She asked me if I knew who Lacey was."

"Why the hell would she ask you that?"

"Man, you not going to believe this, but Lacey has been hanging out with Kelly."

I damn near swerved off the road at the mention of the two names I never wanted to hear being mentioned in the same sentence.

"No, you can't be serious," I said, rubbing my forehead.

"When Jessica mentioned it, it totally threw me for a loop. I told her she used to work for the company. I asked her how she knew her and she said she was at Kelly's place before the move and Lacey stopped by. She told Kelly that Lacey looked mighty familiar but couldn't figure it out at the time. Jess remembered seeing her at the job, but couldn't recall her name. Come to find out Lacey was going by her hyphenated name 'Renae' only."

I leaned back on the headrest unable to speak. What are the odds of some shit like this happening?

"Oh man, this isn't good."

"Jessica is curious as to why Lacey wouldn't disclose the fact she used to work at the company or even mention that she knew who you were."

I shook my head in disbelief as I sighed. "How the hell did they even connect? Lacey is so out of Kelly's league."

"Jessica said Gigi introduced her to Kelly. Gigi's best friend is Lacey's sister."

"I can't believe this, man. I've seen Lacey and she's never once mentioned it."

Darnell chuckled. "And you really think she would? Man, it's a choke-hold move; a revenge tactic."

I hit the steering wheel. "If I were to see her right now, I'll probably be sitting in a jail cell."

"It wouldn't resolve anything, bruh, so it's not worth the thought. You mentioned you'd seen her recently. Are you still messing around with her?"

"No. I saw her a few weeks ago at this spot Carlton and I were at."

"Well I just wanted to make you aware of what's going on. If Jess is asking me about it, I can only imagine the questions that will come from Kelly. Just trying to give you a heads-up, bruh; this situation can turn ugly."

I thanked him for letting me know and he was absolutely right—things could get ugly.

I thought about the week before with Kelly being in a funk. Could this have been the reason? If she knew about this, why hadn't she asked me about it? As with most women, I'm sure she was waiting on further evidence before she made her strike. At any rate, I couldn't let this deter me from my plans of the day. However, I needed to prepare myself if this situation blew up. I definitely underestimated Lacey on this one, but it goes to show you never know who knows who.

After rushing in and out of Target with my mind going full throttle about everything Darnell had told me, I tried to remain cool as I walked back in the house. The kids were up in full swing. I grabbed Kimora from her high chair to clean her up.

Kelly walked in from outside with a look of exhaustion.

"Babe, how about you go chill out for a minute."

She exhaled. "I'm just about done. Casey will be coming over in a few to help with everything else."

She went upstairs as I continued to get the kids taken care of. I prepared them for their baths and set out their clothes for the day.

It was eleven thirty when I heard the doorbell ring. I walked in our bedroom as I could hear Kelly yelling from the bathroom that it was probably Casey.

I peeked out and opened the door. "Hey, Casey."

We greeted each other with a hug.

"Hey, Derek. Man, this house is really nice."

"Thanks," I said as she walked in. "You know your girl has gone above and beyond to make the inside just as beautiful as the outside."

She patted me on the back. "Yeah, I feel for your wallet." She chuckled. "How have you been doing?"

"Pretty good. How's life in Texas?"

"I'm making the most of it, but I'm hoping to get a transfer in the next few months."

"That's cool. Well, Kelly is in the bathtub, but I'll go ahead and show you around."

I gave her the tour of the house as she admired all the work that I had to give Kelly the credit for doing. When we got to the kids' playroom, she was in awe of the wall murals in which I could finally boast I'd done myself.

Soon after, Kelly came downstairs and I went up to start getting dressed.

My mind told me to call Lacey and ask her exactly what the hell was going on. Was her idea of getting close to Kelly some sort of scare tactic? Whatever the case might be, I planned on confronting her about it, but I wouldn't be bothered with it today.

After I showered and dressed, I gave myself a look over in the mirror. I could hear voices coming up the stairs as I opened the door.

Mrs. Jackson was walking up the stairs holding Kaylee's hand. I gave her a hug when she reached the final step.

"I would've thought you'd get a ranch style versus all these stairs," she said, exhaling deeply. "I'm definitely getting too old for this. It's a beautiful house though."

"Thank you," I said.

I continued to show her around the upstairs area while Kaylee was more interested in showing her the playroom.

"Derek," Kelly yelled from downstairs.

"Yeah," I answered and started down the stairs.

She walked towards me with a perplexed look. "One of the legs on the pop-up tent keeps slipping down. Can you take a look at it?"

I walked outside and noticed Carlton and Maria had arrived.

"You guys didn't have to come so sharp; it's just a backyard boogie," I said as I gave Carlton the brother handshake and a hug.

Carlton punched me jokingly in the arm. "You know we gotta look like money everywhere we go." He winked.

Maria stood as we exchanged hugs. Her hair was pulled back in a bun and she wore a brown belted off-the-shoulder jumpsuit with her tan snake-skin red bottoms. Maria always made sure she was the epitome of a mannequin at a high-end store.

"The house is absolutely beautiful. I'm so proud of you and Kelly." She beamed.

"Thanks, Maria. She's done a great job with the decorating even though she's damn near drained my accounts."

She smiled. "You can never put a price tag on quality and good taste. I can tell she was trained well."

Surely Maria could afford to say such a thing since she was sitting on millions and her house was like a fine arts museum.

"Oh that she was." I winked. "Well, excuse me, I need to go over here and fix this tent."

I fumbled with the leg of the tent and hoped I wouldn't break out in a sweat by doing so. I wasn't the most handy man but I always did my best to at least try. Once the leg popped up and latched into place, I stood back to admire my work and prayed it wouldn't humiliate me by collapsing.

As more guests arrived, I helped Kelly bring out the food and, before we knew it, the party was in full swing. Everyone loved the house and the way we'd set everything up for the party. Kelly clung to my arm as we mingled with everyone, and when they gave their admiration for the decorating, she didn't boast but gave us both credit.

Kelly stepped away to check on the kids, and I signaled over to Carlton.

"What's up," he asked.

"Darnell called and told me this morning that Laccy has been hanging out with Kelly."

His eyes grew big. "Man, get the fuck out of here. Since when did they become friends?"

I shrugged. "I have no idea, but obviously they've been hanging out for a while. Jessica brought it to Darnell's attention because she knew she recognized her from somewhere and then she recalled seeing her at the company. So she's trying to figure out why Lacey hasn't said anything about it to Kelly."

He rubbed his forehead. "And Kelly knows this now?"

"She hasn't said anything to me, but if Jessica knows, I'm sure she does too."

"This is crazy. I know Atlanta can be small, but damn, what are the odds of a girlfriend and a lover connecting like that?"

I shook my head. "I've got to have the worst luck in the world on that one. I couldn't deal with this today, but I wanted you to see what was up."

"You know I have no problem doing that. She really makes me question her mental stability sometimes."

I frowned. "Really? Is it customary for her to do shit like this?"

"I don't put anything past Lacey, but you know lately she's been real chill so I thought she was finally mellowing out. Are you still proposing to Kelly?"

"That's the plan. Got the ring right here in my pocket."

He patted me on the shoulder. "That's right, go ahead and proceed with your plan. In the meantime, I'll handle Lacey and make sure she knocks off whatever it is she's plotting in her mind."

As we mingled, laughed, ate, and opened our gifts, which were mainly money and gift cards, we took the time to thank everyone for coming out. I let Kelly take the lead on the speech as I could feel my nerves taking over as I prepared to propose.

After she was done, she went to go do something when I grabbed her hand.

She gave me a puzzled look as I started to speak to everyone.

"I'm truly blessed and humbled for everything in which I have, and settling in this house with my family has brought me great joy. I'm not going to go on a tangent about all I've gone through in the past because I'm just grateful to be at this point with a beautiful home, my kids, and this beautiful lady standing to the right of me."

I could feel my knees tremble as she blushed through all the "oohs and ahs" from everyone.

I kneeled on one knee to a round of applause and screams.

"Dang, can ya'll give a brother a chance to get it out first," I said with a smile.

Everyone laughed. Kelly's eyes filled with tears as I looked into her eyes.

"Kelly Michelle Waters, are you ready to do this? Will you be my wife?"

She nodded as the tears fell from her eyes. "Yes."

I placed the ring on her finger as she cried and fanned herself. She left me kneeling as everyone flocked over to admire her ring. As I got up, she turned towards me and gave me a kiss as everyone erupted into applause. Everything felt so right and I saw a glow on Kelly's face I hadn't seen in quite some time.

As the ladies bombarded Kelly to gawk at her ring and wish her congratulations, I huddled with the guys. A party that was only supposed to last for two hours turned into an afternoon and evening event.

Denise offered to take the kids back with her in order to give Kelly and me some uninterrupted celebratory time. Once the last guest left the house, Kelly and I lay out on the floor of the family room.

"I am totally drained," said Kelly as she stretched her arms over her eyes.

I crawled near her and kissed her on the cheek. "Hopefully not too drained where you can't make love to your fiancé." I winked.

She rolled on her side to face me with a smirk. "I guess I could give you some since you've laced my finger with such a beautiful ring."

"Well damn, I would hate to think what I would get if I didn't put that beautiful ring on your finger."

She rubbed my cheek. "You totally surprised me today; I honestly had no idea."

"Mission accomplished." I smiled. "I was nervous as hell doing that."

"Yeah, I felt you trembling," she said, chuckling. She rolled on her stomach and pushed herself up with her knees then extended her hand to me. "Let's go take a hot bath so you can soak them old bones."

"Oh really now," I said as I took her hand and stood up. "Let's see what you think about these old bones tonight when I'm making you moan," I said with raised eyebrows.

We retreated to our bedroom. As Kelly went into the bathroom to run bath water, I could see the light on my cell phone, which meant I had a message. I had a missed call from Carlton. I checked my text and it read, *"Handled…let me know if she starts making waves."*

Carlton's reassurance that the matter with Lacey had been taken care of made me feel a bit at ease. I didn't want to draw suspicion by texting back and forth, so I didn't respond to his text.

I entered the bathroom where Kelly had lit some candles with the tune of Teddy P's "Turn Off the Lights" playing in the background. She was already reclining back in the tub with her eyes closed as I undressed and slid in across from her.

"So you going to bathe with the ring on, I see," I said.

"It isn't going to turn, is it," she jokingly replied.

I leaned back. "If it does, we going to have some problems."

She rubbed on my legs. "We got a lot of gift cards and checks."

"You can keep the gift cards, just give me the checks." I laughed.

She playfully swatted me on the leg. "No, we will deposit the checks in a joint account. We need to start preparing for our wedding."

Women kill me! I'd just spent over two thousand on a damn engagement ring and now the decision of the "wedding" had come up. Could my pockets recuperate first?

"When are we trying to make this wedding for?" I asked with a side eye.

She pouted her lips and gave me a blank stare. "I hope you don't think I'm trying to be engaged for a year."

Yeah, indeed I was hoping for a year; hell, two if I could stretch it that long. The last thing I wanted right now was for an argument to ensue and I to miss out on an opportunity for some loving.

"All I'm saying is we need some time to financially rebound from the house and all the purchases we've made. I don't know about you, but I don't like my account being under a certain dollar amount."

I could tell my response was not satisfying her need to know exactly when.

"I understand we've made some big purchases lately, but my parents have set aside money for my wedding since I graduated college."

I'm sure they have, I said to myself. I drew her in towards me and looked her in her eyes.

"We will figure this all out, but as of right now, let us enjoy this next step we are taking. Okay?"

Her confused look gave way to a half smile as I leaned in and kissed her passionately. "Now let's hurry up and bathe so we can really celebrate."

Even though her half smile indicated "this conversation will do for the moment," I was willing to take it. I was too horny to argue and too tired for further conversation. All I wanted to hear was the music of our bodies meshed together.

When we got out of the tub, she went to the closet while I prepared myself for some bedroom action. She walked out holding something behind her back.

"Since you wanted to know what was up with my missing period, here's the answer," she said, handing me the stick of the pregnancy test.

I sat up and flicked on the nightstand light as I adjusted my eyes to read it. One line, not pregnant—it read.

I gave it back to her as I grinned. "Who says by morning that we can't change that?"

She shook her head as she went in the bathroom to throw the test in the trash. She came back out and got in bed. I pulled her on top of me.

"Why don't you show me how much you love me?"

"How much I love you or how much I love it," she said, grabbing my penis.

I grasped. "Whichever one is going to make my toes curl."

She kissed me on my chest, which was always a good starting point. I moaned as she drew circles around my nipples with her tongue. She grabbed my penis and slowly stroked it, diverting all her attention to my lower region.

I awaited the touch of her tongue on the tip of my penis as she continued to stroke it. I wanted to yell "put your mouth on it now," but instead I let her do whatever necessary to get herself ready.

Just as her tongue wrapped around the tip, the doorbell rang. What the hell? She tried to move away as I quickly grabbed the back of her head to continue. The doorbell rang again. Fuck!

I looked at the clock—nine o'clock. Who the hell would be so rude as to come over without calling first? At this point, I was irritated and ready for whoever it was to go away.

"Are you going to see who it is?" she whispered.

"Damn it," I said as I got up from the bed.

I walked over to the window and peeked through one of the blinds. My heart raced as I recognized the car in the driveway to be Lacey's. What the hell is she doing here? I could hear Kelly getting out of bed.

"Who is it?" she asked.

I couldn't speak; I couldn't even move. All I wanted to do was evaporate like water in the plush carpet of my bedroom.

She looked out the window and looked back at me with a perplexed look.

"That's Renae," she said. "Why wouldn't she call first?"

She grabbed her housecoat and ran down the stairs. As much as I wanted to run behind her, I couldn't move. I heard the chime of the front door open as I threw on my pajama pants and t-shirt. The more I moved towards the bedroom door, the more I realized that tonight everything within my relationship would be blown to pieces.

CHAPTER 25
LA'TIA

Over the past few weeks, I'd had a lot of time to think about my life; where I wanted to go and how I planned on getting there. When I received the message about my mom's visitation, I was elated that she wanted to see me. I hadn't seen her in nearly three years and it was finally time I made peace with her. I wanted her to see that I was doing well for myself, and also for her to meet her grandson.

Before the visitation with Rita, I'd put a lot of thought into the offer Carlton proposed. He wooed me with materialistic things and money, while spending nights with me giving me the sexual attention that I craved. Despite all his generous acts and the amazing sex, I'd been successful in not falling in love with him. Truth was I wouldn't allow myself to feel it; I saw the relationship for what it was and didn't need any further complication.

When it came time to meet Maria, I took a shot of Patron beforehand to shake off the nerves I felt mounting. I knew she was going to intimidate me and make me feel like bubble gum under the bottom of her Christian Louboutin shoes. She arranged for us to meet at her offsite office.

Her office was housed in the Buckhead area in a beautiful Victorian-style building. From the foyer to the marble floors, you knew the tenants of the building had to have some serious money to afford the rent.

I took the stairs to her second-floor office and felt myself trembling with each step. I stopped to take a moment to gather myself, then continued to her office door. I knocked and within seconds there stood the female who was with her the night at the club. She gave me a smirk as she looked me up and down. Without even a "hello," she opened the door and turned for me to follow her.

Maria was on the phone, but motioned for us to come in. When I walked in, Maria extended her hand to the seat in front of her desk. The chair looked like it came from some antique store, with its high back and velvet golden cushions. Her assistant went to the nearby refrigerator and retrieved two bottles of Fiji water, which she laid on coasters nearest to us. She then turned and walked out, closing the door behind her.

Maria ended her phone call and without saying a word opened her bottled water and took a sip.

"The never-ending drama of the business world." She grinned. "Did you have any trouble finding the office?"

"No, pretty straightforward," I answered with a straight face.

I could see her giving me the look over as she gulped more of her water. I sat unfazed knowing I was looking pretty damn hot. I even took out my weave, so my naturally long hair could be on display.

"Well, let's get down to business. Carlton wants you to carry our baby and I want you to understand that this is strictly a business transaction."

I nodded as she continued to speak.

"I don't know if you've developed feelings for Carlton, but make no mistake about it, there is no divorce between us," she said, leaning forward with her hands interlocked on her desk.

I looked directly at her with a grin. "To think that would be rather naive of me. I know what a business proposal is and I don't expect nor want anything as far as a relationship."

She smiled. "So tell me a bit about yourself."

I looked up at the ceiling as I sucked my teeth, then diverted my attention back to her.

"Let's cut the bullshit, Maria. A woman of your caliber I'm sure has done her homework, so let's not play games."

She chuckled as she leaned back in her chair. "Awww…you're a feisty little spitfire, I see. Well, you know what, I have done my homework. But I'm just interested in what you have to say about yourself. You know we tend to get half-truths out of people when it comes to who they really are."

I could feel my leg twitching as I tried not to let my anger show at the mind game she was playing.

I smiled. "Is this an interview for a position? I feel like I'm being interrogated here when I've already been given the job."

She laughed. "Oh dear, now you really sound naïve. Nothing is ever official until you sign on the dotted line and, furthermore, no job is given without my approval." She twirled side to side in her chair. "So tell me, what happened with Noah's father?"

I wanted to say "none of your fucking business," but I had nothing to hide when it came to that situation.

"He was killed," I said without further explanation.

"The drug-dealing world can be a cold game. It's so unfortunate that your son will never have that relationship with his father." She sighed. "What is your relationship like with your mother?"

I rolled my eyes. I felt like I was at a psychologist's office. "We don't have the best relationship, but it is what it is."

She crossed her arms as she continued to lean back in her chair. "Do you think that lack of a relationship has made you who you are?"

With squinted eyes, I was ready to unleash. "I don't understand how any of this is relevant to the subject matter at hand. I'm a woman that has endured a lot in my life, but all I know how to do is keep pushing and live my life the best way I can. Now, I really wish you would cut to the chase."

She gave me a big smile. "Young lady, even a job wants a background check on their workers to understand who they are as a person. You being a carrier of such precious cargo, I need to understand you."

"Excuse me, but it's not as if this child is going to have any of my DNA; I'm just the carrier."

"True, but still I need to know you for myself. How many married men have you slept with?"

I stood as I ironed out my clothes and reached for my purse. "As far as I'm concerned, this meeting is over."

Maria stood behind her desk. "Just know if you leave here today, there is no deal."

I walked closer to her desk and leaned forward. "Fuck you and your deal," I said with a smirk.

I then headed for the door and turned towards her. "Have a good day, Maria. I hope you find a woman who lacks confidence so your intimidation can actually work. That's definitely not me."

As I stepped out of the office, her female assistant gave me a cold look. I smiled at her and mumbled the word "bitch." I felt liberated as I walked out of the building and to my car. At that point I knew that I had to go with my gut instinct and make some serious changes.

Carlton called and asked if he could meet with me and I calmly told him no. There was nothing he could say or do that would make me reconsider the offer. I couldn't subject myself to further scrutiny of being a single mother doing whatever I needed to do to provide for me and my son. I couldn't live a lie and continue in such a meaningless relationship.

I'd been avoiding Carlton for nearly two weeks and spent the majority of my days looking for a job. When he stopped calling me, I felt relieved and only hoped that meant he wouldn't try to see me at the club.

The day I visited Rita, I couldn't handle my nervousness. I cried before I even got there as Noah looked at me with his big brown eyes wondering what the hell was going on. Even with the rocky past between Rita and me, bottom line was she was my mother and I loved her still. I didn't know if her rehabilitation would mean much for our relationship, but I prayed that it would be the turning point she needed.

Once everyone arrived, I got the opportunity to meet Janen. I found her to be strikingly beautiful with an eccentric look. I could sense her nervousness as well with meeting all of us, but after a few moments of drama brought on by Carlita, she blended in nicely.

When she invited me out for the evening, I didn't want to go. However, since this was an opportunity for me to form a relationship with her, I figured I might as well take her up on the offer.

That night, I felt like something wasn't right; a feeling I couldn't shake stirred within me. I couldn't pick out a suitable outfit and changed three times before giving in to what I had put on last. My mind was going full-speed ahead wondering how things would go since it wasn't just Janen, but others who would be there with her.

When I arrived and saw Janen, the feelings before started to subside. She was so inviting and I started to relax. However, the minute I saw Jessica's face and her reaction in seeing me, I realized why I'd felt as I did earlier on. Being face-to-face with Jessica, the wife of a man I'd been involved with and lied to, I couldn't handle the reality staring back at me.

The look of confusion on Janen's face further made me feel like shit. She was totally oblivious to the mess she'd brought together. After Jessica had her moment of anger and disbelief, I explained to Janen the situation as briefly as I could. She herself couldn't believe it nor formulate the words to say. Janen was clearly caught in the middle of a situation involving a sister she'd grown up with and a sister she'd just met less than twelve hours ago.

In shame, I apologized to Janen and rushed to valet to get my car. With the long line of people waiting in valet, I was ready to go and retrieve my own car. Janen walked outside and asked to speak with me. We walked off to the side and she leaned against the building with her eyes closed and her hands over her head.

"This has been one helluva day and this is the least thing I expected as the end of it," she said without making eye contact.

I shook my head. "Janen, I don't really know what to say. Of course I didn't know Jessica was your sister or I wouldn't have come here."

She looked at me with tears in her eyes. "You know when Jess went through all that with Darnell, she never really said who you were and I respected that. But I also knew that the whole situation caused her a great deal of pain, so I cursed and wished all kind of bad karma on this trifling-ass woman who caused my sister so much pain."

I deeply exhaled as I turned to check my spot in valet. I couldn't ignore the emotions she felt now or even then; who wants to see anybody they love being hurt?

I nodded my head. "You had every right to feel that way, Janen. What I did was wrong—I knew it then and there's no denying it now. That bad karma you wished on me—yeah, I got that too, but I can only blame me. Listen, Jessica is your sister and I know I could never compare to the chemistry you guys have considering we just met. I don't want to further complicate things, so if you don't want anything to do with me—I accept that."

My car came around as the valet guy looked around for me. I held up my hand as he nodded towards me.

There were no other words between Janen and I; the situation was just too complicated. I told her good night and headed to my car without once looking back. I got in my car and had a breakdown. I didn't want to go to work; all I wanted to do was go home. I called the club and told them I was too sick to come in, which wasn't far from the truth.

Once I got home, my cell phone rang. I saw it was Rachelle but I didn't feel like talking so I hit the "ignore" button. I sent her a text saying I didn't feel good and would talk to her later.

I undressed and got in the fetal position in my bed. No music, no TV; only the stillness of the night with the lighting from the outside peeking through my blinds.

It had been three days since that night and I'd still not gone back to work. Carlton sent me a text asking if he could come by and I finally responded stating that he could. I'd given much thought about my life over the past few days and if I planned to move forward, I needed to find closure in my present situation.

I'd laid Noah down for his nap when I heard the distinct ringing of the phone alerting me someone was at the gate. I didn't bother to ask who it was as I hit "9" to allow access.

I closed Noah's door and made my way to the living room. The doorbell rang as I opened it and in walked Carlton. He handed me a fresh bouquet of flowers. I didn't even bother to put them in water but laid them on my breakfast bar and proceeded to the living room.

I sat in my lounge chair as he sat on the sofa with his legs crossed and his hand rubbing his chin.

"You really had me worried about you, Tia," he said with a concerned look.

"Thank you for giving me the space I needed. I don't doubt your concern, but I wasn't in a good place to talk to anybody."

"After speaking with Rachelle, I figured you really needed time to yourself since you weren't even talking to her."

I shrugged. "Sometimes you don't need your friends to help you get through situations. I had to do things on my own terms."

He uncrossed his legs and leaned forward. "Well I'm sure all this is not by accident. After your meeting with Maria, things seemed to go left."

I grinned. "Oh Maria, yeah, she's an interesting piece of work. I wasn't feeling her intimidation games and I'm not about to become anyone's victim if I can help it."

"Come on, Tia. You women are naturally competitive with each other and you had to know this wasn't going to be a meeting of tea and laughter."

"Nope, I didn't expect that at all. But as big a bitch as she was being, she made me realize the most important thing and that's losing my self-respect. I've always thrived off being an independent woman and living life on my terms, but my actions have indicated differently. I've been on my own since I was seventeen, and when my first love showed me a lifestyle of living financially comfortable with all the trimmings to match, I couldn't see myself going below that lifestyle. I settled for him being a drug dealer so I could continue to live in my luxury apartment, travel, and buy all my expensive brand-name clothes. And when he went to jail, I took interest in a married man thinking that might be my meal ticket while my man was doing time. Got caught up in that not only physically, but mentally too as he was the kind of man I wanted in my life. He was the only married man I'd ever been with; but besides being with him, which was wrong—I made the mistake of opening up my heart to him. In that moment I realized you never give a man what he hasn't rightfully earned. Sex is nothing compared to what you experience and go through when you open up your heart."

Carlton looked at me with a look of compassion. As if I were some lost girl who needed a hug. I didn't need his empathy; I needed him to understand where I was in my life.

"Tia, we've all done things in life in which we are not proud. I'm not judging you and that has never been my intent."

I bit my lip as I looked towards the ceiling. "I know you are a genuine person, Carlton, but this situation is unhealthy for me and the path in which I want my life to go. When you make mistakes in life, it's a moment for you to grow and move from it. I feel like I haven't grown much in that area. I've guarded my heart, but I've allowed myself to be bought when I'm not up for sale. I'm devaluing myself in order to live the lifestyle that I once was accustomed to and it's not right no matter how I try to flip the situation."

Carlton ran his fingers through his hair. "OK, so you're declining the offer and want me out of your life."

I nodded my head. "You may think your wife is OK with you doing what you do on the side, but she's not. I can tell she loves you, but she's lost a bit of herself through whatever she's gone through medically. And through that, she doesn't want to take the risk of losing you too."

Carlton sighed as he closed his eyes. "I get your logic, Tia, and I appreciate your honesty. Maria is a good woman, but I can't help who I am as a man. I'm not making excuses for myself, but it is what it is. Some women would never accept that side of me as Maria does and that's why we have the openness in our relationship that we do. I know you may not get that and even some of my closest male friends don't either, but that's just the way it is and it works."

He stood up and looked down on me with a smile. "It's been real, Tia."

I stood up and extended my hand. "Good luck, Carlton."

He looked at my outstretched hand then took it in his hand and kissed it. "You're beautiful, intelligent, and hella sexy. The man you're looking for is out there—be patient."

I smiled as I opened the door. He took a look at me, patted me on the shoulder, and left. I closed the door and from there, I deemed that as one closed chapter of my life.

My cell phone rang. I raced back to my room and answered quickly.

"Hello."

"Tia," said the muffled voice. "This is your uncle Robbie."

"Hey, Unc. Are you sick?"

He sniffed. "No, the rehab called me and they've rushed Rita to the hospital.

"What?" I said. "Did they say why?"

"She overdosed. They found her in the bathroom passed out."

I rubbed my fingers through my hair as I paced the floor. "Oh my God! What hospital is she at?"

"She's at Grady. I'm trying to get down there but I don't trust my car and I don't want to get stranded."

"Let me see if Noah's grandmother can watch him and I'll call you back. Did you call Carlita and Janen?"

"I tried Carlita, but I got a busy signal. I left Janen a message."

After our phone conversation, I called Sharon and she agreed to watch Noah for the night. I packed a bag for Noah, grabbed my purse, and rushed out the door.

My mind was going full throttle thinking about Rita and praying she would be OK. When I last visited her, she had a look of sadness on her face even though she tried her best to be in good spirits with everyone there. I could only imagine the clarity she got from being clean and how the guilt of her not being accepted by her own mother and failing her children must have made her feel unworthy. I believe that when people make a conscious decision to change their lives for the better, then it can be done. However, an idle mind is the devil's playground and it was apparent she allowed that being to seep into her mind.

I dropped off Noah and within minutes I was pulling up at Robbie's. When I parked in the driveway, he and David came rushing out to the car. From the look on Robbie's face, you could tell he'd been crying and was deeply concerned about his baby sister.

The ride to the hospital was very somber as everyone's attention was clearly on Rita. My cell phone rang—it was Janen.

"Tia, I received Robbie's message. Are you down at the hospital?"

"Robbie and David are with me and we're heading down there now."

"Is it OK if I call you back in the next thirty minutes to check on things?"

"Sure," I said.

I hadn't heard from Janen since the night at the club nor had I reached out to her. I felt bad about how things had gone down, but I couldn't forge a relationship with someone who was not willing to forgive me for my past mistakes.

We reached the hospital and I let Robbie and David out at the emergency entrance while I found parking. My nerves were on high as I parked the car and checked my face in the mirror.

I got out of the car and headed into the hospital. As I walked through the metal detectors, I could see that the waiting area was filled to capacity. I walked over to a corner where Robbie and David were standing.

"What's the deal?" I asked.

"The front desk lady said they have too many people back in the area, so as soon as some of the visitors come out, one of us can go back."

I looked around the room and there was not one chair available. Hospitals always made me uncomfortable and it didn't help I was a germaphobe. As a wave of visitors came through the automatic double doors, the attendant called for Robbie.

David started to follow Robbie. "David, how about you stay with me?" I said.

He looked from me to Robbie as he walked down the corridor. "OK," he said and stood beside me.

Two chairs opened up and we both rushed over to claim them. I looked over at David who was clearly upset. His leg shook uncontrollably and he fidgeted with his fingers. I grabbed his hand and rubbed it.

"It's going to be OK, David," I said as I looked at him.

"I hope so," he said, looking down at my hand.

We sat and waited for what felt like hours before Robbie came back out to join us in the waiting room. David immediately stood when he saw him. From the look on Robbie's face, I could tell whatever news he was about to deliver wasn't anything good.

David motioned for Robbie to take a seat as he stood awaiting the update from him.

Robbie cleared his throat. "Rita has had three seizures since she's been here. They are trying to stabilize her heart rate now."

I hung my head as I fought back tears. "Can I go back there?"

"I think so, but I must warn you, she doesn't look good at all. They also said she suffered a mini stroke, which could've happened well before she got to the hospital."

I sighed as I prepared myself to see her. As I walked through the double doors and the white sterile corridor, all I could think about was how I had to make the same dreadful walk when my paternal grandmother was last hospitalized. It felt as if I was walking the Green Mile as I finally turned the corner to witness the straight chaos of the emergency room.

There were beds in the hallway filled with sick people who moaned and screamed for help. As I approached the nurses' station, I could hear the cry of a visitor as an orderly escorted her back to the waiting room. I tried to keep my emotions together, but the scene was enough to make you shed tears for every soul suffering there.

The nurse pointed me to where Rita was as she zoomed past me to take care of a patient. I slowly walked in the room and gasped as I saw Rita connected to so many machines. The look on her face, even with her eyes closed, reflected one of weariness and pain. I walked over to her bedside and rubbed her hand.

"Mama," I whispered as I leaned over her bed.

Her eyes fluttered as she fought to open them.

I rubbed her uncombed hair. "Mama, it's Tia. You don't have to open your eyes. I just want you to know I'm here. Can you hear me?"

She slowly nodded her head. I could feel the tears gathering in my eyes.

"I love you so much. Even with all we've been through, I've never stopped loving you."

Her eyes slowly flickered open as a tear fell from her right eye. She tried to smile, but was overcome by pain.

"Mama, do you need me to get the nurse?"

She shook her head. "I'm tired," she whispered.

The tears fell even more so and I couldn't stand to look at her. I walked to the nearby window and let all the pain I felt inside flow like a stream down my face. I didn't need her to see me undone; I needed to be strong for her. I wiped my eyes and walked back to her bedside. Her eyes were closed and her mouth was moving, but I couldn't make out what she was saying. I stared at her and prayed that she would pull through this storm she faced.

My time was interrupted when a nurse and doctor came in and informed me that I'd need to return to the waiting room. I didn't want to leave her; she needed someone with her. I gave her a kiss and whispered in her ear that I loved her. I left the room, walked past all the moaning bodies in the hallway, and headed down the corridor without once looking back. All I wanted was to get out of here as I motioned to Robbie that I was stepping outside.

I decided to go ahead and give Janen a call to update her. I gave her the news of Rita's condition and how she was when I went back to see her. There was silence on the other end as she struggled with the words to say. We ended our conversation with her stating that she would try to catch a flight up tomorrow and would let me know.

I tried calling Carlita and got the same busy signal Robbie told me about earlier. I didn't know what was going on with her phone, but felt she needed to know what was happening.

Robbie came out and wrapped his arm around my shoulder as we embraced.

"She told me she's tired," I mumbled.

"Even if she didn't tell us, we can tell by her face. Her lying up in that bed like that reminds me of our mother."

I didn't know much about my maternal grandmother other than the fact they had a rocky relationship. Rita would always call her Queen Bitch and as kids we never visited her. Robbie always said that their mother was mean to Rita and it stemmed from Rita's dad ending their relationship after she gave birth.

"Is David still sitting in there?"

"Yes, he's going nuts and wants to see her. I can't have him going back there alone so I'll give them a few minutes before we head back. You going to be OK?"

I nodded. "I'm a lot stronger than I look."

We headed back in and David stood up so I could sit down. He and Robbie headed down the corridor to see Rita. I texted Rachelle to let her know what was going on and that I'd call her tomorrow.

I went to stand to go out and get some fresh air when the PA system came on announcing "CODE BLUE." My hands started to shake as I walked towards the corridor. I wanted to see for myself that everything was OK with Rita. But I stopped, unable to move. When I started for the door again the attendant informed me I wouldn't be able to go back. She explained that the visitors back there should be on their way out as part of procedure. I stood by the door until they opened and David walked through as if he'd seen a ghost. I called for him, but he walked right past me and out the door. I looked for Robbie and didn't see him, so I nervously followed David outside where he sunk to the ground in tears. It didn't take him to tell me—I already knew. Rita was gone.

CHAPTER 26
KELLY

When my doorbell rang after nine o'clock all I could think about was cursing out whoever was being so rude. After noticing Renae's car, I threw on my robe and raced down the stairs. I could see her pacing on the porch through the sheers of my side window. I slightly opened the door with a frown.

"Renae, what the hell are you doing here this late without calling?" I asked.

As she looked at me, I could see she'd been crying as her eyeliner left a trail down her face.

"I'm sorry for stopping by this late, but I really need to talk to you."

"And you couldn't call me first?" I asked with irritation.

Renae looked away. "I know this is inappropriate, but I wasn't thinking clearly. I wanted to talk to you face-to-face before I left town."

I opened the door all the way. She stepped in and looked around.

"This is nice, Kelly," she whispered.

"Thanks," I said as I walked back into the family room.

I flicked on the light and she took a seat on the couch. I stretched out on the chaise and faced her. I needed answers myself and hopefully with whatever she had to say it would all be said without me even asking.

"So what's up?" I asked as I yawned.

She had a look of discomfort on her face as she spoke. "I came to Atlanta for a fresh start on life, but quickly realized how I can't do that when I'm still doing the same shit. My family and I have always been at odds; I'm clearly the outcast. I've always marched to my own beat and didn't give two shits about what other people thought of me. I've lived a rather heartless life and done things I'm not proud of."

As she spoke, my mind kept wondering as to what exactly she was trying to get at. As much as I was curious about her, I wasn't in the mood to hear her life story.

She continued. "To make a long story short, I haven't been truthful about a number of things."

Great and here it is, the moment I've been waiting for.

"When Gigi introduced us, I was mesmerized by how beautiful you were. Then as we talked more and I asked Gigi about you, she told me you had a daughter. That's when it all clicked and I realized you were dating Derek. I used to work for the company months ago."

I chimed in. "And your real name is Lacey-Renae."

Her bewildered look let me know she didn't think I even knew that much about her.

"Yes," she said. "How did you know?"

I leaned forward as I stared at her. "Jessica told me you looked too familiar and she wouldn't let it go. So when she went to visit her husband, she remembered she'd seen you there and inquired about you. I've known that bit of information for weeks, but I've been trying to figure out why exactly you wouldn't say anything about it."

She looked around. "Is Derek here?"

I frowned. "Yes. Why?"

"Can you have him come down?"

I gave her a side-eye stare. "Why is that necessary?"

"Because what I have to say involves him and I prefer that he take part in this conversation."

Instantly I started boiling on the inside and felt my ears burning. Her wanting to involve Derek only could mean one thing. I yelled for Derek to come downstairs, but in less than two seconds he was already walking in with a look of guilt.

"Well, seems like you two already know each other, so why don't you do me the favor of letting me know what the fuck is going on here."

Derek stood in the corner propped on the wall looking as if he were lost for words.

"Since I'm sure he's in shock by all this, I'll go ahead and say it. Derek and I were intimate when you guys broke up."

I looked from her to him with a look of rage in my eyes. The next thing I knew I flew off the chaise and lunged at Lacey as she sat on the couch. I gripped the little bit of hair she had and yanked her ass to the floor and punched her right in the mouth. Derek raced over and pulled me off as Lacey delivered a kick directly to my stomach. Balled over in pain, I fought to get Derek off me so I could kick her ass.

"Derek, get off me right now," I said in a winded voice.

"Look, calm down, Kelly. We can't talk this through if you're going on like this."

"Fuck you and that bitch!" I cried.

I slapped him and fell back on the couch to catch my breath. She'd managed to crawl over into a corner sobbing like a baby.

I looked at Derek as he stood over me. "And you had the nerve to propose to me today knowing damn well that your ass hasn't been faithful. How could you? Wait, don't answer that," I said as I fought to stand up straight.

I started to slowly walk, as the pain was still there, but I refused to back down. Before I could get halfway near Renae, Derek grabbed me by my waist. I turned towards him and kneed him as hard as I could in his private area. He dropped to the floor and bellowed in pain. Lacey immediately stood and reached in her purse. I had little time to react as she pulled out a gun and pointed it towards me.

"I'm trained and licensed; don't make me use this," she said as she pulled back the hammer.

I froze in place and could barely speak as I stared down the barrel of the snub-nosed .38 revolver. I couldn't believe this was taking place in my home after such a great evening.

"I came here to talk to you woman-to-woman, not to be punched and beat on. I will shoot you before I allow you to do that," she said in a raised tone.

I held up my hands. "All I want to know is why. You straight played me as if you were trying to be a friend and now in an effort to clear your conscience before you leave town, you decide to tell me."

With her gun still pointing towards me, she moved behind the couch.

"I took a liking to you, Kelly. You were everything that I wanted to be but fell short of. I couldn't tell you because I knew it would hurt you, but you needed to know the truth and I knew he wouldn't tell you. I'm so sick of men not being held accountable for the shit they put us women through."

Derek sat on the floor and looked at her as she spoke. "Lacey, you can't stand there and say I led you on. You knew we were on the outs and I told you point-blank that I didn't want a relationship."

She glared at him. "I'm not talking to you, Derek."

He leaned his head back on the wall. "All I want to know is if this thing is still going on," I asked.

Lacey lowered her gun and placed it in her purse. She looked from Derek to me. Derek held his head down and avoided eye contact.

I shifted my weight and put my hand on my hip. "That's a question that requires a response, or should I assume a silence indicates that it's been ongoing."

Lacey looked at me. "For a while we were, but not anymore."

I turned my back towards them as I fought the urge to turn into an angry black woman. I wanted to beat the hell out of Derek for portraying this "perfect gentleman" role knowing he was just as deceitful as his brother.

"When you say 'a while,' what does that equate to?"

"Maybe two months after you were officially back together."

I turned to face her with my arms folded as I sucked my lips. The tears I tried to hold back once again came streaming down my face.

I dried my eyes. "Get the hell out of my house. NOW!"

Lacey didn't budge, but continued to stand in the same spot as if there was more she needed to say.

"GET THE FUCK OUT OF MY HOUSE," I screamed.

She turned and gave Derek a mincing look as she slowly walked to the door. I stood where I could see her walk out. Once she left, I ran to the door and locked it. I slid down to the floor as I cursed myself for being so naïve.

It was amazing how your life could change so quickly. I was ready to take that step towards marriage because I wholeheartedly loved Derek and everything we'd been able to build together. Now I questioned everything and felt heartbroken that I'd allowed myself to reach this point. I didn't know where to even begin to pick up the pieces, but for right now, I wanted to wallow in my self-pity and thoughts.

CHAPTER 27
JANEN

Life since I'd left Atlanta from Rita's visitation was rather uneventful. After the whole clash with Jessica and Tia, I couldn't help but feel I'd rehashed old feelings. While I was oblivious to Tia being the culprit of Darnell's affair, knowing made me leery about forging a relationship with her.

I spoke to Jessica and she was calm about the situation. She said, "You can't chose your family, but we can chose who we deal with."

After leaving the drama in Atlanta, I cleared my mind and went on to L.A. to surprise Tony. I'd spoken to him about my night out in Atlanta with Jessica and Tia and he couldn't believe it.

To ease the mood, he discussed some ideas for our first year anniversary. I grew excited hearing his input and appreciated him taking the lead on planning. I looked forward to our much-needed time away.

On the four-and-a-half-hour flight, I corresponded with his assistant to make sure everything was intact. I wanted everything to be right and couldn't wait to see the look of surprise on his face. I took a nap after wrapping up some business, and before long, the attendant was on the P.A. announcing our approach into L.A.

I retrieved my bags from baggage claim and caught a cab to the Crowne Plaza Hotel in Redondo Beach. I'd made reservations for the following evening at the Chart House as well as a private gondola ride at the pier.

I arrived at the hotel and the staff greeted me with friendly customer service. Everyone eagerly gave me pointers on some fun things to do for the rest of our trip. Once I arrived to the suite overlooking the ocean, I marveled at the beauty of God's creation. This couldn't all come together at a more perfect place.

I put my bags in the closet and took a quick shower. Afterwards I put on this cherry-almond body oil that Tony loved and slipped on a short halter dress. As I looked at my watch, I realized he would be arriving in the next thirty minutes. I decided to call him.

"Hey, babe," he answered.

"Hey, love. How's your day going?"

"Great, it's just about over. I'm waiting on the shuttle now to take me back to the hotel."

"Any plans for the day?" I asked, pacing the room.

"I was invited to play a round of golf, but I prefer to relax. What you doing today?"

"Oh, nothing special, I'm missing you terribly."

"Why don't you check on some flights and fly out here within the next day or so?"

I smiled at his suggestion knowing my presence here today would surely be as shocking and romantic as I envisioned.

"I'll do that."

"OK, babe, well the shuttle is here so I should be at the hotel shortly. I'll call you back."

With that I started to go around the room to make sure none of my stuff was lying around. I called the front desk and asked the young lady if she could call me when he came in.

I'd forgotten to do so earlier but I sent Jessica a text letting her know I'd arrived. She replied back with a smiley face.

Before long, the phone rang—Tony had arrived. As I rushed to the blinds-style closet in the sitting area, I tried to control my breathing as nervousness and excitement kicked in. Then it dawned on me—I'd left my cell phone on the coffee table. I darted out, picked up the phone, and pushed the button to turn it on mute. With perfect timing, I situated myself back in the closet when I heard voices outside the door. I figured it could have been Tony talking to housekeeping since they were in the hallway when I arrived. However, the voice followed him inside, and because of the angle of the closet I couldn't see the entryway. Then I heard a laugh that instantly made my eyes buck. What the hell was she doing here?

I watched attentively as Carrie took a seat on the couch while Tony threw his suit jacket around the desk chair. He removed his laptop from his bag and connected it before taking a seat at the desk. Instantly I wanted to hop out of the closet and put fear in both their hearts, but something told me to be still—not to make a move just yet.

I could feel myself growing hot in the tightly enclosed space. Carrie's presence left me wondering why Tony didn't tell me she was here. My thoughts were interrupted by their conversation.

"So, where's that wife of yours? Is she still hung up on reconnecting with the family that obviously didn't want her?" Carrie asked with a smirk.

Tony shook his head. "She's back in Miami. Why are you asking questions about her as if you care?"

My thoughts exactly, I said to myself. Messy bitch!

She shrugged her shoulders. "Your wife is rather selfish, Tony, and you know it. You've been dealing with a lot and it seems like her only interest is this other family."

"How about you worry about your relationship and not mine? You don't like Janen and, for the life of me, outside of her being black, I don't see why you don't."

She chuckled. "Oh, so now you're trying to call me a racist? Her color has nothing to do with it. Have you ever stopped to think that maybe I don't like her because I don't think she's good enough for you?"

At this point it took everything in me not to hop out of the closet like the Incredible Hulk. Good enough for him? I knew the bitch never liked me. Her actions were all self-motivated and I had a feeling I was about to get more than I bargained for.

"Carrie, you're overstepping your boundaries. What the hell you mean she's not good enough?"

She stood up and sat on the edge of the couch closest to the desk. "Well, for one, she's not here for you like I am. Anytime you're having a rough day, I instantly know it and I do things spontaneously to cheer you up. She doesn't do that; a wife should be attentive to the needs of her man. Besides, it's no secret how I feel about you and I love making you smile. You brush me off without addressing my feelings. I've shown you how much I love and care for you, but you've never given me an opportunity."

Tony twirled in the chair to face her. "Carrie, do you realize we were damn near raised together and my parents treated you as if you were their own? I've always seen you as a little sister and even back then, when that moment happened between us, I told you it could never happen again. It didn't feel right then, so what makes you think I would've pursued something further?"

She leaned forward in an attempt to kiss him. He pushed her away.

"Wow! Carrie, if you can't get a hold of your emotions then I'm going to ask that you leave."

By this time, I'd heard enough and seen enough. Once and for all this bitch would be put in her place. I flung open the doors of the closet and stood with my arms folded. The looks on their faces were priceless as Carrie quickly ran to the corner on the opposite side of the desk behind Tony. Tony sat with his hand over his heart.

"Janen," he stated as if he thought I were a ghost.

Remaining calm and poised, I took a deep breath. "Yep, it's me. Surprise! So, huh, Carrie, you seem to have had a lot on your chest today, especially about me. How about you talk that shit like a woman to my face?" I said, walking towards her.

Tony stood up from the chair and blocked my path.

"Janen, babe, let's not take it there. I understand you're upset and for good cause, but this isn't the way to handle it."

I looked at him with a frown. "This bitch basically sat up here and downplayed me as a wife so she could try to seduce you and you think that's not worthy of an ass-whooping. What if you witnessed that with me and another man?"

Carrie nervously stood in the corner. Her face turned red as she trembled like a leaf in the wind.

"Look, I'll just leave," she said nervously.

I raised my hand. "Oh no, don't leave on my behalf. Let's discuss your whole motive of coming to L.A."

As soon as she tried to get around the desk, I lunged at her so quickly that it took Tony by surprise. With her long blonde hair in my grip, I twisted it around my hand like a rope and pulled her down to the floor. She screamed as I banged her head against the floor.

Tony pulled me up off her, but I still had her hair locked tightly around my hand. She screamed and scratched me as I pushed my knee in her side.

"Janen, let her go now," he said through clenched teeth.

As she wept in pain, I knew there was no way she could win this fight. I gave her hair one final jerk before turning her loose. Tony pushed me into the bedroom where I fell back on the bed in tears.

"I need you to sit here and calm down," he said as he pointed at me with his finger.

I didn't have the strength to argue. I leaned back on the bed and gathered myself. Even though she deserved it, I couldn't help but feel disappointed in myself for allowing her to take me there. I'd wanted to put her in her place ever since she came into my life, but I knew I could've handled it differently.

I heard the door close as Tony came back in the room and leaned against the wall. I reclined back on my elbows as I stared at him.

"I knew there was something more between you two and you've always denied it," I said.

He held up his hand. "That happened when we were twenty, Janen. Well over fifteen years ago; I haven't been with her again since then."

I sat upright and raised my voice. "I don't give a damn if it happened when you were fifteen. The point is I asked you and you said no. You've known that this 'sister' of yours has wanted more from you than a friendship and has been chasing you for years, but I'm not supposed to know that when it's clearly obvious by her actions."

He massaged his neck as he rolled it around in a circular motion. "Look, I apologize for not being straightforward with you about what happened in the past, but she's never come on to me like she did today."

"Let me guess, you must've told her about the problems we've been going through lately, so she decided to come out here and make her move. That's the oldest trick in the book, Tony."

"Look, you saw and heard for yourself I'm not and have never been into her like that. Now I was wrong for not being honest with you from the start, but I've never led her to think otherwise."

I shook my head. "You were also wrong for not once mentioning her being out here. Exactly when did she get here?"

"Two days ago, but I didn't see her until yesterday. I know after today, if not right now, she'll be on the phone calling my mom about this and…"

"Does it look like I give a damn who she tells? I was angry and all the penned-up frustration towards her I've battled with finally surfaced. She disrespected me and you think I'm not going to defend myself. Again, I would surely like to see how you'd react if the shoe was on the other foot."

We went on and on for hours about the situation until I grew tired of discussing anything related to her. In true fashion his mother did call and Tony politely told her that it wasn't her business. Obviously Carrie had called, making herself sound like the victim.

All in all, my trip to L.A. wasn't a total drag as we spent some much-needed time together having much-needed conversations. For once, he sat attentively and listened as I talked about my reunion with Rita and meeting my other siblings. We were like lovebirds for the remainder of the trip, which reminded me of our early dating days. There were no phone calls from Carrie or anybody else that spoiled our time together.

Back in Miami, Tony was being recognized tonight at a private ceremony at the latest resort opening on Miami Beach. All day I'd been prepping my look, as some of Miami's elite class of residents would be in attendance, which, for me, meant potential opportunities.

I slipped on my black tailored pencil pants and my multi-colored fitted peplum shirt. I had a fresh twist out and my face was made up fashionably to give my look a defining pop. I gave myself a look in the mirror and had to high-five my damn self. Girl, you look HAUTE!

Tony stepped out from the closet and gave me a look over.

"You going to have all eyes on you tonight." He smirked.

"Then you should feel extremely proud that while they looking, you're the one taking me home." I winked.

My cell phone rang as I struggled to get my shoes on. Whoever it was would have to be called back later. Within seconds the house phone rang, which meant car service was downstairs. I gathered my purse, gave myself a final look over, and headed out.

Once we were in the car, I checked my phone to see who had called—it was Robbie. I checked my voicemail; he had left a message stating that Rita had been rushed to the hospital due to a drug overdose. My heart started beating rapidly as I hung up the phone and nervously tried to call Robbie back.

Tony, noticing my change in mood, asked me what was wrong and I explained to him the situation. He urged me to call Robbie back to get further details. When I called him, he didn't answer. The only other person's number I had was Tia's and I hadn't spoken to her since the night at the lounge. I called her and she explained that she, Robbie, and David were en route to the hospital and she would keep me updated.

Tony wrapped his arm around me in support as I took a deep breath. While I didn't know Rita long, she was still my mother and I prayed she was OK. I gathered myself as we pulled up for the dinner.

Throughout the night I kept checking my cell phone trying not to miss a call from Tia. She called and reported that things didn't look too good. I tried my best not to let the news damper my spirits. I told her I would look into a flight tomorrow, but I knew this would be something I needed to discuss with Tony since our anniversary was approaching.

As he went up to accept his award, I couldn't help but feel extremely proud of his accomplishment. He'd worked hard over the years and to see him getting the acknowledgment truly excited me.

After the dinner, we didn't stick around for much longer. I excused myself to the restroom when my cell phone rang. It was Tia and I almost didn't want to answer.

"Tia," I quickly answered.

"She passed away," she sobbed.

I leaned against the wall as I batted my eyes to hold back tears. "I'm sooo sorry to hear that. I know it's tough, but stand strong, Tia. How are Robbie and David?"

She sniffed. "Robbie broke down worse than us both. David is definitely shaken up. When we went back there, once they'd removed the machines, he just held her hand and stared at her. We had to plead with him to let her go so we could leave."

"I can only imagine. Do you all need any help with the arrangements?"

Tia sighed. "Robbie said he only had a small policy on Rita, which would be enough for the preparation expenses, but not the burial. I've been trying to contact Carlita since earlier and can't get in touch with her, but, yes, we'll need help in a financial sense as well."

"OK, I'll call you tomorrow and let you know when I'll be in town. Until then, just keep me updated."

I threw my cell phone in my purse and gave myself a look over in the mirror before rejoining Tony. Luckily he was waiting for me outside the restroom area.

"You OK?" he asked with a concerned look.

"She just passed," I responded.

He immediately hugged me and I needed it.

"I'm here for you, babe. If you need to go to Atlanta, we will go."

I nodded my head and felt the tears rolling down my face as he mentioned that "we" would go. I appreciated his support and attentiveness towards the situation since talking to him about the visitation.

Two days later, we were both heading to Atlanta. While I went to Robbie's, he stayed back at the hotel. When I pulled up, I noticed a candy-apple-red Cayenne Porsche in the driveway. Before I could approach the door, David was already standing on the porch.

There was a sense of sadness on his face, but he smiled upon my approach to the staircase. He held out his hand as he helped me up the stairs. I extended my arms to hug him as he accepted.

We walked into the house and down the hallway to the kitchen area. I'd never been in their house, but you could tell from the décor it was definitely a man's house. Carlita was sitting at the kitchen table texting away on her iPhone while Tia was finishing up washing dishes.

After hellos were exchanged we all sat down to discuss the arrangements. Carlita sat sideways in the chair looking at her freshly manicured nails as if she were already bored with the conversation.

Tia grabbed a notebook from the counter and looked around. "So the funeral is set for Friday at 11:00 a.m., but we still need four thousand to cover the burial and headstone."

I sighed as I held my head down. Tony and I discussed a financial contribution to the expenses and I allowed him to take the lead on how much without any objections.

"Well my husband and I will contribute fifteen hundred of that amount. We have our anniversary trip approaching, so that's the best we can offer."

Tia smiled. "No problem, that's definitely a help. Thanks, Janen. Carlita, do you think you and your husband will be able to make a sizeable donation?"

Carlita frowned. "And what exactly are you contributing?"

Tia rolled her eyes. "I'm not married; I'm a single parent, so my finances are limited. I will contribute to getting the food for the repast, but I can't contribute anything that would put a dent in the remaining amount."

Robbie looked at Carlita and shook his head. "Why are you so selfish? Your mother is dead! Why can't you leave the past behind and help give her a proper burial?"

Carlita threw her hand up to indicate stop. "Wait just a damn minute! You don't know what my finances are like. Yes, I have a husband, but I don't just go spending money without first consulting with him. If there's a money issue with burying her, why not cremate her and spread her ashes at the drug houses she loved to visit."

My mouth flew open as I looked from Carlita to Robbie to Tia. David got up from the table and went to his room. We heard the door slam.

I decided to speak up as I could see anger in both Robbie's and Tia's faces.

"Look, Carlita, let's get through the logistics of what needs to be done without insults and disrespect."

Carlita frowned as she turned towards me. "Girl, please, we've known you a month and you think you can come and direct. Let me make this known for you and everybody else that's sitting at this table looking at me like I'm the devil. My life was never easy with Rita and she never once apologized to me for all the shit she put me through."

I could see Carlita fighting back her emotions as she paused to gather herself.

"I'm not trying to come and take over, Carlita; I'm here to help. You're right, I don't know you guys nor the circumstances you've endured, but Rita is your mother."

She looked at me as if she were about to spit fire from her mouth. "Huh, some mother she turned out to be. Maybe to you a burial is sufficient, but I think her burning suits her best."

Tia stood and started towards Carlita. Robbie pushed his chair back and grabbed her.

"There ain't going to be no fighting up in here," he said to Tia as he restrained her.

Tia stared at Carlita and breathed heavily. Carlita, on the other hand, leaned back in her seat with her arms crossed with a "yeah right" look on her face.

"Rita gave you the most attention out of all of us and you sit here like your life has been the worst. You have no idea what I went through," said Tia as she paced the floor near her chair.

Carlita shook her head. "Boo woo, Tia. Let me say all attention ain't good attention, believe it. Your precious mother used me to support her habit, that's why I got so much attention. I don't recall her doing that to you, because I'm sure you would be on my side if she did."

Robbie looked at her with a puzzled look. "What the hell are you talking about? Rita always dressed you nicely and paraded you around like you were her pride and joy. You were so beautiful and…"

"And she did all that parading me around so when I got older, she could trick me off to her dealers. Yes, you heard me right; the shit started when I was fourteen."

Tia gasped as I sat in amazement, unable to move as my eyes were fixated on Carlita.

"I don't believe that one bit," Robbie said as he got up from his seat.

Carlita stood up and grabbed his arm. "Unc, you know I love you and respect all that you did in trying to help raise us. I would never maliciously defame someone's character if it weren't true. Remember when I'd turned sixteen and Rita and I had been gone all day. When we came back I was sick and you two got into an argument. Every time you tried to see what was wrong with me or what you could do for me, Rita was right there asking you to leave me alone. She said I was suffering from bad menstrual cramps. Do you remember that?"

Robbie looked away and then back at her as he nodded his head.

"Well it was on that day that I had my second abortion. I had two abortions by the time I was seventeen and two STDs." She sniffled. "Imagine how I felt thinking my mother truly loved me, yet would allow these men to demoralize and rape me of my innocence so she could feed her own drug habit. What mother would do that to her child? I grew to hate her for ruining me. Soon it wasn't long before drug dealers started looking at me as if I were their property. Rita used me and didn't give two shits about how this could affect me later in life and, trust me, it has."

All you could hear were sniffles in the room. Carlita had stunned us all by her news. With her revealing such a past, it gave clarity as to why she came off so cold. I had to take back my earlier thought of her because I now saw what it all stemmed from—years of physical and mental abuse.

Tia walked over to Carlita and gave her hug. Seeing them embrace and cry in each other arms made me feel so blessed and thankful. My purpose of looking for my biological mother was for closure and I'd gotten that and more. Now it was time for me to move on and shift my focus to what mattered most.

CHAPTER 28
DEREK

The days following the aftermath of Lacey's confession, things were not the same. Kelly couldn't stand being in the same room with me and moved into the guestroom. Trying to get her to talk was pointless, as she wouldn't so much as look at me. I didn't want to argue in front of the kids, so I felt like giving her space was the best option.

The next day I called Carlton to let him know what happened. He didn't seem too surprised by her actions. Furthermore, the same night she'd called Maria and quit as her assistant.

As much as I would've liked to slap Lacey silly for what she did, the bottom line was I had myself to blame. Being the player-type of man had never been my area of expertise. I'd seen many men balance the life of a wife and mistress, girlfriend and a sidepiece, but I always felt it was too much to try to juggle such a complicated lifestyle. I enjoyed being monogamous and knowing that I was giving all of me to that one person. Call it a mid-life crisis, but cheating had its moments; now I was left to deal with the consequences.

I'd called Denise the day before and asked if the kids could stay with her until Saturday evening and she agreed. I hadn't discussed what was going on with anyone other than Carlton. I couldn't stand to hear Darnell say "I told you so," but I was sure if Kelly had told Jessica then he knew.

I dropped the kids off at Denise's and headed home. I pulled up in the garage to see that Kelly was in the midst of leaving. I hopped out of the car and ran over to her car door.

"Can we please talk?" I pleaded.

She stared at me with venom in her eyes. "For what?"

I frowned. "We've been walking around this house like strangers in the street and you have to ask for what. Come on now, Kelly."

She sighed as she cut off the engine and got out. I led the way into the house and took a seat at the kitchen table. She sat at the kitchen breakfast bar, away from me.

"I fucked up, Kelly, and there's no way around denying that. We were on the outs when I met Lacey and I never led her on to think we were going to be together. Once things got back on track with us, I started pulling myself away from her."

She looked at me with a smirk. "You started pulling yourself away from her, but not enough to completely let it go considering you were back in a relationship. You were heartless and selfish in your act, Derek. For you and every other 'think with your dick' man out there who thinks it's cool to trick off on the side, yet when you get caught up in your bullshit, you want to profess how you've fucked up. You damn right you did!"

"Baby, I'm not going to sit here and make excuses for myself, because I can't. I've never once been the type of man that cheats, but I did and now all I want to do is know how we can fix this. It's my fault, I get it, and I know I've hurt you, but I do love you, Kelly."

She got up from her seat and walked over to the table. "I thought you were different, I guess that's what hurts the most. I've thought about what I should do and of course the first thing that came to mind was leave; go back to my townhouse. But I know that this house is an investment we are both in so to abandon ship isn't the responsible thing to do. And furthermore, I don't want to see the kids hurt over this. However, I can't sit and pretend this shit doesn't sting like alcohol on an open wound. I don't know when I'll get over it, but until I do, just give me my space."

She walked away and out the door leading to the garage. I was left to sit and think about all that she'd said and all that wasn't said. Was it a good sign that she was still wearing her ring? Oh, who the hell am I fooling on that one.

The front doorbell rang and my heart raced. Since the night Lacey had shown up at the house, anytime the doorbell rang unexpectedly, I panicked. I got to the door and peeked out—it was Darnell.

I opened the door. "What's up, man? What are you doing here?"

He walked in without invitation. "Why bother asking a question you already know the answer to. Didn't I tell you this shit was going to get ugly."

I shook my head as I closed the front door and headed to the kitchen area.

"Look, man, I know you mean well but I don't need your ridicule right now."

"Your issues are a part of my damn household right about now, so guess what—you're going to hear my mouth because I've had to hear this shit from Jessica all day."

I went to the refrigerator for a beer and slid one over to Darnell.

"I'm sorry, man, trust me, this shit took me completely by surprise."

"Lacey is young and fearless. This chick forged a relationship with your girlfriend. That spells nothing but loose cannon to me."

"Is Kelly with Jessica?"

"Yeah, that's why I'm here. I didn't want to be dragged in the middle of that discussion, so I left."

I sat on the bar stool next to Darnell. "How do I fix this, bruh?"

Darnell took a long gulp of his beer. "A lot of ass-kissing, my man." He chuckled. "But for real, you have to give her space. Right now she's pissed and nothing you are saying is making any sense to her. She has to be willing to accept what has happened and see that you're committed to not making the same mistake twice. Basically, go to work and bring your ass home."

I sighed. "No more hanging out with Carlton, huh."

"I like Carlton and he's a cool-ass dude, but why you think I've not once hung out with him since I've been back in Jessica's good graces? That's a damn setup for trouble. Carlton plays the game by his rules, which are fine with Maria; we ain't got it like that."

"I can't blame what happened on Carlton though; that's my doing."

"Yeah you right, but don't act like Kelly hasn't asked what's up with him."

"True. OK, but back to what I was saying before. What do I need to do?"

"Man, you got to find what works for you. Jessica and I did counseling and even that initially didn't start off well. It takes time and you just have to be patient. Did she give you your ring back?"

I gave him a side eye. "Nope and that gives me a bit of hope."

"Yeah I agree, but then too it's probably about saving face and not having those who know she's engaged question why she's not wearing it."

I ran my hand over my face. "The house doesn't even feel the same; it's like we live here and there's no love and warmth when you walk through the door."

"Yeah, I know that feeling. Trust me, when it takes a turn for the better, you'll appreciate everything you had to endure to get to that point."

"Does Jessica ever throw in your face the fact that you cheated?"

Darnell held his head down. "Thankfully she doesn't. Look, just like you had to get over the fact that she lied to you during her pregnancy, you have to have that same understanding of how she deals with getting over this. This chick was hanging out with her all that time knowing who she was and then to be slapped in the face with the fact you two were intimate; that's a lot."

I looked away in embarrassment. "Yeah, I feel you. I felt like things were truly coming together for us and now this."

Darnell looks at me with a serious look. "If I've taught you nothing else, bruh, remember this. There will never be happiness in a relationship unless there's truth and honesty. This was not some situation that could've been swept under the rug; you would've had to confess at some point or another. The past does have a way of sneaking up on you without warning. I can honestly say through my situation, I learned a lot about myself as well as Jessica. We were both committed to restoring what was lost and broken; you guys must have that same determination. It's not going to be easy, but when you know what you have, it makes it all worthwhile."

I nodded as I acknowledged all that he'd said. My brother had always been there for me and I valued his opinion and advice, even when I didn't want to hear the truth. I knew the road to getting our relationship back on track would be far from easy, but it was the hand I dealt, so I had to accept whatever came my way. I just hoped she has the patience and determination to ride the difficult waves that come with forgiveness.

THREE MONTHS LATER...

CHAPTER 29
LA'TIA

As I stared out of my office window, I was overcome with emotion thinking about how my life had changed in the past few months. After burying Rita, I quit my job at the club. It wasn't a hard decision as it was necessary in my desire to make life changes.

While I was making positive changes in my life, my relationship with Rachelle was on the decline. I loved her to life, but our mentalities were different and I realized that sometimes those we love can be the most toxic to our personal growth. I never wanted her to feel as though our friendship never meant anything to me, because she was like family. However, I had to do things for myself and on my terms without the ridicule and negativity.

Rita's death brought me back closer to my family. I made it a point on a weekly basis to drop by Robbie's and help him out as well as spend time with David. Robbie was such a blessing to David and truly treated him like a son more so than a nephew. I could only be thankful for his love, guidance, and patience in raising a child with a mental illness and still being the father figure in his life throughout his manhood.

Carlita and I were mending our relationship and I'd recently visited with her and her husband. Jeffrey was a nice man and he treated my sister like a queen. Their home was beautiful and filled with all kinds of expensive décor and art. So much so, that I had to keep a keen eye on Noah's every move while we were there.

As far as Janen, we'd only kept in contact through text. We didn't have a relationship and I'd accepted that that was as good as it might ever get.

Since starting my new job two months ago as a customer service manager, I'd put Noah in daycare nearby my job. He loved interacting with the other kids and I loved seeing how excited he was about going to daycare each day. Things were shaping up nicely and I could only be thankful for my blessings.

I looked at the clock then closed my eyes and thought about what I had to do. I grabbed my purse and told the receptionist I would be back in about two hours.

When I got in the car, I took out the paper I'd jotted the address on and entered it into my navigation system. As the directions for my every turn came through the speakers, I felt proud of myself for taking this final step of closing a lingering chapter in my life.

Once I'd arrived at my destination, I took a deep breath before exiting the car. Before I could make it to the building, she was walking out the door and froze upon seeing me approach.

"I didn't mean to startle you, but I came here because I wanted to talk to you," I said with sincerity.

She gave me a blank stare as she started towards her car. "And what is it you want to talk to me about?"

Once she reached her SUV, she hit the remote to place her belongings in the backseat. She closed the door and turned to face me with her arms folded. I could see her jaw twitching as she awaited my response.

"Jessica, I wanted to meet with you face-to-face to give you the apology you deserve. I've had to live with the horrible decision I made then and it's not been easy. But more importantly, I know that in order to truly move on, I needed you and Darnell to know that I'm truly sorry for my actions. It was immature, heartless, and inconsiderate. I accept my responsibility and I was wrong. I hope that you can find it in your heart to one day forgive me knowing that I'm deeply sorry for everything I put you two through."

After standing for what seemed like minutes, I started to turn and head for my car.

"Wait," she responded.

I turned around to face her.

"One thing I learned from all of this is that if we continue to hold on to the hurt and pain of our past, we can't progress. So in my mind I forgave you for what you did, but the night I saw you, I realized I hadn't forgiven you in my heart. I appreciate the fact you were woman enough to come here and apologize so unexpectedly. Honestly I didn't ever think you'd have the guts to do it; glad I was wrong." She smirked.

"I mean it sincerely and I thank you for being receptive to it. Thanks for your time," I said as I turned and headed back to my car.

As I drove away, I let the sunroof back and embraced the sun as it shone on my face. I couldn't help but feel free of the guilt and shame of my past. I had one final stop before heading back to the office.

I pulled up and changed my shoes before getting out of the car. I grabbed the artificial floral arrangement I'd worked on the night before from my trunk and headed through the grass to Marcus's headstone.

I squatted down and placed the arrangement in the mounted cup.

"Babe, I miss you so much," I said through tears. "I've gone through a lot over the last couple of months, but one thing remains the same and that's the hole in my heart. I look at our son each day with such joy in knowing he's a part of you. He's getting so big and I just dread the day when I have to tell him about why you're no longer here. I'm doing all I can to make sure he has a great life. Your mom and siblings have been a blessing to us and Noah absolutely loves them. I just wanted to let you know that I love you so much and I'm ready to finally live my life."

I stood up, kissed my two fingers, and touched the top of the headstone. As much as I missed him, I knew that I had to move on with my life. I'd made a lot of decisions in life that I wasn't proud of, but I was overjoyed that I'd been given a second chance, a new lease on life.

I got in my car and, as tears fell from eyes, I realized these were no longer tears of pain and hurt, but tears of joy. I smiled as I put my car in drive and headed back to the office; inside I finally felt free.

CHAPTER 30
KELLY

"Yes, I'll have the contract drawn up immediately and sent overnight to your office."

My assistant walked in with a bouquet of flowers as I wrapped up my phone call with a client. After I concluded my call, she stood with the flowers in her hand and a smile on her face. I was irked by the fact she didn't just sit them on my desk like she'd done all week.

"Yes, Jasmine," I asked as she stood near my desk.

"Either your clients really love you or there must be trouble in paradise," she said.

I adored Jasmine, but I didn't fancy her nosiness, especially when it came to my private affairs.

"That's none of your business. You can leave them right there on the desk and exit."

Jasmine put the flowers down and rolled her eyes as she left my office. I got up and closed the door behind her. I paced the floor before walking over to read the card from the flowers.

"Baby, I miss us. I know things have been difficult between us but I hope you see that I'm committed to making this work. I don't want us to be over; I need you."

I sighed as I rubbed my forehead. Even after talking to Jessica about it and trying my best to move past the situation, I still felt stuck. I loved Derek and I wanted a future with him, but I wanted to make him feel the pain and misery I was feeling.

Every night I retreated to our guestroom, I entered into what I considered "the cell." It was where I felt confined in my feelings and thoughts; it was becoming a dreary place for me that I couldn't stand. I did everything I could to just go in the room when I was sleepy, but the minute I walked in, sleep was far from my mind. So many nights I wished Derek would come into the room, pick me up from the bed, and move me back to our room, but it didn't happen.

We were now in a place where we could stand to be in the same room together and interact with the kids as a family, but the distance between us was undeniable. To everyone that didn't know, I played the happy soon-to-be-wife, when inside I didn't know if I would get to that point. I wore the ring, but felt it had no purpose other than for show.

My phone rang as I took a deep breath and answered. "Kelly Waters."

"Kelly, it's Gigi."

It had been quite a few weeks since I'd heard from her, as she'd gotten a promotion and moved to our Kennesaw location.

"Hey, girl. How's it going?"

"I'm going crazy! This office is a wreck and my boutique is opening next week."

"Whew—don't envy you there."

"Tell me about it. Look, have you heard from Renae? Her sister called me looking for her due to a death in their family and she hasn't been able to reach her."

I hadn't told Gigi about what had transpired between us and didn't want to get questioned, so I refrained from doing so.

"Last I heard she was moving to Chicago and I hadn't heard from her in weeks."

"That girl is infamous for her disappearing acts, but oh well. Anyway, are you planning on coming to my opening next week? Did you get the E-Vite?"

"Yes, I responded this morning; I'll be there."

"OK, great. Nice talking to you; see you soon."

I hung up as Jasmine stood halfway in the door. "You have a call from Derek."

"Tell him I'm busy," I responded.

"He said it's urgent," she said as she quickly closed the door behind her.

I rushed to answer the phone thinking it could be something with the kids.

"Hello," I answered.

"I need you to get the kids from the daycare. My dad has been rushed to the hospital."

"I'm sorry to hear that. Is he going to be OK?"

Derek sighed. "He's non-responsive, so I don't know what's going on right now. Darnell and I are on the way from the office. I'll call you as soon as I find out more."

We hung up and I immediately contacted my boss and let him know that I would need to leave early due to an emergency. I called my mom on the way out and she agreed to the kids coming over.

I called Jessica as I headed to get the kids; she answered on the first ring.

"Hello."

"Hey, are you on the way to the hospital?"

"Yes, I just dropped Tianna off at my mom's. What about you?"

"I'm picking up the kids now to take them to my mom's house. Have you heard anything?"

"No. I spoke with Denise and she said she and her mom were in the waiting room and hadn't gotten any updates as of yet. I'm pulling up now."

After picking up the kids and dropping them off, I said a prayer as I drove to the hospital. Their father's health had been on the decline since his stroke a few years ago, but his children did all they could to make sure he had the best home health service, to alleviate some of the burden from their mother.

When I arrived at the hospital, chills instantly went over me. I walked in the waiting room as Derek walked over to greet me. I instantly extended my arms as we embraced. I rubbed his back and whispered, "I'm here for you."

The doctor came out and spoke to everyone, stating that Mr. Walker had suffered yet another stroke and that his heart was very weak.

As Darnell and his mother went back to visit with him first, I sat with Derek hand-in-hand. The last time we'd been this close together was the night of our housewarming. Every bit of romance and affection had been nonexistent until now. He was off in a daze; worried about his father. I didn't know exactly what to say, but I knew just being here for him was the best thing I could do. When his mother was escorted back out to the waiting area in tears, I couldn't help but shed tears along with her. She and Mr. Walker had been married for over forty years and to see a person you've loved for that long deteriorate health-wise I was sure was a hurtful process.

Derek excused himself and went back to his dad. Jessica came over and sat next to me.

"You OK," she asked.

"Yeah, it's seeing Mrs. Walker in tears like that. She's such a strong lady," I said.

"No matter how strong a person appears, we all have a breaking point. How are things with you and Derek?"

I rolled my eyes. "It's sad but this is the closest we've been to each other in months. I've been so stubborn, Jess, and in my heart, I'm ready to forgive him."

Jessica waved her hand. "Girl, you being stubborn is no surprise, but you letting this situation drag on is ridiculous. You are wearing this man's ring knowing in your heart you're ready to forgive, but you can't open yourself up to just saying it. Kells, life is too short. We all make mistakes and fall short, but if you love someone and want to see it work, you've got to find a way to move on."

I nodded my head as Darnell and Derek stood in the hallway visibly upset. Denise joined them as they all talked. A few minutes later, Derek walked over and took his seat beside me.

He wiped his face and shook his head. "That was tough. My old man not looking good at all," he said.

I rubbed his back. "I can only imagine how tough that is to witness. What's next?"

He threw up his hands. "It's a wait-and-see kind of deal. Pops has been through so much and I know he's tired. I hate to say it but it'll be a miracle if he pulls through this."

We sat in silence as Darnell came over to us.

"Hey, why don't you two go ahead and go home. Denise is going to take Mom back to see Daddy and then she's taking her home. I'll stay up here and I'll call you if there's any change."

After staying for another hour with no change, Derek and I left. I called my mom and she insisted that the kids stay since things were so touch and go.

At home, Derek took a shower and came downstairs to join me in the kitchen.

"You hungry?" I asked.

He shook his head. "I don't have an appetite."

I put the bowl of salad back in the refrigerator and stood at the bar where he was seated.

"I know you are hurting right now, but know that you are not in this alone."

He looked at me with sadness in his eyes. "Are you saying all this out of sympathy for me?"

I bit my lip as I looked away. "No I'm not." I sighed. "I know it's not been easy these past few months and I realize I've only made things even more difficult than it had to be. While I'm hurt over what happened, I know within my heart I can forgive you because I love you."

Derek grabbed my hands. "And all I've wanted is the opportunity to show you I'm a better man. I want us to get back on track and, you know what, if you're ready to get married—let's do it. Life is so precious and I don't want to waste another moment holding off on what naturally feels right."

"I'm not looking to get married tomorrow, but it's nice to know you are ready for that step. I'm going to suggest we do some pre-marital counseling though."

"Whatever it takes—I'm game."

I leaned in and gave him what I planned as a peck on the lips. But the moment our lips connected, we locked in the most passionate kiss ever. As I looked into his eyes, I saw his sincerity and love for me. I knew he was sorry for what he'd done and I'd punished him enough.

One thing I'd learned was your very own actions can inflict the most pain to yourself. I'd had to endure a lot of self-inflicted pain, which made me a stronger person. With Derek I'd become a better person and I truly loved the woman I'd become. Through it all, I felt proud of myself for standing in the midst of adversity without walking away. I believed in our relationship and I was ready for the next chapter of our lives.

CHAPTER 31
JANEN

As I rested my head on Tony's chest, I thought about how far we'd come in our marriage. We'd celebrated our one-year anniversary in Jamaica with drinks in hand on the beach by day and candlelight dinners and a lot of bedroom action at night.

Since Rita's funeral, I hadn't communicated much with Robbie. My business started to pick up, which left little time for other things outside of my marriage. I'd learned all I needed to know about my biological family and I was content on letting things flow as is.

Tia and I occasionally texted with basic pleasantries, but I think we both realized we would never gain that closeness as sisters. Jessica and I had a long talk and she didn't want me to base my relationship with Tia over what'd transpired with them. It was hard to look past that, especially when it came to trust. There were no hard feelings, but I preferred to keep things as they were.

Tony got up to use the bathroom when the phone rang. Normally our house phone only rang when we had a delivery. I answered the phone and there was silence.

"Hello."

Silence again, but I could hear the person breathing on the other end.

I rolled my eyes in disgust. "HELLO," I screamed.

"Janen, this is Carrie," she said in a shaky voice.

I sighed. "And what exactly do you want, Carrie?"

She hesitated and once again there was silence.

Growing irritated by her pauses, I hung up the phone. I hadn't mentioned Carrie's name nor had Tony since the L.A. incident. As they say, "out of sight, out of mind" and in her case, I was content with that.

Tony peeked outside the bathroom as he brushed his teeth. "Who was that?" he asked.

"Carrie," I said. I lay back on the bed as I looked at his facial expression.

He turned around to rinse his mouth at the sink. Once he was done, he came out and sat on the bed.

"Babe, she wants to talk to you," he said.

I sat up and stared at him. "There's nothing she can say to me at this point."

"Oh, but there is. She owes you an apology; what you choose to do with it is on you."

"How long have you been back talking to her?"

He sighed. "She called me two weeks ago in tears and apologizing. My mom initially told me I was wrong for shutting her out as I did, but I had to put her in her place on that. Carrie gave them a half-ass story as to what happened in L.A. and they sided with her."

"No surprise there," I said, rolling my eyes.

"Hearing what I had to say as well as admitting what transpired years ago between us, put a lot of things in perspective for them. They don't hate you, Janen; they simply didn't understand the half-truth given."

"So have you forgiven her?"

"Yes I have. I don't like harboring ill feelings toward anyone. It's too draining and unnecessary. I can forgive and move on."

I was irritated and couldn't believe he could be so quick to forgive this so called "sister" who came on to him sexually and disrespected his wife.

"I guess that means you'll be back embracing her like nothing happened," I said with irritation.

"No it doesn't. I can forgive and move on by feeding a person with a long-handled spoon. I'm married to you and have to be respectful of the fact that you don't trust Carrie and I totally get it. I'm not going to do anything that will jeopardize the trust within our marriage; it's not worth it."

"And I appreciate you acknowledging that, but you're making it all about me. Do you feel like you can trust her after that?"

He shook his head. "She's made our relationship uncomfortable. Plus I love you too much. She didn't have a chance then and she doesn't have it now."

I blushed as I pulled him in for a kiss.

"How dare you offend my fresh breath like that with your morning breath," he joked.

I kissed him on the lips anyway then headed in the bathroom to freshen up. I closed the door and pulled open the drawer with all my belongings. I fished through it until I found what I was looking for. I smiled as I looked at it.

Once I finished brushing my teeth and washed my face, I walked out of the bathroom to find Tony posed naked on the bed. I instantly laughed at his silly pose.

"Oh, you find me humorous, huh." He smiled.

"Oh not at all," I said, looking him up and down. "Close your eyes."

"Awww…you trying to get a lil freaky, huh," he said with his eyes closed.

I placed the item on the side of him.

"Now open them," I instructed.

He opened his eyes. "And you're still clothed?"

I chuckled as I pointed to the spot next to him.

He did a double take as he looked down at the pregnancy test with two dark blue lines. He sat up in bed and stared at it as if it were going to change again.

"Got anything to say?" I smirked.

He grinned at me. "Damn, I thought you made me the happiest man when you accepted my marriage proposal, but this takes the cake," he said.

He stood up and pulled me in towards him.

"I was so filled with emotion yesterday when I took the test. When it showed positive, I felt like the luckiest woman ever."

"Woman, you did this yesterday and I'm just now finding out? Oh, so that explains that good loving I got last night."

I slapped his chest. "Oh, so it's not good all the time?"

"Babe, you know you put some extra stank on that thang last night. Had me feeling like I was losing my virginity all over again."

We laughed as we embraced.

"I'm so happy right now, honey. Thank you for being such a wonderful husband. You've made me better."

"You're welcome, babe. I love you and can't wait to take on this next journey in our life together."

"I couldn't agree more." I smiled.

The past few months had its share of ups and downs, but my happiness today wouldn't be possible if I didn't battle the storms I faced. I'd learned to be a better daughter, sister, wife, and now I was on to the challenge of motherhood. My life was shaping up to that fairy tale I'd always dreamed of—being happy.

CHAPTER 32
DEREK

When my father passed away, I experienced nearly the same grief I felt when Karen passed. I knew my father was tired and he lived a full life unlike Karen, but still my relationship with him was irreplaceable.

Darnell, being the oldest, took care of all the arrangements along with Denise. I couldn't be a part of that grueling process after dealing with that before. I plastered on a happy face for the sake of the kids, but inside I felt dazed.

One thing that comforted me during such a difficult time was having Kelly here lending her understanding, love, and support. I'd tried going into the office since Darnell wasn't going in, just to be a presence and that was mainly all I was. I couldn't focus on much of anything, and seeing the framed pictures of my father with his many clients from his earlier years throughout the building didn't help either.

The day of the funeral I finally felt as if I could get through it without shedding a tear. My father was loved by many; family, friends, and colleagues all spoke highly of him during the service. I felt overwhelmingly proud of the path my father paved for our family.

The Jacksons came to attend the service and were staying a few days to spend time with them. I was thankful for their involvement in the kids' lives and for always looking out for me.

The day felt so long and during the repast, all I could think about was taking a hot shower and going to bed. The past few days were draining enough, and now that my father had been laid to rest, I was hoping my mind could be put at rest.

With Kaylee and Kayden with the Jacksons, and Kimora with Kelly's parents, it gave us some much-needed time to ourselves. We'd been through so much over the course of four months and throughout, she still stood by me.

As we walked through the garage door leading into our home, I grabbed her by the waist and pulled her into me.

"Thank you, babe. I don't know how I would've made it through without you."

Kelly wrapped her arms around my neck. "I'm glad I could be here for you. I know things have been rough, but we're working through it and I'm thankful for that."

I squeezed her tightly in my arms and took in the smell of her favorite perfume, Delicious.

We headed upstairs to wind down for the evening. I went to the computer to check my email. During my days at work, unable to focus, I decided to plan a vacation for Kelly and me as a surprise. I'd shared the details with her parents, Jessica and Darnell, and Casey, so they could make arrangements as well because I planned on marrying her there. I wasn't the most detailed person when it came to planning, but I could honestly say I put a lot of time and effort in ensuring this would be romantic and beautiful.

When Monday morning rolled around, I'd already arranged for Kelly to receive a bouquet of her favorite flowers along with a card announcing our trip to Cabo. I made sure to clear my calendar around the time of her delivery to her job just so I could hear the excitement in her voice.

Things were back in full swing and while I thought about my father often, I was at peace with his departure. I worked feverishly to get caught up on outstanding work from last week.

My phone rang and my assistant mentioned that the caller on the line refused to provide their name. My first thought was to let it roll to voicemail, but since I was in a good mood, I decided to take it.

"Derek Walker," I answered.

"Derek, please don't hang up it's me…"

I immediately recognized the voice, and the smile I wore on my face turned into a scowl.

"You have some fucking nerve calling me," I said through clenched teeth.

"I would appreciate if you give me five minutes of your time. I'm not trying to harass you, but I do have something to say."

I put the phone down as I closed my office door.

"You have exactly five minutes," I said, looking at the clock.

"First of all, I want to apologize for the scene at your house. I didn't intend on taking things where they went, but Kelly brought that on."

"You came to our home unannounced and decided to tell her about our affair and you thought it was going to be peaceful. Obviously you knew it, too, since you came equipped with a gun. Be glad I have something to live for, because in that very moment, I wanted to choke the shit out of you."

"She put her hands on me and I pulled out my gun to control her with no intent on using it. I'm a licensed gun carrier, so I stay strapped, especially at night. But anyway, I apologize for having to go there."

"Apology not accepted. You are a malicious and spiteful bitch," I said, irritated.

"I'll take that because I understand your anger. I came with the intent of being honest about something I should've told her from the beginning. You never would've told her because that's what you men do. Do your dirt and carry on like nothing has happened. In your mind, proposing was going to be just the thing to help you ease your conscience and make her happy. See, that's what pisses me off about you men. Women love you with all their might, you half-ass them and then try to compensate for your faulty ways by winning them over with what you know they want. It's manipulative and it's deceiving. I came clean with Kelly on my own terms because I knew she would probably never hear the truth from you. I was leaving Atlanta and had nothing to lose by telling her the truth, but what I gained was the opportunity to right a wrong and become a better person from it."

I didn't need to hear anything further from her. "You've said what you called to say, now do me a favor and never call me again. If you do, I will have your number traced and get a restraining order for harassment."

She chuckled. "Have a nice life."

And with that, the phone line went dead. I hung up the phone and sat in silence. I knew how fortunate I was to have Kelly's forgiveness; I was sure in the back of her mind she was a long way from forgetting. I could only take things one day at a time and the state of our relationship at this point was steadily on the rebound.

As my phone rang, I instantly smiled judging by the time.

"Derek Walker," I answered.

She squealed in the phone. "Derek Walker, you are something else. I can't believe you planned a trip for us; damn, I'm starting to like this new you."

"If I could take you around the world and back, I would. Glad you're excited. Well, did the flowers even interest you?"

"Oh my bad, yes, they are stunning and have my office smelling so good. You know you got these heifers in here jealous."

"I'm sure they're thinking I done messed up again or something." I chuckled. "Baby, can I ask you a question?"

She hesitated. "Sure."

"Will you marry me?"

I could tell she was blushing as she answered. "Yes, Derek. And you know what, I thought about our wedding and you're right, we have spent a great deal of money with the house. I'm OK with waiting until next year."

I smiled. "Thanks for understanding. I don't want us to get in over our heads."

"Well, babe, I have a meeting to get to but I wanted to say thank you so much; I'm super excited and in need of a vacation."

I hung up the phone and Darnell was at the door. I motioned for him to come in.

"Everything all right?" he asked.

"Couldn't be better. Did you guys get your travel arrangements taken care of?"

"Jessica jumped on that immediately. She's always looking for ways to spend money." He chuckled. "Listen, bruh, I wanted to let you know that I'm proud of you. We as men have to go through our growing pains to really appreciate what we have in life."

I sighed. "Yeah, that's true, but I've learned and I'm not trying to experience that again."

"Right on. Maria called and invited us to some club for a birthday celebration for Carlton next weekend. You down?"

I looked at him with a smirk. "If it's the club I'm thinking of, you might want to send your regards and decline."

Darnell had a perturbed look on his face. "What are you talking about? How dangerous can a birthday party be at a club? I'm sure since it's Maria we're talking about, I'm sure it's upscale."

I got up from my seat and walked over to the door. "Bruh, let's discuss this over lunch. Believe me, even upscale has a way of bringing its own kind of trouble; a trouble you ain't ready for." I smiled.

I patted him on the shoulder as we headed out of the office. As we rounded the corner, I saw a framed photo of my father in the lobby when he first opened the company. I stood and beamed at the young man who reminded me so much of myself. I was proud of who I'd become as a man and only hoped I could continue to live in a way that made my father smile from heaven.

GROUP DISCUSSION QUESTIONS

1. Even though La'Tia discussed her dislike for Marcus not keeping his promise to her. Why do you think she allowed him to remain in her life? Could you identify with her reasoning?
2. Do you agree with Kelly's logic of wanting to be married first before investing in a home with Derek? Do you see a change in Kelly's persona from the first novel?
3. Did you find Tony's disagreement with Janen finding her biological mother justifiable?
4. How did you feel about the friendship between Carlton and Derek after finding out about Carlton's marriage?
5. La'Tia considered Rachelle to be her best friend even though their values differed. What is your opinion of Rachelle?
6. Was Kelly justified in treating Gigi as she did upon finding out the truth about her relationship with her ex?
7. Lacey appeared to be a free spirit and lived life on her own terms. Do you feel she was out to destroy Derek's relationship with Kelly? Or upon getting to know Kelly, do you think she grew fond of her and genuinely wanted her to know the truth?
8. Once Janen learned of why her mother gave her up for adoption. Should she have accepted it and moved on completely without further interaction?
9. What were your thoughts on Carlton's business proposal to La'Tia? How would you have handled the meeting with Maria?
10. It is not uncommon for families to have dysfunction and due to it become disconnected. With Robbie, David, and Carlita, what are your thoughts on each of the characters and their contribution to the storyline?
11. Would you have stayed with Derek after his situation with Lacey was revealed? Do you feel Kelly gave him another chance out of obligation?
12. In your opinion, how did each of the characters evolve from their first introduction in the previous novel (Love & Deceit Affairs of the Heart)?

ACKNOWLEDGEMENTS

I would like to thank God for being the head of my life and blessing me with the talent of writing. I am so thankful for yet another journey in being artistically creative and producing a body of work for your reading enjoyment. I appreciate all my readers that supported me on my first novel, Love & Deceit Affairs of the Heart, and all your feedback and admiration for the characters within the book. I hope with this follow-up, I did not disappoint. My goal in writing has always been to entertain, but also bring forth realistic situations. Thank you for supporting my movement!

I would like to extend thanks to my graphic designer and friend, Marrio Marshall for yet another great cover design. I thank you for your patience and your willingness to work with me in my moments of indecisiveness (smile).

I would like to thank my mother, Darlene, for being my number one salesperson and supporter. To my family, it would take another page for me to individually acknowledge each of you, but from the bottom of my heart – I LOVE YOU AND THANK YOU!

To all my Facebook and Instagram friends that shouted me out and told a friend about my book – THANK YOU!

Last but not least, I thank my husband for introducing my book to other acquaintances which allowed me the opportunity to share my book with my first book club. *Champagne Divas Book Club* – you fabulous ladies are the best! Rhonda, I can't thank you enough for allowing me to share my baby with you all and become a member of such a great group of women. Also thank you Yvonne and *The Literary Ladies* for your support as well.

In closing, I've had so many people expressing their interest in writing a book and how I've inspired them to do so. It takes courage to create stories and present it to readers not knowing what kind of feedback you'll receive. My advice to anyone looking to write is to BELIEVE IN YOURSELF! You must also have confidence in your craft to not let the opinions of others hinder your desire to move forward. Keep striving and live life to the fullest by pursuing your dreams. Best wishes!

www.ingramcontent.com/pod-product-compliance
Lightning Source LLC
Chambersburg PA
CBHW031948070426
42453CB00006BA/139